About t

Bruce Lewis, son of Professor Herbert Price Lewis, grew up in West Wales. He spent his formative years either on, or in, the sea at Aberystwyth. Eventually sent to school in 'land-locked' Wiltshire, he nonetheless remained true to his ambition to join the Navy. However, during the early days of World War Two it became clear that only in the air would Britain be able to keep up a constant attack against the enemy. So, on his 18th birthday, he volunteered to fly with the RAF. As a Flight/Sergeant (later promoted to Flying Officer), he flew with Lancasters of 101 Special Duties Squadron, Bomber Command. He survived 35 operations.

In 1946 he became the first British Air Force of Occupation newscaster with BFN in Hamburg. This was the beginning of a long association with broadcasting, both BBC Radio and Television, and ITV. He wrote *The Technique of Television Announcing,* a standard work on the subject. He also created one of Britain's first Independent Radio Stations.

Bruce Lewis met his wife, Miki, when she was a WAAF engaged in Signals Duties on the same wartime squadron. They have 5 sons and a daughter and divide their time between their two modest homes, one in the Cotswolds, the other in the hills of Andalucia.

FOUR MEN WENT TO WAR

THE STORIES OF

Odell Dobson
AMERICAN AIR GUNNER

George Paine
BRITISH PARATROOPER

Helmut Steiner
GERMAN PANZER DRIVER

Antonio Benetti
ITALIAN SKI COMMANDO

BY BRUCE LEWIS

with a foreword by
Frank Richardson

ARROW BOOKS

Arrow Books Limited
62-65 Chandos Place, London WC2N 4NW

An imprint of Century Hutchinson Limited

London Melbourne Sydney Auckland
Johannesburg and agencies throughout
the world

First published by Leo Cooper 1987
Arrow edition 1988
© Bruce Lewis 1987

Printed and bound in Great Britain by
Anchor Brendon Limited, Tiptree, Essex

ISBN 0 09 958830 7

CONTENTS

ILLUSTRATIONS

"Every man thinks meanly of himself for not having been a soldier."

Samuel Johnson in Boswell's *Life*
10 April, 1778

FOREWORD

by Major-General Frank Richardson

The four soldiers' stories told in this book will stir vivid memories of similar experiences in many survivors of the Second World War; and perhaps cause readers who have never been called upon to go to war to ponder on their own ability "to survive and triumph over extraordinary circumstances", as Mr Lewis puts it. Everyone will sympathize with the "abiding dream of home" which all four shared; but what moved these "quite ordinary men" to volunteer for active service?

Today the threat of 'Mutual Assured Destruction', which has contributed to the deterrent effect of nuclear weapons, understandably leads to the proliferation of organizations dedicated to the preservation of peace – even peace at any price.

It seems unlikely that any national leader could again inspire that fanatical devotion and eagerness to march under his banner achieved by Hitler. Having experienced how even a foreign visitor to Nazi Germany, in the peaceful environment of skiing centres in 1937 and 1938, could feel the magnetic impact of those eyes staring from the ubiquitous posters with their reminder that '*Der Deutscher Gruss ist Heil Hitler*' I felt no surprise on reading of Helmut Steiner's youthful determination to join a combatant unit, forging the signature of his father, a victim of Nazi persecution. But it is interesting to recall that in the same city of Cologne another boy was resisting Hitler's evil influence, as we can read in Heinrich Böll's *What's to Become of the Boy?*

It has been said that the Italians are too intelligent, civilized and cultured to make good soldiers, and the story of Antonio Benetti is interesting in this connection. He displayed considerable powers of leadership in successfully leading his ski commando through mountainous country to safety in neutral Switzerland, but it was hardly a contribution to the war aims of Mussolini, to whom his devotion was barely luke-warm. Neither, of course, was his successful avoidance of the uncivilized business of combat, by reaching an accommodation with his enemy, relying on the comradeship which exists among skiers and 'mountain men' of all nations. The peaceful, almost idyllic interlude in the Valday mountains, like the 'Christmas Truce' in the First World War, illustrates the readiness of front-line soldiers to fraternize with the enemy – fellow-men enduring the same perils and hardships. During the Peninsular War instances were frequent, when both sides had to draw water from the same source, or met whilst foraging for food or firewood, and French brandy was swapped for English tobacco. The original Desert Rats had an almost affectionate regard for the splendid men of the *Afrika Korps* - before Montgomery arrived to send them packing. At the end, Montgomery's non-fraternization order, designed to let the Germans know that this time their army had been decisively beaten, was readily accepted by men who had seen Belsen and Buchenwald. But can we doubt that, if Rommel had survived his Führer's malignant vengeance, he would have soon been attending Montgomery's Alamein reunions, enjoying the same welcome as was extended to the German general Von Lettow Vorbeck after the First World War? He might even have ended up in command of both German and British troops as did another German general who had plotted against Hitler.

If there are lessons to be learned from the stories of these four men and their subsequent friendly meetings, it must be in the field of morale. The morale of the soldier, which Field-Marshal Montgomery called the greatest single factor in war, may be said to have three elements – the soldier's personal morale; his morale as a member of a small group; and his morale as a member of the regiment – *Esprit de Corps*. Personal morale may grow from differing national roots, while the importance of the small group of comrades is surely universal. It is illustrated in the stories of the American Odell Dobson and the German Helmut Steiner – the crews of bomber planes and tanks being totally dependent for their efficiency, and often for their survival, on each man carrying out his allotted role and being prepared to take over that of a wounded comrade. George Paine, the cheerful Cockney, relied heavily upon the comradeship of his mates, whether in making a good thing out of looking after the needs of others or in trying to escape from a prisoner-of-war camp.

Kameradschaft – comradeship, is the god of the German Army. In the British Army comradeship is taken for granted and our god has always been Regimental Spirit – *Esprit de Corps*. For a long time I have felt that our most valuable contribution to the strength of the Western Alliance could lie in the fostering of what I call *Esprit de NATO*; acting as a catalyst to help in breaking down national jealousies and suspicions. Expounding this theme in my book *Fighting Spirit*, I wrote:-

Because our country has fought both by the side of and against so many of the armies of the alliance, we are well equipped to develop the theme of cousins, whose relationships, as families, growing up through nursery and school days to adulthood, may pass through phases of childish dislikes, boyhood friendships and adult enmities, to the comfortable tolerance of middle age.

To become really good allies in this spirit nations must learn not only to see themselves as others see them but to see those others as they see themselves. The British are not particularly good at either of these exercises. Napoleon complained of our "complacency" and Tsar Alexander I, who became our ally, admitted that he hated "the British tone of superiority". It was probably feelings like this which led General de Gaulle to put his foot down on our grandiose plans to celebrate, with the renascent German Army, the 200th anniversary, in 1959, of our joint victory over the French at Minden. This blow to the burgeoning of *Esprit de NATO* was compounded by his ordering the NATO headquarters out of France. This was attributed to his dislike of American dominance; and Alistair Cooke had said that de Gaulle was 'paranoid' about our special relationship with the United States. But our special relationship had once been with Germany, and not all that long ago.

When in 1836 Sir Archibald Alison wrote, in *Blackwood's Magazine*, that "Germany . . . from original character, common descent and mutual glories is the natural ally of England," few would have thought to contradict him. Four years later our Queen married a German prince and some eighteen years after that her daughter married the Crown Prince of Prussia. Perhaps a slight softening of our Germanic front began when Queen Victoria was charmed by the somewhat flirtatious gallantry of Napoleon III (a bogus Bonaparte, whose real father was the Dutch admiral, Verhuell) and the undisguised enjoyment of visits to Paris of her son – later to be known as Edward the Peacemaker. But the inauguration, in 1904, of the *Entente Cordiale* was to be followed in ten years by war with our 'natural allies'. John Mander, in his book *Our German Cousins*, dates the "transfer of popular affection from Germany to France" as somewhere around 1871.

Dr Johnson's opinion that: "Every man thinks meanly of himself for not having been a soldier, or not having been at sea" applies to nations as well as to men. Even Switzerland, the least aggressive of countries, maintains an efficient army. Nations, like boys and men, like to think that they could give a good account of themselves in a fight; they treasure and take pride in the memory of times when they did so. In *Fighting Spirit* I gave many examples of the sort of things we ought to know about the martial feats which our allies like to remember – too many to be recounted here. An example of where we ourselves need to take a balanced view concerns one of our proudest martial memories – Wellington's victory at Waterloo. We are justly proud of the prolonged stubborn resistance of the splendid British infantry; and we always acknowledge the crucial role played by courageous old Blücher and his Prussians. But how many of us know that in Wellington's army, which bore the brunt of that long day, the British troops were actually outnumbered by Netherlanders and Germans? Napoleon claimed that but for the heroic resistance of a Netherland brigade at Quatre Bras there would have been no battle of Waterloo, as he would have "conquered as at Friedland", and marched straight into Brussels. The Germans in Wellington's army were our own superb King's German Legion, whose heroic contributions to Wellington's victories in the Peninsular War and at Waterloo we should never forget – but how many of us really know about them?

So much for the past. What about the present? The world today can hardly be called peaceful; but it is justly claimed that the nuclear deterrent has at least staved off a third world war for over 40 years. In the awful event of it failing to continue to do so how would those of military age respond to the call to arms? Would campaigners for peace at any price in our country and in those of our allies score a greater success than the Peace Pledge Union appeared to do at the Cenotaph in 1986? The world has changed to an astonishing extent since the four heroes of this book decided to 'go for a soldier'. Britain has become a multi-racial society and is still striving to come to terms with that radical change in our island race. Hints have been dropped in high places that it may be time that some black faces were seen below the bearskins of Her Majesty's Brigade of Guards. Would our coloured compatriots prove to be as ready to fight for their country as they are to represent it in sporting activities, winning many gold medals for Britain? Here we should certainly remember with pride the great deeds of our fine Indian Army – and remember also that a black tribe – the Hadendowa of Sudan – have a unique distinction – they broke a British square.

INTRODUCTION

These tales are not fiction. They recount the real-life stories of men caught up in the Second World War. It is an advantage that these episodes were told to me only after a lapse of four decades when the participants could view the events with a dispassionate eye – no longer caring to create an effect.

Indeed, my most difficult task has been to draw these veterans out, to overcome that natural reticence they share with others whose deeds exceed the common experience. C. C. Colton was right when he said: 'The greatest friend of truth is Time, her greatest enemy is Prejudice, and her constant companion is Humility'.

Odell would hardly have *invented* his feelings of guilt when he failed to prepare his fellow crewman's gun for battle, anymore than Helmut was courting the modern reader's approbation by telling me of his bitter disappointment at being refused service in the SS. George, too, could so easily have skipped over the occasion when he failed in his duty as a soldier by not shooting a German infantryman lined up in his rifle-sights; while Antonio displayed a transparent honesty by refusing to cover up his philosophy of avoiding conflict whenever possible.

At the time of writing, all these men who went to war continue to lead active, busy lives. When I first got to know them they were strangers to one another, although three live within a few miles of each other in Southern Spain. The American, Odell Dobson, was also in this region, on holiday, when I first met him. I only wish he had been around when I had the pleasure of bringing the three residents of the Costa del Sol together in a restaurant near Marbella. By a happy coincidence it was George Paine's 70th birthday. Helmut Steiner and Antonio Benetti were delighted to raise their glasses in celebration – in fact the old soldiers, once implacable enemies, behaved as though they had been close comrades for years.

It was strange how I came to meet these men. For many years I had worked as a broadcaster in British television and radio, when suddenly the media and I grew tired of each other. My wife Miki bravely agreed that we should try an entirely different sort of life, working on the Costa del Sol. After selling our much-loved millhouse in Northumberland, we headed south to the sun and set up a sailing and water-ski club near Marbella. It was completely unlike anything we had tackled before, but we learned quickly.

We were lucky too. There was plenty of family muscle to help us with the boats – each of our five sons and our daughter weighed in willingly for varying periods throughout the three years we spent in Spain. Overall it was a happy and amusing time. The way of life suited us well. Raising sails, launching catamarans, hauling in the speedboat, we reached unimagined peaks of physical fitness, became deeply suntanned and, most important, threw off all the accumulated cares of 'rat-race living'.

With fewer preoccupations, it became easier to listen to what other people were saying. The imagination was stimulated in a way that was clearer, more vivid and exciting than at any time since childhood. It was surprising, too, how many of those holiday-makers who strolled out of their 5-star hotels and wandered down to our crushed-marble beach, wanted to talk, to confide to us the most intimate details of their lives back home.

They came from many countries and any number of backgrounds. In a way it was like enjoying the world tour we had never been able to afford. We talked with men who owned banks; with a New York cop spending his savings on the holiday of a lifetime; pop stars who sang and composed beneath our grass sunshades; a Welsh judge – holder of the Victoria Cross; a Spanish baker – who, when a pilot in the Civil War, dropped bombs on Málaga; a German, still proud at having shaken hands with Adolf Hitler – he produced a dog-eared photograph from his bathing trunks to prove it; film stars; racing drivers; smugglers; and a constant stream of ordinary people from all over the world.

There were groups too, like the players and soloists of James Last's orchestra; the Everton football team, over from England to play Seville; and of course the organized tourist parties. It was the arrival of one such party, the staff of the claims department of a large insurance company on vacation from Alabama, that led to my meeting with Odell Dobson.

Odell was the president in charge of the group, a huge man of John Wayne proportions. Unlike the rest, he took no interest in sunbathing or water sports, but sat quietly under the palm-leaf awning of our beach hut, a rather tired man enjoying a well-earned rest. I seem to remember being particularly busy at that time. It was, after all, a strenuous operation with water-skiing, catamarans, paddleboats, gondolas, beach beds and the teeshirt shop, all demanding continuous attention.

A couple of days went by before Odell and I got into conversation. I remarked on how well his son handled his sailboat. Patrick was with the US

Army stationed in Germany. He had taken leave to travel to Spain, joining his father, mother and sister Lise on holiday. It was talk about the American forces that led Odell to tell me that he had seen service during the Second World War as a waistgunner on a B24 Liberator operating over Germany. This interested me very much, because I had flown as a wireless operator/air-gunner in RAF Lancasters at the same time. I had often tried to imagine what life was like for aircrew flying in American bombers. During the war, with our people flying at night and the Americans raiding by day, there was little opportunity to meet and compare notes.

As the days passed, the whole amazing story unfolded, almost in serial form. Odell, with his measured Southern drawl, related every detail of his terrifying experiences – including the most vivid description I have ever heard of a shell-shattered bomber in its death throes – as witnessed from *inside* the aircraft.

On the evening before the Dobsons' holiday ended we all went out for a meal. Optimistically I had put a notebook in my pocket – but this was a family occasion, so I was unable to check on facts and figures, place names and dates. 'Odell,' I said as we parted, 'I had hoped for an accurate record of everything you've told me, but there's been no chance to jot things down.' 'Don't worry,' he replied, 'when I get back to the States I'll record it all and send it to you – if you really want it.'

He was as good as his word. The tapes arrived in due course. In a letter Odell said, 'I am sure there is nothing special about my experiences; a lot more men went through much more than I ever did.' Readers will be able to judge for themselves.

Tristram, our youngest son, then twelve years old, attended an excellent little school at nearby San Pedro de Alcantara. The lessons were in English, but the flavour was international. In his free time Tristram lived for swimming and fishing. Every Monday throughout the long summer holiday he went on day trips aboard the *Flamingo*, a local shark-catcher, and revelled in the excitement of the chase. This treat cost him nothing. A German restaurant owner hired the *Flamingo* on this day each week for his own fishing party and kindly extended a regular invitation to our son.

Meanwhile, early one morning our number three son, Byron, an ex-paratrooper, and I were hauling the speedboat into the sea. 'Met an interesting character last night at a party,' Byron said. He went on to tell me that this man, George Paine, had also been a paratrooper and had fought at Arnhem.

Only a few days elapsed before I too met George at a party. What this tough, witty, bright little Londoner had to say convinced me that we had another strange story on our hands. In a marathon session some time later, George unfolded his extraordinary adventures. It was dawn the following day before we came to the point where George Paine made his final escape from the enemy. This time I had recorded every detail.

On the way home an idea began to take shape. I had personal accounts from men serving with the two principal Western Allies in the Second World War. If I could only get hold of similar individual stories from a German and an Italian, allies on the opposing side, the set would make a unique record.

By now it was the last Monday before the start of the autumn school term. As usual we collected Tristram as he disembarked from the *Flamingo*. Luis Proetta, his Gibraltarian headmaster, was with us. As the fishing party came ashore, Luis nudged me; 'You know those war stories of yours? Well, what about talking to Helmut, the German restaurateur? I believe he has a fantastic tale to tell – if you can get him to talk.'

Next day, in the headmaster's office, I began to question Helmut Steiner, a stocky, blue-eyed, fair-haired, 'short-fused' man. It was hard going. He kept flying off at tangents – justifying his actions and those of his nation during the war with a fierce intensity. It dawned on me that here was a man, a one-time brave soldier – loyal to his beliefs and his country – who had been deeply affected by subsequent events and the humiliation of defeat.

It has taken a long time and numerous meetings to piece Helmut's experiences together. I am still far from sure I have heard the whole story, but what I have heard moves me deeply.

The season finished. The tourists went home. We packed the boats and gear away for the winter. I called on a Public Relations man of our acquaintance. I wanted to thank him for the help and advice that had eased our progress through the first year of business in a foreign land. As we talked, the subject of my son Byron's military service came up. 'I find that very interesting,' said the PR man, 'I too was a soldier during the war.'

He was Antonio Benetti, a tall, elegant, athletic Italian. Within days I had my fourth story! In contrast to the others, Antonio skipped lightly over the gloomier incidents, which I am sure were more numerous than he cared to reveal. Instead, he dwelt amusingly on a plethora of humorous events, stretching from Italy to Russia and back again. It was the only way Antonio could bear to regard a war that he, and the majority of Italians, viewed as a disgraceful profanity – a profanity imposed on his country by her vain-glorious leader, Benito Mussolini.

If there are common themes linking these four men who went to war, then it must be the manifestation of dogged courage, enterprise in adversity and, above all, the ability of quite ordinary men to survive and triumph over extraordinary circumstances. There was one other thing they all shared and that was a dream – the abiding dream of home. And, unlike millions of their comrades, they did come home – in the end.

ODELL DOBSON

AMERICAN AIR GUNNER

O N THE NIGHT of 10 September, 1944, we were alerted for an attack on an ordnance manufacturing depot near Hanover.

Between 4am and 5am (on 11 September) twenty-four crews were briefed. Around 7.30am all twenty-four aircraft took off.

Just across the Rhine about 11.55am the formation was attacked by twenty to thirty Messerschmidt 109s for about five minutes. Several of the enemy aircraft were camouflaged with white stripes to simulate American P51s. The enemy attack was pressed home vigorously, coming in singly . . . most of the ME109s were firing 20mm time-fused shells, some of which were noticed to explode before hitting our planes. The attack occurred at a time when our formation was temporarily without fighter support.

As a result of this attack four of our ships are missing . . . including aircraft B24 466 of 578 Squadron which was last seen at 11.58am near Koblenz when hit by enemy aircraft. Fire broke out in no 3 engine, after which the whole plane burst into flames, peeled over, spun in and crashed. No chutes seen.

Excerpt from Mission Narrative of 392nd Bombardment Group USAAF and 578 Squadron Report, 11 September, 1944

Two hundred and forty airmen took part in this mission. What follows is the story of one of them.

ODELL FRANKLIN DOBSON was born at 168 Park Avenue, Schoolfield (Pittsylvania County), Virginia on 11 March, 1922. His sister, Frances Marie, followed him into the world two years later. Both their parents worked as factory hands in the local cotton mills. Their father, Robert Franklin Dobson, who had been born in Newport News, Virginia, came of good Colonial Virginia stock, but was regarded as the black sheep of his family. By the time Odell and Frances were born, their father was an alcoholic who suffered from back trouble; his working life was therefore erratic. Their mother, born in Abingdon, Virginia and christened Lucy Widener, could trace her ancestry back to a German immigrant named John (Johann) Widener, who came to Pennsylvania in the late 1750s. John's son Michael served in the Revolutionary War with the Hessian Mercenaries, becoming interpreter to George Washington, who appears to have regarded him highly, referring to him as 'Mikey'. After the war Michael Widener was given land in south-west Virginia, near Abingdon, known to this day as Widener's Valley.

These promising beginnings brought no inherited benefits to the Dobsons in the 1920s and '30s. On the contrary, partly on account of prevailing economic conditions, but mainly through Dobson senior's inability to hold down a regular job, the family was poor. Not that Odell was really aware of their poverty; it seemed quite normal because nearly all the neighbours were equally hard up. When he was fifteen Odell quit school, lied about his age and got a job in the mill to help support his mother, father and sister. From the time he was a very young boy, Odell read everything he could about the First World War. He was fascinated by every aspect of modern warfare and prayed that, if another world war broke out, he would be old enough to participate.

In 1939, the year the Germans marched into Poland, and Great Britain and France declared war on the Nazis, the Dobson family moved to

Lexington, North Carolina. Now seventeen, Odell started work on the night shift in a new mill, thus giving himself time to attend High School. Later, to make life a little easier, he gave up his job at the mill and worked at a bakery instead. The shifts were from 4am until 7am, six days a week, with extra hours on Saturdays and Sundays. As the Second World War engulfed Europe, Odell avidly read all he could in such magazines as *Time* and *Newsweek*. He never missed a speech by the British Prime Minister, Winston Churchill. He impressed the other High School kids by quoting great chunks from these broadcasts verbatim. A programme that always stirred him was Ed Murrow's 'This is London'.

Out of the eight dollars he earned at the bakery, he managed to pay for half an hour's private flying tuition each week. He now had a clear idea what he was going to do. He was resolved to become an Army Air Force pilot. One Sunday afternoon he was listening to the radio when he heard the shattering news that Pearl Harbor had been attacked by Japanese planes and the United States fleet destroyed. It was 7 December, 1941. America was at war. Next day, although still at High School, Odell reported to the recruiting office at nearby Salisbury and tried to join up. The military authorities told him that, as he was under age, he would need written permission from his parents before he could be accepted. His mother reluctantly agreed to sign the necessary papers, but only on condition that he completed his studies and sat for his examinations.

The following June he graduated successfully. Then, a few weeks later on 18 August, 1942 he enlisted in the Army Air Force. It was barely a week before that he had walked dejectedly out of the recruiting office, because – after passing every other test – he was rejected for being 10 pounds underweight, at 145 pounds (10 stone 5 pounds). Odell vowed he would find those extra 10 pounds in one week. He took no exercise and ate everything he could cram down his throat. At 5am on the crucial day he went into an all-night restaurant and bought a quart of milk. Then, reinforced with his drink, he sat down and started to eat eleven pounds of bananas. By the time the recruiting office opened, he still had a few bananas left and was feeling sick. But he staggered down to the army centre. For good luck, as he entered the building he gulped down as much water as he could from a handy drinking fountain. Nearly bursting, he wobbled up to the captain in charge of the outfit and gasped – 'weigh me quick, sir!' The Captain motioned Odell onto the scales – fully clothed. The pointer came to rest at exactly the prescribed weight – 155 pounds (11 stone 1 pound). He was in.

Then he was sent home to wait his turn and six months slipped by before he was called for active duty. Soon he was undergoing pilot instruction in the air; but then came the greatest disappointment of his life. For some reason which he never fully understood, he was 'washed out' as a pilot after his initial flying training. Odell was now in danger of finishing up in some ground occupation. If he were to remain a flyer he had to take drastic action – quick. Officially, at six feet, one and a half inches, he was considered too tall to qualify as an air gunner. But by a fair amount of cunning, which included forgery of a medic's signature on an army document, he beat the system and got himself accepted for training as a 'ball-turret gunner'. This was by far the most cramped fighting position in a bomber, normally reserved for flyers not more than five feet, six inches in height. Fortunately for Odell, he eventually finished up in the waist-gun position of a B24 Liberator – a location in the airplane with adequate headroom.

There was a lot more to the business of air gunnery than he had ever imagined. At Harlingen Gunnery School, Texas, the Army Air Force turned him into an expert – and he enjoyed every minute of it. It was like all the fun of the fair on a tremendous scale. He fired machine guns at fixed targets; he shot skeet (clay pigeons) on a regular skeet range, also from the back of a moving truck bouncing down forest tracks, with skeet suddenly appearing in the air without warning; from ball turrets fitted with Sperry Computing sights – tracking the skeet as it sailed down from fire rangers' towers. They fired 30mm and 50mm machine guns at a variety of moving targets, some mounted on railroad flat cars travelling at speed. Flying in type AT6 advanced trainers, they stood in open cockpits firing at sleeves (drogues) towed by other aircraft. Later they climbed into bombers and did the same exercises from the cramped confines of ball turrets. Odell particularly enjoyed air-to-ground firing practice, in which he aimed at huge boards, like roadside hoardings, floating upright in the sea.

On his final air-firing test, the crucial examination before qualification or failure, he went up in an open cockpit. He asked the pilot to fly him into a good position so he could blast the 'sleeve' full of holes, but it was his bad luck that the pilot, like some of the other flyers there, had screwed up his service career in some way. He had been sent to Harlingen as a form of punishment – condemned to the monotony of flying type AT6s round and round the Texan sky, day after day. Odell's pilot was in no mood to be helpful to a 'sprog' airgunner; on the contrary, he stood off from the target at maximum range. To frustrate the perspiring pupil's efforts even more, he bucked the aircraft up and down, trying to throw him off his aim. When graduation day arrived Odell was in an agony of suspense. None of the trainees had any idea whether they had qualified or not. Standing stiffly to attention on the vast parade ground at Harlingen, Odell's name was one of the last to be called out. He marched forward, saluted and the Colonel congratulated him as he pinned his wings on his tunic. He must have hit the target after all.

*

Within a few days Odell had joined his new bomber crew. They flew and practised as a team until the Army Air Force was satisfied they had reached a level of proficiency which entitled them to go to war. Setting course for England, they headed out across the Atlantic from Goose Bay, Labrador, in their four-engined B24 Liberator. A short time after their arrival in the United Kingdom they were flying operational missions over Europe from 578 Squadron base at Wendling in Norfolk.

Their baptism of fire was sudden and violent. From the sheltered environment of the United States they had travelled over three thousand miles to be hurled into the bloodiest air battle of all time. This was real war with a vengeance. On one of their early operations, a mission to the Baltic sea port of Kiel in Northern Germany, their airplane was badly shot up and damaged before reaching the target. It seemed debatable whether the bomber was sufficiently airworthy to fly back to England. Bill, the navigator, plotted a course to neutral Sweden and advised the pilot of the new compass heading. But the captain, First Lieutenant C.A. Rudd, chose to ignore it, continuing on their original course until they reached the target and the bombs were dropped. It was then they decided to attempt the long struggle home. The rest of the group had pulled away from them and they were alone and unprotected. Crippled, they flew out over the North Sea at 12,000 feet, less than half the normal operational height. They staggered straight over the island of Heligoland – one of the most powerfully armed batteries in Europe. It seemed as if every gun on the island had opened up simultaneously. But somehow it survived that mile-thick curtain of exploding steel. On and on it droned, sinking ever lower towards the sea. At last they saw the coast of Scotland ahead. Within minutes they had coaxed her, broken and all but finished, safely down onto an emergency airfield. Odell's crew had lived to fight another day, unlike their rugged old Liberator, which never flew again.

When they returned to base, by train, 'Rudd's Ruffians', as the crew were known, were faced with an irresistible temptation in the form of 'Ford's Folly'. The old girl had quite a history – she was the first B24 Liberator to be built by the Ford Motor Company of America. Early into battle, she had flown more missions than any other American bomber in the European theatre – seventy-nine raids at that time. She was a wreck and should have been written off. Yet when the 'Old Man' offered her to Rudd, he agreed to fly her. The bait was just too tempting to be ignored. 'Push her total up to a hundred missions,' said the Squadron Commander, 'and you and your crew can take her back to the States on a War Bonds tour.' The idea appealed to the men very much. They would be wined and dined and fêted like heroes by their fellow countrymen – and women! After all they had made enough fuss of the 'Memphis Belle' – starred her in a movie and all that kind of stuff – and *she* had only done twenty-five missions when they sent *her* home. So they figured old 'Ford's Folly' would go over pretty big in the States when the time came.

It was the second Sunday in September, 1944. All the enlisted men from the crew of 'Ford's Folly', with the exception of Odell, were away from the base on day pass. Odell had decided to stay around and take it easy, so he was far from pleased when pilot and navigator, Lieutenants Rudd and Dawson, strolled into his hut late in the afternoon and asked him if he would help them swing the compass and calibrate the instruments on their bomber. Irritably he threw down his book and followed them out to the hard stand where 'Ford's Folly' was parked. It was dark long before they had finished their work, yet they were not particularly concerned, because it was after 5 o'clock and no battle order had been posted, which normally meant no operational flying on the following day. On this occasion they were wrong. At 10 o'clock that night they were told that 'Ford's Folly' was scheduled for a raid in the morning. Earlier that day it had been too cloudy to verify the sun compass, there had been no chance to carry out a flight test and guns and turrets had not been checked. As Odell said later, 'If Rudd had been smart, he would have refused to fly the ship on that mission.' The First Lieutenant would not have been alone in backing down – the Group had called for maximum effort, but only twenty-four out of forty-eight aircraft took off the following morning.

As usual, after pre-flight breakfast, they were briefed. Here they were told that their target was an ordnance manufacturing depot near Hanover. It was still very early in the morning when Odell went over to the flights to oil and instal his guns in 'Ford's Folly'. Sergeant Modlen, the nose-turret gunner, was a 'washed-out' navigator who acted as standby for Lieutenant Dawson, the regular navigator, in the event of an emergency. Part of Odell's duty was to check the nose-turret guns for Modlen while he attended the navigators' briefing. Odell fixed Modlen's guns, but did not bother to check the electrical circuit to the nose turret. Then, feeling tired, he took a blanket and went for a nap in an adjoining wheatfield while he waited for the rest of the crew to show up. Just before take-off, always a time of tension, the flyers were more than usually apprehensive – it was mission 13.

Nervousness was cloaked by flippant observations; Maynard, upper turret gunner and engineer, said 'This is not mission 13, it is mission 12a.'

'No,' cut in Roger Clapp, the radio operator, 'don't kid yourself, we are taking off on mission 13 and this is the one where we go down.'

On a superstitious impulse Odell slid through the 3×5 feet camera-hatch back onto the ground. He scrubbed his feet several times back and forth on the grass at the side of the runway before climbing once more into the aircraft.

Shortly after take-off, as they were forming up, Modlen, the front gunner, called up, 'Dobby, the radical on my gunsight won't light up. Did you pre-flight my turret?'

'Sure I did', Odell lied, knowing the pilot and all the rest of the crew were listening on the interphone. The crew had always taken a great pride in its operational efficiency. Back in the Overseas Training Unit at Casper, Wyoming, the previous March, they had been awarded their own bomber on completion of the course, one of only three crews, out of a total of forty, to receive this privilege. Since then, as operational experience increased, there had been a tendency to back off on some of the routine checks, to become slipshod. Odell cursed himself for being a stupid, lazy slob. He advised Modlen to take the small bulb out of his 'trouble light', (the movable inspection lamp) and use that to replace the defective one. In a moment Modlen was speaking again: 'Dobby, there ain't no bulb in the "trouble light".' So, on that trip there were no sights on the aircraft's front guns. Afterwards, Odell's only consolation was that, as far as he knew, there had been no head-on attacks by fighters that morning.

Odell started to get his own gun ready. On a B24 Liberator the 50mm flexible machine guns mounted in the waist of the bomber were fired through large open windows on both sides of the aircraft. The ammunition boxes had belts of 500 rounds and these rattled along flexible metal chutes to feed the guns. During firing the noise and vibration were unbelievable. Odell discovered that the hooks that attached the chute to his gun were missing. He had some safety wire in his 'para bag' and used that to fix up the chute. Then he checked his gun and got it firing satisfactorily. Meanwhile, Sergeant Hoganson, the right waist gunner, was having problems of his own. The chute fitted on his gun all right, but the apparatus that kept the gun steady while firing came off in his hand. Odell had a precious spool of nylon cord, the first he had ever been able to acquire. He used this to bind up the contraption as firmly as possible. By this time Odell was in an ugly mood, cursing the lousy job done by armourers when supposedly preparing an aircraft for a raid. He was relieving his frustration by swinging his gun around with considerable violence when, all of a sudden, he knocked his front sight off. To top it all, just as 'Ford's Folly' crossed the Belgian coast, the motor operating the hydraulics for the tail turret caught fire and burned out. This put the most effective gun position out of action. Odell was shocked by this latest mishap. If all this could happen to the guns, he mused unhappily, what about the state of everything else connected with this wreck of an airplane? The motors themselves sounded pretty rough to him.

As they flew over the Ardennes, Odell knew they would soon be swinging north, heading up towards Hanover. He was sitting on one of his 'personal bombs', an empty ammunition box. He usually carried one or two of these heavy wooden containers to chuck out over the target. As he stared out of his open gun position, he realized they were stationed in one of the most vulnerable sections – lower left squadron, with only 'Tail-end Charlie' behind them.

Suddenly someone yelled 'Fighters'. They were all around, ME109s – the sky seemed to be black with them. Odell fired at one enemy plane. It broke away right under the Liberator, so close he could see the German in his cockpit. The enemy pilot was wily enough not to finish up on the bomber's tail, where the gunner would normally have the best shot at him. Tail gunners had no worries about deflection; they just laid the sight on the fighter's nose and blazed away. Their attacker was not to know Sergeant Place was sitting impotently behind his guns, the tail turret useless.

The Messerschmidts kept coming in on a pursuit curve. They started their attack about three or four thousand feet ahead and a thousand feet above, then rolled over and started firing as they closed in. Odell thought he had hit the next ME109 that came in. As the fighter broke away it was trailing thick black smoke and he felt sure it was going down. Then he recalled being told about the synthetic fuel the Germans were using, apparently made from coal and God knows what. When their pilots hit the throttles for maximum power while breaking away it was no wonder they made smoke with that stuff in the cylinders.

'Hoggy', the other waist gunner, was doing well. He exploded an attacking fighter and punched Odell on the shoulder to look round and see it so he could verify it later at squadron interrogation. Odell had already seen him blow another one out of the sky just a few seconds earlier.

The next one looked as if it was coming straight for Odell; the yellow nose cone was pointing directly at him. This time he was certain his shells had smashed home; the fighter was burning all along the wings. Odell waited for the enemy to explode. Then, as it came in closer, he realized that the flames were only flashes from the ME109's wing guns as it fired at him. Next moment a 20mm shell, maybe from the gun in that yellow nose cone, hit Odell's gun and exploded. Most of the white-hot metal fragments hit him in the chest, but one piece struck him clean between the eyes. It cut through his hard rubber goggle frame and entered his head right at the top of his nose. The force of the explosion knocked him down on the deck. Although he did not know it at the time, the shell had smashed both his legs. Everything went black. He could not see, but was still aware of what was going on. Over his headphones he was conscious of Spencer, the bombardier, telling Rudd that he should salvo the bombs to lighten the aircraft, because by that time both motors on the right wing were out of action; no 3 was feathered, while no 4 was windmilling and burning. Try as they could, they were unable to get the prop to feather completely on no 4.

Every few moments Odell heard someone on the interphone yell out, 'More fighters coming in!' In fact there was a continuous babble of voices and Hoggy said several times, 'Dobby's been hit. Dobby's been hit.' Then Dawson, the navigator, cut in: 'Get off the damned interphone, Hoganson'. He wanted everyone to be quiet so no essential orders would be missed. Unknown to Odell, Mainard, the upper-turret gunner, had been hit and possibly killed in the first fighter attack. His canopy was shot away and Roger Clapp, the radio operator, saw him slump forward and then slither out of his turret, down onto the floor below. Roger put Mainard's head in his lap and tried to put a bandage over a gaping hole in his skull, but the gunner never spoke, or even opened his eyes.

The situation was more than desperate – two engines knocked out and only Hoganson's waist gun still firing. Odell could not figure out how Hoggy kept going the way he did. After a while, Odell was able to see out of his right eye. There was blood running out of his head and dripping into the severed half of his goggles dangling on his left cheek. He tried to raise himself up, but did not get very far. Hoggy was still firing, but then he was hit and fell down on top of Odell. He struggled back up, holding on to his shoulder, turned round and tried to charge Odell's gun to get it firing again, but it had been completely knocked out in the explosion. Then Odell watched Hoggy swing back to his own gun and fire at another fighter: he hit it for sure. In a moment Hoggy was struck again and collapsed onto Odell a second time. Incredibly, he got back up. His oxygen mask was hanging off and blood was pouring down his face. He fired at the plane he had just hit as it dived past the Liberator's right wing. The Messerschmidt was burning from its wing roots all the way back past the cockpit. It was heading straight down to earth. Then a 20mm shell hit Hoggy in the head and he fell down for a third time. He did not get up after that. Odell could see the flames streaming out of no 4 motor. He was sure the bomber was going to blow any second. Struggling out of his flak suit, he clipped on his parachute and crawled to the camera hatch which he managed to open. Lying close to the opening Odell prayed that, if the airplane exploded, he would be blown clear. Still connected to the interphone, he heard Rudd, his Captain, saying: 'Hang on boys. I'm going to hit the deck.'

As they started to descend, Odell guessed they were around 27,000 feet. The big bomber was diving steeply, when, for some reason he could not understand, 'Ford's Folly' began to climb at an acute angle. It stalled with all the power coming from the two remaining motors on the left wing. It rolled over to the left and started spinning. The first two or three turns of the spin were fairly flat, but then it nosed over and began to go down fast with the flames streaming from the right wing. Odell knew that, if he were to get out at all, this was his last chance. The centrifugal forces were pinning him to the deck, but he managed to pull himself over the hatch. Just before the slipstream caught him and pulled him out, he had time to take one last look inside the aircraft. Back near the tail Place had climbed out of his tail turret and was sitting with his back to a bulkhead; his oxygen mask was off and blood streamed down his face. Hoggy was lying where he had fallen, his eyes glazed, but, as Odell looked at him, his friend half-raised his hand for a moment, then it fell back to his side. There was nothing that Odell could do to help. The next second he was gone.

Odell slowly moved his head from side to side, trying to break through the haze that kept blurring his consciousness like mist on a mirror. To say that he was *in* pain suggests suffering in a certain area of his body, a concentration of hurting in one place, but it was not like that. Pain emanated from so many parts of him that his body was *all* pain – pain that stifled coherent thought and inhibited action. His whole body was a throbbing, pulsating mass of agony. His right eye fell open involuntarily. His gaze drew in his immediate surroundings as though viewed through a gunsight – objectively, detached. He was in a small, dimly-lit room with dull green paint on the walls. What light there was came from a window high up in the wall above his head. It had rusty iron bars inserted vertically on the outside of the dirty panes of glass. He was in a cell, but not a locked cell. He turned his head to the right; a heavy wooden door with a small metal grill stood wide open. He had a restricted view of the passage beyond. Vaguely he discerned voices coming from the office he knew was located on the other side of the corridor. Opposite, over in the left-hand corner of the cell, was a low narrow doorway, with stone steps leading down into utter darkness and only God knew where. With a sudden chill of fear, he remembered how they had first brought him in here. Half-carrying, half-shoving, they had thrust him into this cell. Then, as he stood there bewildered, the big man with the high-pitched voice had suddenly hurled himself at Odell, projecting him straight into the doorway above the stone stairs. He had looked down into the darkness below and experienced one of those rare moments in life when only one decision is possible. Smashed, crippled and weakened as he was, he knew he had to summon all his remaining strength for the desperate struggle to keep out of that black hole. He put up his hands and gripped the doorposts on either side of him. He hung on with the wild determination of a man who had no alternative as the big man tried to push his prisoner down those steps. Odell's great fear was that his mutilated legs would again collapse under him, as they had done many times while his captors had been bringing him here. If that happened now, he would fold into a helpless heap and roll down those steps to meet whatever fate his attacker had in mind for him. In the event other things intervened to save him. The smallness of the opening in relation to his own size was one thing. His 6 feet 1½ inch frame, padded out with bulky flying kit, had certainly slowed down his assailant's efforts to force him through the confined space. More conclusively, one of the other men had come back into the cell. Why this made any difference to the situation, Odell had no idea. All he knew was that there had been a muffled conversation behind his back, then the two men left.

Now he was sitting on a wooden bench, the daylight filtering down through the dirty glass. His head was slumped on his chest, but he kept his right eye open. He studied his knees, covered in the green canvas of his flying-suit; he looked beyond his knees to his feet. One foot wore a flying boot, while the other seemed to be covered in a sock, but he could not be sure. With complete detachment, as though those feet had nothing to do with him, he noted that they both stood in puddles of coagulating blood. With almost academic detachment, he decided that those puddles looked jellified. Maybe it was time to release some new blood over them and freshen them up a little. Slowly and carefully, in great pain, he slumped further forward until his head was almost resting on his knees. He gently pushed up his left trouser leg, exposing a crudely tied tourniquet encircling his leg below the knee. Carefully he untied the knot and loosened the bandage. To his satisfaction fresh blood began to flow over his foot and drip down on to the puddle. He was aware that at least two-thirds of his shin was missing. After a few moments he retightened the tourniquet and turned his attention to the other leg, this time releasing pressure over an area of torn flesh above his right knee. More blood coursed down his leg and ran into his surviving flying boot, now squelchy with gore. After replacing his scarf which served as a tourniquet on this leg, without haste he pulled down the zip on his flying jacket. He wanted to inspect a part of his body he had been unable to examine earlier. Putting his hand inside his shirt he cautiously felt his ribs. As his fingers moved down over the right side of his chest, he felt them sink into a mass of soft, broken flesh. He could see that his shirt was torn and stained in blood. He withdrew his hand and examined it without emotion. He recalled the first time when, as a boy, he had shot a rabbit. After returning home with his prize, he had proudly skinned and gutted the animal in his mother's kitchen. When he had finished his messy work, his fingers were stained red. They had looked the same then as they did now. He knew he should check the condition of his head. Blood had been running down his face and he remembered how, earlier that day, he had felt blood trickling into his broken goggles as they dangled on his left cheek, below his sightless eye. He had been worried about that eye. Why was it all sealed up? Was it damaged beyond repair? But he was weaker now. He had taxed himself heavily, easing and adjusting his tourniquets. Pain was gaining mastery over him and, although his head was slumped so low, he lacked the will to raise his hands to his face. His arms were hanging down beside his legs, while his bloodstained fingers rested lightly on the floor of his cell. He drifted away into semi-consciousness where he hung in a limbo of suffering.

Just over three hours ago Staff Sergeant Odell Dobson of the 392nd Bombardment Group of the USAAF had been viewing the ground below him as he hung from his parachute, convinced that he was suspended up there in the clear September sky, neither ascending nor descending, but swayed by the illusion that the little German town of Treis was rushing up to meet him. He figured he had done reasonably well so far. Having been sucked feet first through the camera hatch, he had rolled and tumbled through the thin air. He had not forgotten his drill. He waved his arms above his head, as advised in the Instruction Manual: 'This will straighten you out and ensure that you fall feet first. If you fail to do this and pull your ripcord while you are tumbling, there is a danger that you could roll up in the canopy before the parachute has a chance to open.' Odell also remembered what his Squadron Commander had said: 'If you bail out when there is a lot of shooting going on, you shouldn't pop your ripcord while you're up high – it's just possible you could get yourself shot.' That morning there had been enough shooting going on to jog Odell's memory on that score. So he went on falling for as long as he dared and only pulled hard on the metal release handle when he felt himself in danger of passing out. He heard a sound like a bell ringing and imagined it was the noise made by the pilot chute as it left the pack. Then he lost consciousness. When he came round, he looked up and was immediately filled with a feeling of sweet relief – the white canopy billowed above him. He even noticed there were some words printed in blue round the edge of the chute. He guessed he was now about 12,000 feet above the earth. In a detached state he looked on as aircraft were shot out of the sky, both bombers and fighters. One fighter, he did not know whether it was American or German, fell through the air in a manner he had never seen before. At one moment its nose was pointed towards the ground and the next instant the tail was headed straight down, and so it tumbled, end over end, and never spun once in the usual way. One of the big four-engined B24s was going down. It could have been 'Ford's Folly'. He had no means of telling. With smoke and flame trailing from the starboard wing, it disappeared over a hill and hit the ground somewhere beyond his field of vision. It seemed to him that all around there were funeral pyres of burning aircraft.

He was bitterly regretting one thing he had failed to carry out according to the book. His parachute harness had not been adjusted so that it fitted snugly to his body. As a waist gunner he spent hours on missions standing at the open side-window of his bomber. Tight, restricting straps under his crutch were no aid to comfort in such conditions. Habitually he flew with the leg straps dangling around his knees and today was no exception. Now, with the pull of the chute, he had settled ever more deeply into the harness; the chest strap had risen until it was pressing against his chin. He speculated that, if the harness had had an inch or two more slack, the strap that was causing him so much discomfort could well have broken his neck, or even ripped his head clean off when the chute jerked open. As it was, although he could glance upwards, or sideways, he had the greatest difficulty in looking down, which, right then, was the most crucial direction. He had noticed that his left flying boot was missing and that blood was dripping from his foot. Yet he could wriggle his toes and move his legs, which brought him comfort. He was more or less certain he had got away with only a few cuts and scratches, at least as far as his legs were concerned. More seriously, for some reason he was unable to see out of his left eye. He moved his hand over his face. It was caked in blood and fresh blood was oozing from somewhere above his eyebrow. As far as he could tell the eyeball was still intact, but at that moment he was hardly in the best position to carry out a proper examination. He knew he had been hit in the head, but was unsure what damage had been done.

The little town was rushing up towards him at a tremendous pace. As he swivelled his right eye sideways, he could see several people in the streets looking up at him, like toy figures in a model village. Then he had drifted past the houses and was sailing fast over a small wood. All the stories he had heard about flyers making successful jumps from aircraft, only to finish their descent tangled upside down in trees, impaled on stakes, drowned in reservoirs, or electrocuted against high-tension power lines, came rushing into his mind. But then the trees were behind him and he saw with relief that he was going to land in an open field.

A man was guiding a plough drawn by an ox, while a woman encouraged the beast with a switch. For a moment he thought he was going to land right on top of the ox, but he skimmed over the group and touched down in soft, sandy soil about a hundred yards further on. He made such a gentle impact on enemy territory that he was dragged less than his own length. He immediately released the chest lock of his parachute harness, threw the straps off his shoulders, stepped out of the webbing, left the chute lying on the ground and, determined if possible to avoid capture, started running. He ran eight or ten paces and fell down. He got to his feet, staggered a few more feet and fell again. He made two or three further attempts to struggle across the field, but it was no use and he finally collapsed, unable to rise any more. At first he thought it was because of the uneven ploughed ground, but now he was not so sure. A dreadful alternative had occurred to him – a disturbing possibility that there could be something wrong with his legs. He apprehensively rolled up his trouser legs and saw the truth at once - he was not going anywhere under his own power. Fear, frustration and a sickening sense of anti-climax overcame him as he looked at the gory, mangled mess. It hardly needed close inspection to see that a large part of his left shin had been shot away. Shrapnel had torn through the flesh of his other leg higher up, but seemed to have missed his kneecap. All in all it was remarkable that he had managed to take even those few erratic steps on landing. It was a lonely experience sitting there between those soft, sandy furrows. Only minutes before he had been flying in a bomber, absorbed in the job he had been trained to do, surrounded by the men who shared his perilous way of life. Then disaster had struck with overwhelming suddenness, and now, as far as he knew, he was the only survivor from the crew of 'Ford's Folly', crippled and alone in hostile territory.

He raised his good eye to seek out the man and woman who had been ploughing the field. There was no sign of the woman. The farmer had moved over to a wagon piled with substantial-looking stakes. It stood in a sunken track lying below the level of the field. As he watched, the man selected one of the biggest stakes and then, holding it lance-like, started charging towards Odell as though the future of the Third Reich depended on him alone. 'Just like they told us,' he thought grimly. He had heard hair-raising accounts of what had happened to some allied flyers after they had fallen into the hands of vengeful German civilians. Not a few had been beaten with sticks or jabbed with pitchforks. Hysterical villagers had caught men from an RAF bomber crew and strung them up by wire from telegraph poles. Some American flyers, lying helpless and injured near a town called Furzheim, had had petrol poured over them and were then set on fire. If circumstances made it impossible to evade capture, then allied aircrew were advised to put themselves in the hands of the military. It had been found that disciplined soldiers of the Wehrmacht generally behaved responsibly towards their prisoners, unlike some German civilians. All this went through Odell's mind as he drew his .45 from its shoulder holster, jacked a shell into the chamber and pointed the weapon at his would-be assailant. He figured his chances of survival were slim if the farmer really intended to drive the stake through him as he sat there helpless. The best he could do was take a shot at him and try to even the score.

The man kept on coming until he was no more than twenty-five feet away. Suddenly he stopped, his eyes staring wildly at Odell, who now realized for the first time that he was facing an old man. The farmer's eyesight must have been defective, because it was only at this last moment that he noticed Odell was holding a gun. Exhausted though he must have been, the old man swung round and headed back the way he had come with a speed that even exceeded his approach. He scrambled down onto the sunken road and disappeared below the bank. After a short time, his face reappeared over the edge, where it remained, staring across the field at Odell. He knew that people from the nearby town would soon come pounding into the field. He pictured the old man excitedly gesticulating towards the 'enemy', warning them to keep their heads down, because the swine was armed and dangerous. If one of them also had a gun, he could shoot Odell like a winged partridge sitting defenceless on open ground. Odell figured he had one slim chance. Somehow he had to persuade the old farmer that he meant him no harm and then surrender to him without delay. The immediate problem was communication. Like all allied flyers, he had been issued with a small phrasebook containing useful words and expressions in most West European languages, including, of course, German. Unfortunately he had left it in his bedside locker back in England. There was only one German word he could remember and, for better or worse, he decided he might as well use it. '*Kamerad!*' he shouted as loudly as he could. '*Kamerad!*' After an agonizing delay, Odell was surprised to see the old man rising slowly from his hiding-place. 'Maybe he's wondering if I am a friendly Hungarian flyer or something,' he thought. For good measure he called out again: '*Kamerad!*' The farmer was coming back across the field towards him. Slowly this time and, surprisingly, he had forgotten to bring his stake. To ease the old fellow's anxiety, Odell slipped his .45 inside his unzipped flying jacket.

'*Wer bist sie? Amerikanischer Flieger, nein?*' Odell got the message.

'Yes, I'm an American.'

His questioner decided to narrow it down: '*Kanadischer, nein?*'

'No,' said Odell, 'American, from the United States. You were right first time.'

During this brief exchange the old man had moved round to Odell's blind side. With a deftness that belied his years, he reached into Odell's jacket and removed his pistol. Then he gripped the collar of the flying jacket with the same hand that held the gun. Odell could feel the barrel pressing against the back of his head. The farmer was babbling away excitedly and tugging at the fur collar. Odell had no idea what he was trying to do, or how he could calm him down, but he knew he was in real danger of being shot with his own weapon; it was cocked and had one in the chamber. The way the old man was jumping around, it would have been the easiest thing in the world for the gun to have gone off, killing either the farmer or his captive. Whichever way, the future looked bleak. Then it dawned on him what the old man was trying to do. He was attempting to remove his flying jacket. Unzipping it, Odell managed to struggle out of it with some difficulty and a great deal of pain. At once the man gripped his shoulder-holster and pulled it over his head.

Surrender had been accomplished. As Odell had anticipated, it was none too soon. Within a few minutes the mob arrived. A group of between fifteen and twenty people, mostly men, surrounded him. Odell could not help noticing one particularly large man who looked about forty. He was dressed in a gamekeeper's jacket, dark-coloured breeches and jackboots. His big florid face incongruously sported a tiny Hitler moustache. His hands were unusually large. He kept gesticulating wildly, thrusting his enormous fist within inches of Odell's face and yelling angrily: '*Terrorflieger! Terrorflieger! Töte ihn, Töte den Mischling!*' Although expressed in German, Odell understood the mood behind the words only too well. The huge German filled him with apprehension.

Odell slumped to the ground, a pitiful broken heap of bloodstained misery, while the locals jabbered incessantly. At last a decision was reached – they took the ox from the plough and harnessed it to the wagon. The big man was shouting at Odell again, ordering him to his feet. It made no difference that his victim was, for obvious reasons, quite incapable of complying with this order. Realizing that his instructions were not going to be obeyed by this arrogant American swine, the fellow stood over him, quivering with rage. Suddenly, he bent down, grabbed Odell roughly under the arms and hauled him to his feet. Before he could protest, the man had spun him round and shoved him hard in the direction of the cart. In agony Odell tottered a few short steps before collapsing with a groan into a ploughed furrow. Again he was dragged upright, again shoved forward and again he limped a foot or two, then fell heavily once more into the earth. Twice more this torture was inflicted on him. Each time the big man pulled him up, Odell was convinced that what little was left of his shin was about to snap under his weight. They were still some distance from the wagon and Odell felt sure that if this treatment continued he would never reach it in one piece. The big man was about to jerk him on to his feet yet again when a new voice broke into the proceedings. A young man in uniform had arrived on the scene. Though no more than a lad, he spoke with indisputable authority. '*Lass den Mann allein,*' he barked at Odell's tormentor. To Odell's surprise the big man moved away without a word and he was left lying on the ground, covered in soil and dirt. He knew he had to have medical attention soon if he were to survive, yet no one in the crowd seemed to share his anxiety. They did show some curiosity when he broke open his emergency medical kit, extracting the tourniquet and tying it, as best he could, above the wound on his left leg. Then he removed his white silk flying scarf and fastened it as tightly as possible above the right knee. He was aware that dirt must have got into his wounds, particularly those in his head, which had hit the ground every time he had fallen. He drew another bandage from the pack and was trying to tie this round his head and across his forehead when a strange thing happened. An attractive girl, aged about twenty, with blonde hair, detached herself from the mob. She squatted beside him and gently helped him adjust his bandage. As he stared at her, his left eye suddenly popped open. His vision was unimpaired. Then, with the lad in uniform on one side and the girl on the other, they carried him to the wagon. Someone threw his parachute alongside him. He drew it over his legs to protect himself from the flies that were now swarming round his wounds. He was bumped and jolted to the nearby town of Treis, which lay about fifteen miles south-west of Coblenz. He was taken to the Burgomaster's office and then pushed into the adjoining cell. It was here that he resisted attempts of the bully to force him down the steps.

Odell was thinking about his small phial of morphine. All aircrew were issued with these pain-killing devices for use in emergencies. It was still there in his first-aid kit. Back on the squadron they used to say: 'If you get hit and there's no medical attention, there's a danger you may go into shock, brought on by pain and loss of blood.' Then the medics told them: 'You should wait until you reach a point where you think it is impossible to bear the pain from your wounds one moment longer. Do nothing at this stage, but allow at least another two hours to pass before injecting yourself with morphine!' Strangely enough, these harsh instructions did not bother Odell. For hours he had suffered almost unbearable agony. Yet in spite of this, he still retained an irrational horror of jabbing a needle into himself. He looked at his watch – it was 4 o'clock. He would wait another two hours.

He gently ran his fingers over the area of his left eye. He dislodged some caked blood and it again flicked open. He concentrated his gaze on his parachute which lay in an untidy pile on the passage floor outside his cell. Through the open door he could see a pigtailed schoolgirl holding part of the canopy in her hands. She was admiring the quality of the material. In wartime Germany such fine silk would be unknown to a child. Odell watched as she held the shroud to her cheek. Recollections of another instruction came to his mind: 'Allied flyers should do their best to destroy their parachutes if they come down in enemy territory'. At that time Luftwaffe aircrew were issued with inferior chutes manufactured from broadcloth. Morale naturally perked up if a captured RAF or USAAF model happened to come their way. Softly he called to the girl. She looked at him shyly, but with no sign of fear. This time Odell overcame the communication problem by smiling and making a scissors motion with his fingers. She understood at once and scampered away along the corridor. Soon she returned with a large pair of tailor's scissors and, after another inquiring glance at her benefactor, who nodded encouragingly, she started cutting away with a will. Carried away by visions of new dresses and underwear, she soon reduced the main panels of the canopy to manageable pieces. Odell looked on with approval as he saw the chute being destroyed beyond repair.

He was not prepared for what happened next. He heard the door of the office open on the other side of the corridor and then the sound of heavy footsteps coming towards them. The big man gazed down at the busy little *fräulein*. For a second or two he failed to take in the significance of what she was doing. Then he exploded: '*Der Fallschirm! Gott in Himmel!*' Startled by his voice, the girl looked up, terrified by the expression of uncontrollable anger on the man's face. His voice rose to a scream as he stamped his booted feet on the bare floorboards and let forth a torrent of invective. The girl began to cry, but the sight of her tears seemed to enrage the man even more. Slumped helplessly in his cell, Odell was horrified to see him draw back his huge fist and smash it with such force against the girl's body that she was sent hurtling along the passage and out of his line of vision. To Odell this was the outrageous act of a callous and cowardly man. He was astounded to learn later that the man was the girl's father.

This incident cast him into even deeper depression. In between lapses into semi-consciousness, he somehow found the will to attend to his tourniquets at regular intervals, determined to look after himself, however long the Germans chose to neglect him. He had lost so much blood, his mouth was parched. Thoughts of the soda fountain at his favourite drug store back home began to fill his mind. Fantasizing about long cool drinks, his imagination lingered sensually over the memory of their taste. But soon his thoughts came back to reality, his swollen tongue a cruel reminder that his captors had not even had the humanity to give him a drink of water. He felt in his pocket – it contained a Mars bar and a packet of chewing gum. He decided to keep the chocolate for a future occasion. He was not hungry anyway. The chewing gum was a godsend. Popping a couple of strips in his mouth, he soon generated some saliva. But his body was in torment, his legs swelling steadily, his chest black from the bruising impact of the exploding shell. A splinter of steel was lodged against a rib, and more steel lay embedded in his head beneath the tightly knotted, bloody bandage. Waves of nausea swept over him. He was ill with pain. His inhibitions about using the needle faded. Now he longed for the relief morphine would bring. He looked at his watch – a little after five, one hour to go. The next sixty minutes seemed interminable. Barely one of those minutes passed without Odell suggesting to himself that this was the moment to carry out the injection. How could waiting for such a short time more make any difference? Surely, with the agony he was in, the instructions to delay did not apply? Yet still he hung on. At a little after 5.45 pm he heard voices in the corridor and the sound of footsteps coming and going. Thinking he detected the noise of some activity in the street outside, it occurred to him that the Germans might be preparing to move him somewhere else. Removing the phial of morphine from the first-aid pack, he held it in his hand. It was possible that, if the Germans discovered it, they might take it away. He would wait no longer. As he broke the protective shield over the needle, his body experienced chilling sensations. He was going into shock. Working as fast as he could, he depressed the plunger slightly and waited for the first drop of liquid to appear at the point of the needle. This would make sure no air bubbles entered the bloodstream. No liquid appeared. Odell pressed again. Still nothing. With growing alarm he pushed the plunger further and further until it reached its limit. There was no morphine. He crushed the tiny metal container between finger and thumb until it resembled a used toothpaste tube in miniature. The thing contained nothing but air. The anti-climax was almost too much to bear. Odell had screwed up his will and, defying pain, waited with fortitude for the relief he believed the morphine would bring. Now at the end of it all – nothing. Why was the phial empty? Who was to blame? Was it a lazy laboratory worker? A negligent inspector? Or could it possibly be a drug company deliberately defrauding the United States Government? Odell pictured sorely wounded American servicemen in every theatre of war jabbing themselves with syringes labelled morphine and trusting their pain would soon subside. He thought about the effect of air being pumped into a man's veins and swore to himself that, if ever he got back to his country, he would raise hell at the highest level. Maybe he had just been unlucky. Maybe he was the only man on earth ever to receive an empty phial of morphine. Either way his thoughts were no comfort to him and his physical agony was as real as ever.

About 7 o'clock that evening they took Odell into the street and loaded him on to a faggot cart. With two youngsters pulling, he was wheeled through the small town, accompanied by a policeman in a green uniform and an older civilian who carried a rifle. The policeman had taken Odell's watch and his cigarette lighter – he also carried his .45 in its holster slung over his shoulder. Many Germans lined the route. He must have looked a poor sight lying on that cart, begrimed with dirt and caked in blood, with his trouser legs rolled above his knees exposing his unattended wounds. The flies pestered him unremittingly. Among the onlookers, the women were more voluble than the men. Shrill voices hurled abuse, while their sharp, pointed gestures left him in no doubt as to the fierceness of their hatred. The men, for the most part, watched stoically, their faces betraying little of their feelings. Yet Odell thought he caught a glimmer of sympathy in the eyes of one or two of the older fellows. The faggot cart came to a stop outside the railway station. People surrounded him, chattering and pointing. Looking over their heads he could see a three- or four-storey factory on the other side of the station yard. Workers were leaning out of the windows staring across at him. In spite of his situation, he had the satisfaction of thinking that he was helping to slow down the enemy's war production. (It was disappointing to learn later that the company only manufactured cigars!) On the move again, the cart was bounced and bumped across the tracks in order to reach a train which had drawn up at the furthest platform. Progress was so violent that Odell expected to be thrown from the cart and onto the cinders. His swollen legs were excruciatingly painful. He had had more than enough of this ride. From his prone position he was unable to see who was manoeuvring the cart across the rails, but he figured it was still being dragged by the two lads who had wheeled him through the town.

Raising himself on one elbow, he turned his head to shout in protest at the erratic handling of the cart. 'How you doing there, Dobby?' Odell stared in blank amazement. The words were spoken in a warm friendly American drawl. It was the voice of Roger Clapp, his radio operator. A dozen questions sprang to his mind, but the policeman was prodding Roger to get on with pulling the handcart. On reaching the train Odell was lifted into a bare compartment with wooden slatted seats. Roger sat down opposite him, while the old man with the rifle stationed himself in the far corner. The policeman stood out in the corridor, still wearing Odell's .45 slung from his shoulder. As the train pulled away from the station, Odell looked across at his crewmate. Roger had always been something of a character; the extrovert swashbuckler of the crew, he enjoyed striking poses. He was also one for speaking out. 'No pussy-footing around,' he used to say.

Odell recalled what Roger had said just before they had taken off: 'We are taking off on mission 13 and this is the one where we go down.' Roger had often spoken of putting up a fight if he was ever shot down. He had cut his holster off its shoulder-straps and mounted it on a gun belt. He wore it with his pistol tied round his leg and slung low like a cowboy. An old First World War trench knife, with brass knuckles on the hilt, was stuck in his belt. There were always eight or ten clips of .45 ammunition distributed about his body. For his personal pleasure, he carried a full canteen of Webster's cigars and a supply of Old Gold cigarettes. Roger was at all times prepared for the worst. As he looked at him now, Odell was shaken to see the change in his friend's appearance. He could tell at a glance that his arms and equipment had all gone. Gone too was the cocky assurance, the jaunty air of confidence. Roger was at least as filthy and bedraggled as Odell himself. His forehead was red and raw and most of the skin was missing. His hair, which he normally wore well over regulation length and carefully combed, had been crudely hacked away. There were a few knotted tufts sticking out from his head at angles.

In spite of his pain, Odell was hungry for information. Roger told him how he had survived all the fighter attacks without being injured and then parachuted to earth successfully. After that his luck ran out. A bunch of civilians jumped him as he touched down and he made them doubly angry by trying to fight back. They frog-marched him, kicking and struggling, to a spot near the station yard. Here they gave him a real going over, knocking him down and putting the boot in hard. Roger said that, as he lay there, someone sat astride his shoulders and cut off his hair – not with scissors, just grabbed hold of it in bunches and sawed it off with a knife. When he thought they had finished with him, he sat up and called them everything under the sun. Yelling that they were cowardly sons of bitches, he offered to take them on, one at a time. Although they did not understand a word he was saying, Roger guessed they had got the message. Then a big man in jackboots pushed his way through the crowd, strode up to him and kicked him straight in the crutch. They dragged him to his feet and forced him over to a brick wall. Roger stood facing the wall, wondering what was coming next. The big man caught hold of his head with one hand and the collar of his flying jacket with the other and bashed his captive's face into the wall and went on bashing and bashing. Roger could do little more than keep his chin down and take most of it on his forehead. He was sure his brains would burst out of his skull. Mercifully in the end he blacked out. When he came round he was lying on the floor of a small railroad hut. His head was throbbing like a steam engine. Later some men came in and dragged him over to the station. There they pointed to a cart with some sort of bundle dumped on it and motioned him to pull it. 'Can you imagine the shock I had, Dobby, when I saw it was you lying there, all covered in blood?'

While Roger had been talking, Odell's eyes had wandered towards the corridor. The policeman was in intimate conversation with the train conductress. It occurred to Odell that this particular official was not very interested in prisoners of war at that moment. He knew he had guessed right when the policeman, patting the buxom lady on the bottom, led her out of sight down the corridor. Odell went on talking in the same tone of voice. He told Roger that the policeman had just made himself scarce, was likely to be occupied for some time and this was his best chance to slip away. He explained that he intended sliding his escape kit across to him while the old fellow in the corner was looking away. Odell would open the carriage door for Roger because the handle was on his side. Then Odell would roll sideways and fall on top of the old Hun, while Roger jumped out of the train and made his escape. Looking out of the corner of his eye, Odell could see that the old man had no idea what had just been said. He looked down at his bloody legs, knowing he had no hope of jumping the train with Roger, yet glad at least that his friend could make the break. But his radio operator showed no enthusiasm for the plan. His spirit had been beaten out of him. He was weary now, almost beyond words. With a faint shrug of resignation he reminded Odell that all his gear had been taken. Without it he would have no chance. All he wanted to do was crash down somewhere and get some sleep. Odell felt a pang of frustration. It had seemed such a good opportunity, one that might never occur again. But then, looking at Roger, he could see what a rough state he was in. Poor old Roger, maybe he was right. Perhaps he didn't stand a chance. Things being as they were, Odell in no way blamed him for not going. Slowly he slipped his escape kit back into the breast pocket of his flying-suit. It was specially designed to make detection difficult – its perspex case curved to fit his body was less than an inch thick. Yet it contained no less than 5000 dollars, in various European currency notes – all superbly counter-feited. Then there were halizone water-purifying tablets and tablets of high energy benzedrine – known in the RAF as 'wakey wakey' pills. The contents also included maps printed on silk, a tiny compass, fish hooks, a length of nylon cord, a miniature razor and small blocks of concentrated chocolate. 'Oh well,' mused Odell, 'I figure maybe it'll come in useful later on.'

Two hours later the train clanked into Giessen, a town about sixty miles north-east of Treis. The Germans bundled Odell and Roger out onto the platform. People waiting for trains crowded round, studying them with idle curiosity. Odell still had some cigarettes; he took one out and lit it with a match as he sat there on the platform. He managed one deep inhalation before the guard knocked it out of his mouth. The cigarette lay smouldering on the ground. Odell stretched out his hand to retrieve it, but the German got there first. Putting his boot on the cigarette and taking his time, he deliberately crushed it under his heel. Odell slumped down to await events. He did not have to wait long. Lifted up bodily by several men, he was carried into a large bunker under the railway station. Just before they went through the entrance, Odell looked back to see if Roger was following, but there was no sign of him. The bunker was dimly lit by electricity. The walls were bare concrete and the place smelt of unwashed bodies. They propped him on a chair and wrapped his wounds in some white crêpe paper bandages. In half an hour he was out of the place and on his way through the town. This time he was in a wheelchair, pushed by the green-uniformed policeman and a nurse. The town of Giessen was larger than Treis. He had no way of knowing how long this journey through the streets would last, or where they were taking him, although, because the nurse was there, he assumed they were on their way to hospital. Fumbling in his pocket, he fished out another cigarette. This time he had no chance even to light it before the policeman pulled it from between his lips with a curt 'Rauchen verboten!'. Odell put his hand to his head and tried to run his fingers through his hair, but it was matted and congealed with blood. He still had no way of knowing how badly his head had been damaged. This time it was the nurse's turn. She dragged his hand away, then wagged her finger at him sternly. Defiantly, he pulled out his Mars bar and took a generous bite. This time they did not interfere with him and he finished the chocolate in peace.

They pushed him up a broad cobbled road which climbed steadily until they reached a large building with an imposing entrance. It reminded him of an Odeon cinema he had once seen in a London suburb when on leave. The trio trundled into the marble-pillared reception area where huge statues of godlike creatures stared disdainfully down at them. Odell did not like the place one little bit. White-coated men and women hurried about their business and paid no attention to the bedraggled prisoner in the wheelchair. But at least he had been brought to a hospital and now at last he would be getting some proper medical care. If he had known what terrifying experience lay in wait for him, he would have spun his wheelchair round there and then, propelled himself out of the entrance and rattled hell for leather down the cobbled hill. But of course he did not know what was in store and that was just as well.

He was wheeled down a long, broad corridor, then swung to the right through double swing-doors. His escort left him in a large bare room. Bright lights flooded down onto five tables, set out in a row as if prepared for a CO's inspection. The tables were covered with red rubber sheets and Odell noticed that broad black leather straps hung down from the sides of each table. An officer of the Wehrmacht army medical corps hurried into the room and started busying himself setting out instruments on a metal tray. Odell was impressed with his systematic approach and, watching him, his spirits rose a little. A nurse, followed by a medical corporal, arrived on the scene. The nurse was young, with dark hair and unusually large brown eyes. Her appearance would have raised Odell's morale still further, had his favourable reaction not been crushed by the sight of her companion. The corporal was the ugliest man Odell had ever seen. Of medium height and unusually broad, his body was lumpy, as though his uniform had been stuffed with wadding. His arms were so long, they looked as though they had once belonged to someone else, yet his fingers, covered in black hair below the knuckles, were thick and stubby. But it was the man's face that Odell detested on sight. Small black eyes, sunk into folds of white skin, were without a hint of expression. When he smiled, his top lip curled up until it almost touched his stunted nose – and he was smiling then, as he and the nurse walked into the room, displaying an unnatural expanse of wet, red gums above stumpy yellow teeth. He stood in front of Odell for a moment, eyeing him closely, studying him from head to foot. Odell, still in his torn flying gear, was hot, sweaty, covered in blood and filth and altogether uncomfortable. He had been gawped at, yelled at and prodded more than enough to last a lifetime. On top of all that, he was still in almost unbearable pain. 'Now,' he thought bitterly, 'to cap it all, there's this fellow.' What in the blazes was he staring at? Why was he grinning in that repulsive way? And what the hell had it got to do with him anyway?

The corporal nodded to the nurse and between them they lifted Odell up out of the chair and onto the middle table. What happened next was executed so quickly and with such practised dexterity that a moment passed before he grasped what they had done to him. They had strapped him to the operating table. The corporal had deftly secured the broad leather belt across his chest, while the nurse fixed two more straps over his legs, one above the knees, the other below. He was trapped. Odell's anger was now mixed with fear. Struggling to sit up, he only succeeded in hurting himself. A sharp pain shot across his ribs as he pressed upwards against the straps. The nurse spoke to him quietly, using a few words of English: 'Lie still. Do not struggle.' The whole thing was incredible. In the States he had always taken high medical standards for granted. The thought of a patient being placed on an operating table, fully clothed, unwashed and then pinioned, was beyond comprehension. Was this an example of German efficiency? Odell willed himself to relax. The doctor would be here any moment now. Then he would be given his injection and drift away into blissful oblivion. He turned his head and looked towards the officer working in the corner of the room. 'Why doesn't he hurry? Doesn't he realize how I'm suffering?' After what seemed an age, the medical officer finished what he was doing and came towards him. He spoke a few brief words to the corporal, then to Odell's consternation turned and walked out of the room.

Staring up at the corporal's disgusting face, he saw the wet, juicy smile switching on and off as though synchronized with the man's breathing. He noticed that the German was holding a pair of scissors in one hand and long slim tweezers in the other.

'So, Amerikaner, iss time to begin. No?' oozed the corporal. With a chilling shock, Odell realized the truth. It was this corporal, presumably with no proper medical qualifications, who was about to operate on him. His terror grew as it dawned on him that, while he lay there, helpless on that rubber sheet, he was about to be operated on without any anaesthetic. Even the normal precaution of an anti-tetanus shot was obviously out of the question. His body broke out in a cold sweat as the corporal, slowly and methodically began to cut deep into the raw flesh of his left leg. Straining against the straps with every muscle of his body, Odell ground his teeth together in a desperate effort to stop crying out in anguish. The young nurse was standing at the head of the table holding his shoulders. She spoke to him again, softly as before: 'Lie still. Lie still.' Then she took one of his hands and held it. Odell gripped that small hand as though it was his only link with life. All through that nightmare of cutting and probing, he never let go of her hand. Not once did he relax his hold when the corporal drew out the fuse of a

20mm shell embedded deep inside his left leg, or when he removed assorted pieces of flak from his right knee, or when he cut away the flesh on the right side of his body and extracted a jagged length of metal which had nestled against a rib; or even when the German probed into his forehead for another shell fragment, failed to pull it out, gave up and left it where it was.

When it was all over, Odell wearily raised his lids and gazed into the brown eyes looking down at him. By then he could not speak, but hoped the girl understood. Sometimes a man can say 'thank you' without using words. They left him alone then. For a while he lay shivering and cold, although the room must have been warm under the powerful lights. He opened his eyes after a while. This time he saw red gums and yellow teeth unpleasantly close to his face.

'Ello Amerikaner. No so gut, eh?'

'Get stuffed!' breathed Odell weakly. The corporal was in the middle of one of his sickening smiles. 'You like Germany? You like Hitler? You . . . ?' Odell could stand it no more. Somehow finding the strength, he raised his voice and yelled, 'Stuff Hitler! Stuff Germany! And stuff you!' The effort left him exhausted, but in a strange way reposed. He was vaguely aware that the corporal had disappeared.

He was not alone for long. Soon the medical officer was there. In precise English he said, 'Staff Sergeant, I would like you to understand that you are receiving exactly the same treatment as German soldiers with wounds similar to your own. You have only to look around this hospital to confirm that this is so. Furthermore, I strongly advise you that, as long as you are in our hands, you are very careful what you say about our country, or any of our leaders.' Then they wheeled him out of the 'operating theatre' and put him to bed in a little room. He remembered nothing more until the following day.

As the days passed at Giessen hospital, Odell gradually regained his strength. His wounds began to heal and there were no serious complications, although he would carry the scars of his injuries for the rest of his life. The daily diet was a new experience. The previously well-fed American found it hard to adjust to the meagre German wartime fare. He never discovered whether his share was similar to that doled out to other patients in the hospital, or if he was on a smaller allocation as a prisoner of war. On balance he felt he was given as much as anyone in that place, little as it was. That was during the early days of his confinement. Later on, when Red Cross food parcels began to arrive, he was able to supplement his meals with food far superior to that 'enjoyed' by the average citizen in Germany at the time. On his first morning in hospital, they brought him coffee, black bread, butter and jelly. He took one sip of the coffee – it was ersatz and awful – probably made from acorns and to the untrained palate quite undrinkable. He studied the 'wheatbread', spread some butter on it and a little of the jelly. The bread tasted sour. As time passed, this staple diet was to become all too familiar to him. To give bulk to the bread it was processed with sawdust. There were occasions when he discovered quite large splinters of wood embedded in slices of the stuff. The 'butter' was a form of grease made from tree sap. But, to be fair, Reichsmarshal Hermann Goering had warned the German people years before to accept 'guns before butter'. As a nation they had apparently agreed with this policy, so they had no one but themselves to blame.

He was interrogated by a succession of German officers, all keen to learn more about his bombardment group and squadron. He obliged them only with his name, rank and number. When they pressed him further, he parried them in a number of ways. Sometimes he pretended to misunderstand them and repeated his name very deliberately, spelling it out with aggravating slowness, then telling them his rank and number again and again at dictation speed. On other occasions he feigned extreme illness, lying back on his bed while making unintelligible grunts. After a while, when he became bored, he buried his head in the pillow and remained in that position until the Germans left, frustrated and defeated. One day a smartly uniformed *Stabsfeldwebel* (equivalent in rank to an American Warrant Officer, or British Sergeant-Major) came to his room. He wore a high peaked cap, well-fitting tunic and shiny jackboots. He seemed in no hurry to ask questions. Instead he introduced himself as Emil Muelle and said that he lived in a town called Butzbach, about twenty-five kilometres to the south, in the direction of Frankfurt. Odell, wondering if he was supposed to be impressed by this information, maintained an expression of studied indifference. The *Stabsfeldwebel* then enquired about his health. He wanted to know if there was anything he could do for him. Odell, taken by surprise, wondered if this were a new and more subtle style of interrogation. He decided that the man had to be watched carefully and adopted a bantering approach, suggesting that an airplane to fly him back to the States would be very welcome. The German looked amused, but protested that fulfilling such a request under existing circumstances might be difficult. Odell then tried him on a less ambitious plea: Muelle thought he could do something about that. As the *Stabsfeldwebel* walked towards the door, he turned and looked at Odell steadily. Quietly he said: 'This war is bad. It is bad for you, and bad for me also. We all suffer. Your country and mine, they suffer too. It is all so stupid.'

Odell was not overhopeful about the extra food. He figured that if any did turn up, almost certainly there would be strings attached: 'Tell us what we want to know, then you can eat as much as you wish'.

He was quite unprepared for the next visit. On the following day, good as his word, Muelle marched into his tiny ward, accompanied by a Colonel of the United States Army, two other American officers and a couple of German guards loaded down with packages. Colonel Stark explained that he was the Senior Allied Officer at Wettsler PoW Transit Camp, a short distance to the west of Giessen. He told Odell how the *Stabsfeldwebel* had come to the camp and arranged for him and the other officers to visit the hospital. They came bearing gifts – eleven Red Cross food parcels, each of which contained five packs of cigarettes, assorted food and bars of choco-late. A stack of books was dumped beside him on the bed. A new, neatly pressed and folded uniform was laid on his bedside locker. After the miseries of recent days, all this was sheer heaven. To hear American voices and to know that his fellow countrymen were near at hand sent his spirits soaring. Muelle tactfully withdrew, taking the two guards with him.

From Colonel Stark he learned that Allied troops had entered Germany. They had crossed the frontier in the Ardennes sector on the Belgium/Luxembourg border. The date that this had taken place was Monday, 11 September, the day that he had been shot down. At his request the American officers noted his sister's address; Frances Marie was now a nurse at Charlotte Hospital, North Carolina. Within their limited powers as prisoners of war, they promised to do their best to get a message through to the USAAF as quickly as possible, so she could be told that her brother was still alive.

Unknown to them the following telegram had already been sent by a Major-General J.A. Ulio:
Miss Frances M. Dobson, Mercy Nurses Home, Charlotte, North Carolina The Secretary of War desires me to express his deep regret that your brother, Staff Sergeant Odell Dobson has been reported missing in action since 11 September over Germany. If further details or other information are received you will be promptly notified.

24 September, 1944. Odell's sister had two further communications from the military authorities, neither of which was worded in a way likely to ease her anxiety. It was over a hundred days after receiving the first telegram that relief came. A telegram dated 4 January, 1945, read: 'Based on information received through the Provost Marshal General. Records of the War Depart-ment have been amended to show your brother S/Sgt Odell F. Dobson a prisoner of war of the German government. Any further information will be furnished to you . . . ' Four days later the first of Odell's postcards turned up, months after it was written. His short message gave an impression of well-being. He mentioned, almost as an afterthought, that he had been slightly wounded.

Colonel Stark assured Odell that he would arrange to come and see him again in the near future, bringing fresh supplies and keeping him up to date with the latest news. Odell's unfavourable first impression of the hospital was fading. It began to dawn on him that he was comparatively well off – far better than in a PoW camp. By experimenting in his room, he found he could now walk reasonably well, but in front of the nursing staff he always leaned heavily on his crutches and tottered about unsteadily. With returning health, he was beginning to formulate a plan of escape. The idea of getting out of Germany had never been far from his thoughts, even in his darkest moments. Compared with those unfortunate PoWs incarcerated behind barbed wire and guarded day and night by machine guns, he felt sure his own chances of evading his captors were much greater. He wanted to make the attempt while he still had this advantage and he could never be sure when the authorities might decide to move him to a less convenient place.

By now he had talked with Muelle on several occasions and had begun to understand why he was so anxious to help him. Apart from Muelle's complete disillusionment with the war and his conviction that the Nazi doctrine was evil, he also felt he owed a debt of gratitude to the Americans in general and United States flyers in particular. Muelle told Odell about his wife and baby son Roger, and how they lived with his mother-in-law in a three-storey house in Butzbach. One day his mother-in-law had been walking along a street in Butzbach wheeling the little boy in a pram when she heard the sound of strafing and an American fighter plane flew low over the rooftops. In that instant she was so frightened by the noise and the sight of the plane that she froze on the spot. She and the baby made a perfect target, isolated in the middle of the road. The pilot must have spotted her, because the firing stopped and, as the fighter flew overhead its wing dipped, enabling her to see the pilot as clearly as if he had been the driver of a passing car. Mesmerized, she watched as he raised his gauntleted hand, waved, then flew away, leaving them unharmed.

From that time on, Muelle had pledged himself to do whatever he could for American servicemen in captivity. This was no idle promise made during the emotion of the moment – he really meant it, even when it involved considerable risk to himself.

As if guessing what was in his mind, the *Stabsfeldwebel* suddenly asked an astonished Odell if he would like his help in assisting him to escape. Odell assured him that the thought of getting away was never out of his mind; but how could a German soldier possibly get involved in anything so dangerous? Emil brushed aside the question of risk, saying that he 'knew his way around' and immediately outlined his plan. Odell was to climb out of his window under cover of darkness and go round to the back of the hospital. Then he would have to walk down the hill to the railway and follow the tracks to Butzbach. It was a long way, but there was no alternative. Emil would be waiting there to take him to his house where he would be safe. He went on to explain that Butzbach was only a small place, with no industry of any wartime significance. This was the reason, he believed, why it had never been raided by British or American bombers. So Emil proposed that Odell should stay in his cellar which, although it had been designated as an air-raid shelter for a number of people, would probably never be used for that purpose. In the unlikely event of the town being attacked from the air, Emil would take Odell up and hide him in the house, until the 'all clear' sounded.

Odell could see the merits of this scheme. Lying low in his new hideaway for several days, he would be able to rest his legs for a while after his long trek. Once the hue and cry had died down and the heat was off, he could make for the allied lines and freedom. In his enthusiasm, he lost no time in arranging a meeting between Emil Muelle, Colonel Stark and himself to discuss the project in detail. As Senior Allied Officer, Colonel Stark was responsible for any escape ideas.

The Colonel listened as the two men revealed their plan. After they had finished, he lit his pipe and sat for a while in silence. Then he spoke: 'Right, this is how I see it. If you fellows had come to me with this escape idea five months ago, I am pretty sure I would have okayed it. I would have been glad to let you have whatever gear our escape committee could rustle up to help you get through. But now things have changed; the whole situation is different and I have to tell you I am sorry, but you can't go.'

Odell could not conceal his disappointment. 'But why, Colonel? I know I could make it. I'm not worried about the risks. With our armies getting so close, I could be out in a few days. Where's the problem, sir?'

'Well,' said the Colonel, 'in my opinion there are three good reasons why you shouldn't go and you've just come out with the first. Sure, our troops are close, coming closer every day. We've all heard the heavy artillery in the distance. What I say to you is this – why walk, when in a few weeks you will be able to ride? In less than a couple of months the war will be over.'

Colonel Stark was wrong in his estimate, of course, but neither he nor Odell, nor anyone engaged in the mighty forward thrust of the Allied forces could be blamed for thinking this was a reasonable assumption at that time. Who among them would have believed that more than half a year of bitter fighting still lay ahead?

'Now the second point is this,' the Colonel went on. 'You may not know it, but all this locality, which is in the Frankfurt region, is known as a "Death Area" for escaping prisoners. A short time ago an Englishman, supposedly an escapee, was caught with instructions and plans to sabotage various installations in this part of Germany. The Germans have now used this as an excuse to set up their "Death Areas", not only here, but in the vicinity of many large towns all over the country. So you see, Dobson, you could be in real danger of being shot on sight if you cut loose now.'

Odell was beginning to realize that the Colonel had some pretty strong arguments, although he was still not entirely convinced. After all, hadn't he parachuted down into this area and survived? Nobody had attempted to shoot him. Still, if he was really going to be able to ride out in a few weeks, what was the hustle?

Colonel Stark continued: 'I guess that you, Dobson, and a lot of other Americans owe a vote of thanks to our friend Emil Muelle here. He has done one hell of a lot to make our lives more comfortable. Which brings me to my third point. What kind of a "thank you" would it be if you put his life in jeopardy? Even worse, the lives of his family. Can you imagine what the Nazis would do to them if they were caught helping you?'

Muelle was about to interrupt the Colonel, but Odell broke in first: 'There's no answer to that. Of course you're right, sir. Mind you, I had given a lot of thought to the danger Emil would be in if he hid me, but he had more or less convinced me there was nothing to worry about.'

Colonel Stark had put his case and Odell knew that what he said made sense. He consoled himself with the thought that it was no great hardship waiting around for a few weeks until the American Army arrived to liberate him. In the meantime he would use all his cunning to make sure he stayed just where he was, at Giessen hospital.

The point which the Colonel had emphasized about Emil Muelle kept going through his mind. Odell's anxieties for his safety were now fully roused. The *Stabsfeldwebel* seemed to take such incredible risks on behalf of other people, almost as though in a small way he was trying to make amends for all the evil his country was inflicting on the world.

An incident that took place a few days after their discussion of the escape plan did nothing to calm his fears. Two American B17 Flying Fortress bombers collided over the town. A member of one of the crews who miraculously survived the disaster was brought into the hospital. He was a young flyer called Stratton, whose home was in California. He had managed to save himself by bailing out of the bombadier's escape hatch in the nose of the aircraft after the two planes had crashed into each other in midair. Because of the way his bomber was falling, he dropped straight into the propellor blades which sliced off both his knee caps. Later it was noticed that he had orange paint from the tips of the props on both legs of his flying-suit. Yet Stratton was a lot luckier than another flyer who jumped at the same time. He came down on the far side of the town and Emil Muelle went to get him. He found the boy badly injured lying in a street. But an SS man had arrived just before and refused to allow Emil to move him, or tend him in any way. The *Stabsfeldwebel* insisted that the lad had to have treatment as soon as possible, but the SS man shook his head. 'Then what are you going to do with him?' asked Muelle. 'This!' said the SS man, as he raised his gun and shot him dead. Odell heard from one of the hospital staff that Emil had put his own life in peril. After that incident he had expressed his feelings all too clearly for his own good, not only to the SS man, but to higher authority. He had raised such hell that he had become a positive embarrassment to those in power and his name was now prominent on the SS black list. Some of his friends in the medical profession had arranged for him to go into the hospital at Bad Nauheim, just south of his home town, under an assumed name.

It was a rough time in other ways for Emil Muelle. Early one morning he was in the bathroom of his house, shaving. Allied bombers were flying in the vicinity and as a precaution he had insisted that his family should go down into the cellar. Suddenly the only stick of bombs to fall on Butzbach throughout the entire war crashed down into their street, demolishing their home. Emil was saved by a heavy supporting beam which ran across the bathroom ceiling. Shaken, but uninjured, he clawed his way through the rubble, calling out to his family. His mother-in-law had come back into the house to collect a warm coat for her baby grandson. It was at that precise moment that the bombs dropped, killing her instantly. Emil's wife and baby Roger, who had remained in the cellar, were unharmed.

Muelle risked a final visit to Giessen to say goodbye to his American friend, and he explained what had happened, Odell found it difficult to speak, but he told Emil he had written a letter which he hoped might be of use to him, as a kind of passport, when the war was over. This is what it said:

To whom it may concern
The bearer of this paper has helped wounded American soldiers very much, he has been a wonderful friend. He has many times asked for better and more medical aid for the American soldiers in this town. He has risked much to bring us cigarettes and fruit. His wife has sent us candy, fruit and cigarettes. He brought news of the American, British and Russian advance, and has proven to be a wonderful friend. He has declared himself not to be a Nazi and dislikes all of this very much. I ask you, as an American soldier who has been helped by him that, when the war is over, his wife, his baby and himself be allowed safe conduct to his home in Butzbach.
I might add that I am an American flyer and he has offered to keep me in his cellar, rather than send me to a prison camp. Please help him and show him every consideration.
Signed: Staff/Sgt Odell F. Dobson. Army serial no 14101098. United States Army Air Force. October 13, 1944. Giessen, Germany.

Emil read the letter slowly, asking Odell the meaning of certain words and phrases. When he had finished, he folded it carefully and put it in his pocket. He held out his hand but said nothing. After he had gone, Odell reflected that the last thing he had expected to see in wartime Germany was a *Stabsfeldwebel* with tears in his eyes.

When Odell Dobson revisited Germany after the war, he went to see Emil Muelle. He was staggered to learn how many times his letter had come to his friend's rescue. Here is one example: after the war in Allied-occupied Germany, while speeding on the autobahn in a borrowed car, Emil Muelle was stopped by American military policemen. When asked why he was in such a hurry, he produced his letter and explained that he was on his way to Dachau. 'They are holding an enquiry there', Emil said, 'into the alleged shooting of an American flyer by an SS man in a street in Giessen. As the principal witness I am on my way to testify that this is the truth.' He was not detained.

It may have been coincidence, but with the departure of Emil Muelle from Giessen, Odell found that his days at the hospital were numbered. With little warning he was sent by train to Obermasfeld, about sixty-five miles further to the east. This second hospital was situated on an island in the middle of the River Swerra, whose fast-flowing waters were reputed to provide the best trout fishing in Germany. The river also had other uses; through generators installed in the basement, water power supplied the hospital's electrical needs. Odell was pleased to discover that the entire staff was made up of officers and men of the British Army Medical Corps. They had been captured years before, during the campaign in Greece in 1941. This team was headed by an Australian surgeon from Sydney, who ran the outfit with cheerful efficiency. Looking back on his first days in captivity, Odell realized how much better he would have fared if only he had been brought here in the first place.

During his stay at Obermasfeld he made friends with a number of prisoners, including some badly wounded patients. One man had had his instep shot away. Before sending him to this hospital the Germans had operated on him by scraping the remaining bone and then bending his toes back so they rested upside down on the top of what remained of his foot. It had congealed into an ugly blob of flesh. As an athlete, who had once been a keen skier, he had taken his incapacity very hard. After some misgivings, he had accepted the Australian surgeon's advice to have what remained of his foot amputated. He was fitted with an artificial foot and the Aussie assured him that he would have no problems when he resumed his skiing after the war.

Smithy, an infantryman from Baltimore, had sustained horrifying injuries while undergoing his baptism of fire. After enduring the enemy's shelling for about twenty minutes, he decided to stick his head over the edge of his foxhole, to see what was going on. A shell exploded nearby and a piece of shrapnel, some four inches long, pierced his face just below his right eye, tore out his cheekbone, demolished the roof of his mouth and part of his upper jaw; it sliced off a portion of his tongue, went through the bottom of his mouth and out of his neck; still not spent, the jagged splinter of metal ploughed a deep furrow across his chest. To Odell, the intriguing thing about Smithy was that, although he bore his dreadful wounds with courageous fortitude, he raised merry hell over trivial things – such as not having his bed made correctly, or when a busy orderly failed to empty his bedpan immediately.

Odell enjoyed listening to a stocky, red-headed Scot, Jock McCarthy a British paratrooper, as he recounted his almost incredible adventures. Jock had been involved in the Allied landings in Sicily, but had been wounded and captured almost as soon as his feet touched the ground. Later, when a PoW on the mainland, he escaped and spent his time sabotaging freight trains. His speciality was to hop onto slow-moving trains and then uncouple as many box-cars as possible, leaving a collection of separated wagons strung out along the lines. Whenever Jock had the opportunity, he would walk back along the tracks setting fire to those trucks and then retire to some convenient spot to watch the fun as the Germans attempted to sort out the shambles. Jock had escaped and been recaptured several times. On the last occasion he had been experimenting with a system of train derailment which was proving very successful when he was caught yet again. When Odell met him, Jock had long ago recovered from his wounds sustained in Sicily, but was suffering from some unspecified 'stomach trouble' and was daily expecting to be repatriated to Switzerland, classified as a DU – Definitely Unfit for further military service.

One of Odell's most energetic and amusing pals at this place was a Cockney soldier who claimed for himself the title of 'A Walking Bloody Miracle!' He was, too. He had been shot in the right eye by a rifle bullet which had passed clean through his cranium and out of the back of his head. Apart from losing his eye, he did not seem to have been affected. Within a month he was playing cards nightly with Odell, and frequently beating him, which suggested that his faculties were in no way impaired by his experience. His mates kept telling him that the only reason he had escaped death was because there was nothing inside his nut to get in the way of the bullet!

Unfortunately Odell's stay at Obermasfeld was all too short. He had just got into the swing of the hospital routine and settled down to enjoy the fellowship of his new companions when he was told he was on the move again. He was taken to Meiningen, a short distance to the north, where he spent a week in a prison hospital. He learned that this was a staging post, from which those prisoners considered fit enough were transferred to prisoner of war camp. The fate that he had hoped to avoid had caught up with him.

The train clanked slowly past mile after mile of bombed-out buildings. Obscene skeletons of blackened brick and stone gaped silently at the sky. The spectacle was unreal – nothing like this had been seen on such a scale since the world began. The history of war is marked by ruin and devastation – sacked cities, shattered castles, broken churches, homes laid waste. But only now, in the middle of the twentieth century, had man succeeded in lighting a holocaust that had disfigured a whole industrial nation and reduced its towns and cities to a honeycomb of burnt-out shells. There was no movement. Nothing lived, or so it seemed. It was an endless wilderness of destruction. Those stark black ruins marched row on row, as if in mourning for a race that had passed away for ever. This was the devastation inflicted by Britain's RAF Bomber Command, strongly supported later in the war by the United States Army Air Force. All that the mighty Allied air armadas had set out to achieve had been accomplished. Thousands of powerful four-engined bombers, the Americans day after day and the British night after night, had braved the flak and intercepting fighters to burn the heart out of industrial Germany. Watching the sombre scene through the grimy carriage window, he felt no sense of elation. No normal man could rejoice at such a bitter waste of human and material resources. At that moment he felt a deep hatred for Hitler and his Nazi crew who had brought the world to this.

His reveries were interrupted as the train came to a grinding stop. Shouting guards ran up and down the corridors. Four other prisoners shared the compartment with him and there were two more groups of five prisoners each in the adjoining compartment. They had come to a halt in the middle of a vast marshalling yard, with rolling stock stretching as far as the eye could see. Their train stood in an exposed position on a raised embankment. Doors were being flung open as their guards jumped down onto the tracks. Odell could hear the mournful wail of air-raid sirens as the soldiers sprinted down the embankment. Was this a chance to escape? Odell rose to his feet and crossed into the corridor. Peering out of the window he could see some of the guards lying on the embankment with their rifles pointing at the train. Returning to his compartment, he noticed that other Germans had taken up similar positions on that side as well. Not a chance of escape, that was for sure. Whether they liked it or not, the prisoners were going to sit right where they were, waiting to see if the train would be bombed by their own planes. If they decided to jump out, then the German guards were lying there ready to gun them down.

Odell saw them first – a group of B17s, Flying Fortresses, coming in lower than usual. He noticed that the bomb doors were already open. Any moment now they would be dropping their lethal loads. He pictured the crews at their stations – the pilot holding the ship steady, taking instructions from the bombadier as they went into their bomb run, the navigator ready to give the course for home over the interphone as soon as the bombs had gone; the engineer checking fuel levels; the radio operator in a world of his own in his small compartment, receiving a coded message in morse from Group HQ, and the gunners, tense and alert, ceaselessly scanning the skies, waiting for the fighter attack that was bound to come sooner or later. Within seconds the air was vibrating with the crash of gunfire. Heavy anti-aircraft guns were firing from the other side of the tracks, while nearer at hand 20mm and 37mm cannon, mounted in concrete blocks on the top of railroad flat-cars, blazed away at the bombers. While it lasted, the noise was deafening. Odell studied his companions with interest. Two of them had prudently crawled under the seats, while the others were sitting with their hands pressed tightly over their ears. Odell turned back to the window. The Fortresses, with their gracefully curved single tailfins, were passing directly overhead. He could see the bombs lying in rows in their open bomb bays. One airplane was streaming smoke from no 2 motor. 'Good luck, buddy!' breathed Odell, 'Good luck!'

Suddenly it was all over. The firing in the immediate vicinity ceased and the silence that followed seemed unnatural. Then they heard the crump of exploding bombs. The bombers were dropping their loads two or three miles away to the north. He wondered what target could be left amid all this devastation that the Allied Air Chiefs considered worth risking life and limb to attack.

In the fading afternoon light, as the train moved slowly forward, the snow started to fall. Within a short while a white shroud lay over the ruination. It was bitterly cold. The prisoners' only food was black bread smeared with tree-sap margarine. They shivered miserably as they huddled in their unheated compartments. All that night and the following day the train steamed on, heading, as far as they could tell, in a north-easterly direction.

Late on the second night they drew into the station at Stettin on the Baltic coast. None of the American flyers had ever heard of the place. This was ironical, because Odell and the other prisoners in his compartment seriously discussed the possibility of jumping the train when their guard took it into his head to wander off along the platform. If the Americans had realized that the port of Stettin had been the gateway to freedom for a number of British RAF escapees over the years, they would almost certainly have made a break for it. In the docks there were always plenty of neutral Swedish ships. Their skippers had been known to turn a blind eye when British flyers, disguised as seamen or dock workers, had climbed aboard their vessels. But to these prisoners it all seemed hopeless. Odell had handed his escape kit to Colonel Stark for safekeeping. They had no food supplies, no maps, no compasses, no money and they were all dressed in their US flying gear. A blizzard was blowing outside, which reduced visibility to a few yards. What lay beyond their restricted field of vision was a mystery to them. Under different circumstances the PoWs would have been amused when the train continued its journey minus their guard. His rifle remained propped in the compartment. But they were too cold, hungry and depressed to care. Soon another guard patrolling the corridor looked into the compartment and noticed that his comrade was missing. Taking charge of the weapon, he crowded Odell and the others into the adjacent compartment already occupied by Americans. Later that night their guard reappeared. Apparently he had persuaded a motorist to catch up with the slow-moving train.

Odell woke slowly, stretching his frozen limbs in the cold morning air. The blizzard had subsided. He gazed out on a bleak, white vista, broken only by a few snow-capped trees, stunted and forlorn. The train was stationary. He walked into the corridor to stretch his weary muscles and try to generate a little warmth through his body. The guard was there staring through the dirty window. 'Look,' he said, pointing with his wool-gloved hand. Odell turned and looked in the direction indicated by the soldier. There was a large stockade constructed of wooden stakes and heavily enmeshed with barbed wire. The only entrance was no more than twenty feet from the railroad. It was like a place made for cattle, except that it was too exposed for animals. There was no shelter of any kind – no protection from the wind or freezing snow. It was just a large compound, marked out with the barbed wire and stakes. But the stockade was full of people. Men and women, faces white and drawn, drained of emotion or human expression, stood huddled together. Their dark, sombre clothes were devoid of individuality. It was difficult for the mind to grasp they were people at all as they stood cringing from the bitter climate, bereft of identity and stripped of possessions that normally distinguish one person from another. They were silent too, these people, as if the very gift of speech had been taken from them, no longer needed in this new order where only the strong must be heard. And the strong were there all right – black-uniformed, jackbooted, well-fed and brutally arrogant. They strode about the compound, pushing and shouting and beating, like grotesque farmers at a cattle auction, separating the men from the women. The men were being herded into closed trucks at the rear of the train. It was unbelievable how many of these poor wretches were crushed into each wagon before the sliding doors closed with a resounding crash. A large, bullying SS man struggled to separate a couple standing near the compound gate. They were old and the woman was clinging to the man with all the desperation her feeble frame could command – a husband and wife fighting for their simple right to stay together, in defiance of the mindless armed power ranged against them. It was soon over – they were torn apart. The man was marched away to the wagon. As he was being thrust through the doorway, he turned and looked back at the woman. She was so small, so frail, so helpless in the face of her appalling circumstances. Yet at that moment she had a dignity which was both simple and profound. Raising her tiny hand, slowly and reverently she made the sign of the cross. Odell could not speak. He turned and looked into the face of his German guard. To his surprise he saw an expression of weary sadness. 'Now,' said the soldier, 'we are celebrating the birth of the Prince of Peace.' Then the two men stood in silence. After a moment Odell remembered it was Christmas.

More than forty-eight hours after leaving Meiningen, the train pulled into Keifheide on the Polish border. The prisoners and their guards tramped for several miles through a vast pine forest. Odell welcomed the exercise of walking along the snow-covered track, revelling in his temporary freedom. All too soon they arrived at a huge clearing in the forest. In the middle of this area stood the prison camp, Stalag Luft IV – a vast collection of wooden huts surrounded by high barbed-wire fencing which encircled the whole perimeter. To make doubly sure, there was a second fence, equally formidable, a few yards beyond the first. Sentries stood in machine-gun posts elevated on high wooden towers placed at regular intervals along the wire overlooking the compound. These had long been known to RAF men as 'Goon Boxes'. The huge camp was divided into five *lagers*, each housing two thousand men – eight thousand American and two thousand British aircrew. All the American prisoners were enlisted men, NCOs, with the exception of one Jewish flight surgeon, who had flown on a raid 'for the hell of it' and been shot down.

The new arrivals were marched to a reception hut near the main gate. Here they were stripped of all their clothing. They stood in line, naked and shivering with the cold. Eventually a number of German NCOs stamped into the room and searched them with professional thoroughness. When this degrading routine was finished, they were allowed to dress. To the prisoners' consternation, only their lighter garments were returned to them. Personal articles, such as watches, pens or lighters which some of the men had managed to hang onto were confiscated. Odell was relieved of his flying jacket and his summer flying-suit. The loss of his flying jacket angered him particularly. Not only was it a cherished possession, but the pockets were full of the pieces of flak, including the fuse from the 20mm shell that had been dug out of his body. He had become strongly attached to these unusual souvenirs. They also took his lighter which had been recovered for him by Emil Muelle. Raising his voice heatedly, Odell told the nearest German:

'You have no right to take prisoners' uniforms and private possessions. The corporal stared at him blankly, not understanding a word. However, an enormous *feldwebel*, who had not missed a syllable, strode over and stood, hands on hips, glaring down at him. Odell, well over six feet, was dwarfed by this giant of a man.

Although he did not know it, he was confronted by the most hated German on the staff of Stalag Luft IV. Seasoned PoWs had learned to steer clear of the one they called 'Big Stoop'. This grotesque man had a notorious reputation. Many men could testify to his readiness to pummel PoWs about the head with his stick. On one occasion he tied a man to a tree and left him all night in the freezing cold. 'Big Stoop' encouraged those under him to engage in vicious bullying. In the early days at the camp things were at their worst. Prisoners too ill to stand had been bayoneted, hit with rifle butts and bitten by fierce guard dogs goaded on by their keepers. Captive RAF men had managed to smuggle out messages telling what was going on in Stalag Luft IV. As a result Switzerland, the 'protective power', looked into the matter and managed to get some of the excesses curbed. But 'Big Stoop's' enemies had long memories – memories kept alive by a deep loathing for the man who had caused them so much additional suffering. More than one prisoner was biding his time, waiting for the day of retribution.

'Who gives you permission to open your mouth?' asked the *feldwebel* threateningly.

'I just want to know why in hell your men have taken our flying gear. I'll have you know, all that stuff is the property of the United States Government.'

For a moment the *feldwebel* was taken aback by Odell's audacity. Then he roared: 'It is going where it will do the most good. Our soldiers who are now holding back the hordes of Soviet pigs, they need such warm clothes.' Then he added with heavy sarcasm: 'Perhaps we will return them to your defeated government – when we have won the war.'

Odell looked at him defiantly: 'You're nuts! In a month or two you'll see who's won the war and I'm telling you it won't be the lousy Germans. In the meantime, buddy, I want a receipt for all my gear!'

Odell thought the *feldwebel* was going to explode. Then the German drew back his fist and took a mighty swing at him. Odell, knocked off balance, back-pedalled through the door and landed in the slush outside the hut. 'Big Stoop' followed, holding a little red suitcase that Colonel Stark had given to Odell. Without a word he threw it contemptuously on top of the American, turned on his highly polished heel and went back into the hut.

Later, Odell was assigned to C Lager, right in the centre of the complex of huts. In a small administrative building he met the 'Man of Confidence' and other camp leaders. These were senior PoWs who acted as the prisoners' representatives in all dealings with the Germans. They were amazingly well-informed about what was going on in the outside world. The PoWs had the benefit of a daily news service compiled from both BBC and German broadcasts. The radio, in three separate pieces, was concealed on the prisoners themselves. In its segmented form it spent the day travelling round the compound. Then at nightfall the components were brought together and carefully assembled in time to receive the evening newscasts.

Only a matter of hours after arriving at Stalag Luft IV Odell bumped into Roger Clapp, his radio operator. Roger had been carted off to Dulag Luft, near Frankfurt, after he and Odell had parted company. Roger appeared more like his old self. He had recovered something of his debonair manner and his uniform again showed signs of studied individuality. (After the war Roger returned to the United States to face an unhappy future. This normally intelligent young man began to lose his reason. He became a war casualty in a very real sense, spending no less than ten years in an Army Mental Institution.)

That evening Odell was lined up in the compound with other new arrivals, including a small group of US Paratroopers who, presumably, had been sent to this Air Force prison camp in error. They were treated to a homily on the significance of Christmas by a stout German corporal, who did his best to look friendly. He spoke passable English: 'As you will know, it is now too late to post Christmas greetings to your loved ones at home. However, we Germans wish to be as helpful as possible. We would like your people to receive your messages of good will for Eastertide.' Then the corporal started giving them some small cards to fill in, another crude attempt by the Germans to extract information from prisoners. Like all the others, Odell refused the cards, immediately recognizing them for what they were. They had been briefed many times during training sessions to beware of such tricks. Odell noticed that the paratroopers had accepted cards and were preparing to fill them in. Obviously they had not realized what they were doing. Odell stepped out of line and called to the soldiers: 'Hey there, fellas! You mustn't do that – don't go filling those things in. Didn't they tell you back in the army about aiding and abetting the enemy, for God's sake? You guys could get yourselves into serious trouble with our own people after the war. Just hand the damn' things back – and tell them to go to hell!'

An enormous figure loomed above him. It was 'Big Stoop'. For the second time that day Odell was knocked to the ground. As he sat up and shook his head he had the satisfaction of seeing that not a single card was filled in.

The grimness of camp life was alleviated by the ingenuity of many of its inmates. To a newcomer like Odell, the first few days passed quickly enough learning about the remarkably complex organization built up by the prisoners themselves, some of whom had been in captivity for years. In an effort to combat despair, boredom or soul-destroying indifference, an infinite variety of activities had been developed. Concentration on efforts to escape led to the development of all manner of skills: the conversion of uniforms into passable civilian clothes; the dyeing of garments and fashioning of insignia to create imitation German uniforms; the manufacture of 'escape tools' – wire cutters, compasses and even dummy firearms; the forging of documents and making of maps.

Then there were the smooth operators – the 'Traders'. They were always busy bringing pressure to bear on those guards who were known to yield to bribery, flattery and, once they had succumbed, blackmail. Here was an invaluable channel of supply, producing tools, official notepaper, ink and even the temporary loan of document stamps from which exact copies were painstakingly made.

It is a matter of fact that, as a group, airmen, both British and American, made more attempts and succeeded more often in escaping than all other prisoners of war put together. Aircrew prisoners made such a nuisance of themselves that the Germans had been forced to construct these special camps, the Stalag Lufts, in order to contain or attempt to contain their irrepressible 'guests'. It was a consolation to the men to know they were tying up so many enemy troops on time-consuming guard duties. Equally, whenever anyone broke out of camp, substantial German resources both in men and facilities had to be diverted from war activities, and it was then, as a result of these escape attempts, that the Germans finally panicked and established the 'Death Zones' around their principal cities, which gave authority for any escaping airman to be shot on sight. A few months before Odell arrived at Stalag Luft IV, eighty-three RAF men had escaped through an ingeniously constructed tunnel from a PoW camp at Sagan. It was the greatest mass escape of all time. Four escapees, the last four out, were recaptured at the tunnel exit, three others got back to England. All the rest were rounded up over a period of days. Of these, half-a-dozen were sent to concentration camps, about double this number were returned to the Stalag Luft at Sagan, but the majority, fifty-one in all, were murdered on the express orders of Adolf Hitler. In contravention of international law, they were shot by the Gestapo. What Hitler hoped to achieve by issuing such an order is uncertain. If the execution was expected to act as a deterrent, it was doomed to failure. Bomber crews continued their attacks on Germany as aggressively as ever, while in the PoW camps prisoners went on planning their escapes and digging their secret tunnels.

Inevitably there were some PoWs who were not anxious to escape. By temperament some men preferred to lose themselves within their own thoughts and fantasies, shutting out the grim reality of their surroundings by retreating into a world of imagination or indulging in complicated mental exercises. These were the loners, the introverts who wanted no place in a team and only performed those duties that were obligatory to all 'kriegies'.

Such a man was young Jim, the son of a well-known American broadcaster whose shows were sponsored by Lucky Strike cigarettes. For hours Jim would sit in monk-like contemplation, his shaven head bowed, absorbed in deep study of some self-imposed problem. He had the knack of compiling crossword puzzles, a talent much appreciated by his companions.

There was a particularly objectionable 'ferret' who owned a large white cat. The cat would faithfully follow its master on his search duties round the Lager. Some kriegies swore the beast was fitted with radar to assist in the detection of those things which the PoWs preferred should remain hidden. One day in a fit of frustration, as the cat was passing, Jim whipped the animal up, concealed it under his coat and throttled it. That night, avoiding the German Shepherd dogs that roamed the compound after dark, he hoisted its body to the top of the flagpole. Next day all hell was let loose. The Lager Officer, purple with rage and unable to find the culprit, cancelled the issue of all Red Cross parcels. Supplies of coal were stopped in spite of the severe cold. Meals were reduced to a small daily ration of potatoes for each man – potatoes only, nothing more. Jim was taken quietly on one side by his companions and strongly advised to confine all his energies in future to crossword puzzles.

Although the style of living at Stalag Luft IV was low by any civilized standard, it was almost luxurious compared with that suffered by Russian PoWs. Their lot was deplorable. They were clothed in rotten rags which did nothing to protect them from the freezing easterly winds that swept across the open compound. They shuffled along mostly without footwear, their feet bound up in strips of filthy sacking. Pitiful, starving, unwashed, the Russians were herded to the camp each day and assigned the most menial and degrading tasks. Every day two Russians came into the compound to attend the latrines that served the hundreds of men. They were in charge of a vehicle nicknamed the 'honeycart', a gigantic wooden barrel mounted on wheels. By means of a long flexible tube sewage was sucked from the noisome cesspit at the back of the latrine block up into the 'honeycart'. On the one occasion that Odell decided to watch this operation, things went radically wrong. Possibly the wood from which the barrel was constructed had rotted over the years and this, combined with the potent power of the sewage gases, may have caused the trouble. Whatever the reason, the whole 20-foot long contraption exploded, spewing its revolting load not only over the surrounding huts, but also saturating those unlucky kriegies who happened to be in the way at the time. Such an event was no laughing matter when washing facilities were so limited and hot water almost unobtainable.

At Lamsdorf camp, earlier in the war, a British infantryman had contrived to escape in one of these 'honeycarts'. With a packet of cigarettes he bribed the Russian in charge only to half-fill the barrel. Then he climbed inside, while the Russian replaced the lid over the hole at the top. In theory this was an ingenious, if unpleasant, way of escaping from the camp. In practice, of course, gases that were powerful enough to cause an explosion, were more than sufficient to kill a man within moments. Long before the cart had trundled through the main gate, faint cries were heard emanating from the interior of the barrel. A stinking figure, saturated in excrement, was drawn up through the hole, rescued from death by asphyxiation in the nick of time. Escape committees in PoW camps throughout Germany added this method of departure to their list of 'impossibles' – definitely not to be recommended under any circumstances.

The desperate conditions suffered by the Russians preyed on Odell's mind. He was affronted by the unfairness of their treatment. As Allies, he had come to regard them as equals and was filled with admiration for their valiant stand against the Germans. The defence of Stalingrad had assumed the proportions of a heroic legend in his imagination. This image was a reflection of the popular mood of the time among Russia's allies. King George VI had presented the people of Stalingrad with a magnificent sword on behalf of his countrymen to commemorate that city's courageous refusal to bow to the aggressor. Odell's thoughts were uncluttered by any of the political issues that were in later years to confuse and dismay the people of his own country. This was war – matters were clear and simple, at least in the eyes of the enlisted man. These Russians had been trying to do the same job as himself: knocking hell out of Hitler. Like him, these particular ones had been unlucky enough to get captured.

Odell had become friendly with a stocky little navigator from Texas who also lived in C Lager. The Texan shared Odell's sympathy for the Russian prisoners and this feeling was strengthened by his ability to speak their language, which he had studied at the University of Texas, Austin. Learning Russian had also given the Texan an insight into Russia's history and an understanding of her culture. Gradually a plan was worked out which they hoped would help at least a handful of the many thousands of Russian soldiers held in captivity. It was a very simple scheme, but to succeed it needed the cooperation and good faith of every man in the compound. Each morning the Russians assembled outside the camp where they would wait to be detailed by the guards for all the dirty jobs of the day. Occasionally they would be put in the charge of 'trusted' British or American PoWs. On this occasion the square-cut figure of the Texan navigator was seen moving with a purposeful air towards the main gate. As he reached the guard post he yelled to a group of some two dozen Russians to line up in threes. After speaking to them rapidly in their own language, he drew them to attention and marched them into the compound. The operation was carried out with such spirited authority that the goons were quite unaware that an impudent abduction had taken place right under their noses. The Texan paraded his squad in a space between two buildings where they were momentarily out of sight of the Germans. Everything had been arranged – the Russians were quickly guided in ones and twos to various huts in the compound. Then, to their evident surprise, they were immediately treated to a wash, a shave and a haircut. After this they were each kitted out in American Army Air Force uniforms. The transformation was complete. Amazingly, the camp authorities were unaware that anything irregular had taken place.

At roll call that afternoon the Germans were astonished to discover that, even after three counts, they had twenty-four prisoners in excess of their official list. Always on the alert for deficiences, this puzzling *increase* in numbers was an entirely new situation, quite beyond their comprehension. It was already 3.30 in the afternoon, half an hour before darkness.

'You will go to your huts', yelled the Lager Officer, his face shaded in its customary purple hue. 'Tomorrow you will see. We Germans are no fools and you will be sorry to think you can trifle with us so. You can be sure tomorrow will bring us the explanation and,' he stamped his foot in emphasis, 'when it does, you will not like the punishment that will follow. I warn you again, it does not pay to be foolish with us.' Then, amidst a resounding burst of applause from the kriegies, he bounced out of the compound, yelling orders to his minions as he went.

Next morning more than two thousand grumbling and protesting PoWs were herded out onto the snow-covered compound. Their captors lined them up on one side of the huge square. The Germans set up a table in the middle of the area. Then the adjutant made a brief speech: 'We Germans are very thorough, no?' Without waiting for a reply, he went on rapidly: 'We have here on this table a card for every prisoner in this compound – photograph, name, fingerprints and prison number.' A note of triumph was already creeping into his voice: 'When we call your name, you will come forward to this table and be identified.' This meant, of course, that the Germans would compare the photo on the card with the prisoner standing before them and also check the number with the number on the man's 'kriegy dog tags' (the PoW identity discs worn by every inmate on a piece of string tied round his neck). 'After the check,' continued the adjutant, 'each man will cross to the other side of the compound. So, at the end we will sort the sheeps from the wolves, no?' 'NO!' chorused two thousand voices.

Ignoring this mass gesture of no confidence, a German corporal called out the first name. There was no reply. He called again. Still no reply. After several more attempts and by now very red in the face, he was visibly relieved when at last he evoked some response. Reprimanded by the angry Lager Officer the American, with a look of sublime innocence, explained that he found the corporal's accent confusing and so had been unable to recognize his own name when it was called. When he was asked to show his 'dog tags', the ensuing performance was painful to watch – at least for the Germans. Fumbling through layers of assorted clothing, the American politely apologized for the delay, explaining that his hands were frozen and it was difficult anyway to cope with clothing held together with bits of string. So the procedure was repeated, time after time. These delaying tactics were so effective that, by early afternoon, only about half the prisoners had been identified and passed across to the far side of the compound – a thousand men on either side and a handful of Germans clustered round their table in the centre of the square. It was bitterly cold and growing colder. Snow was falling again, covering captives and captors alike. The PoWs had had enough. They had stood for hours in the freezing air, without the opportunity to exercise and with no food in their bellies. As if by a pre-ordained signal, men on either side bent down and began making snowballs. Thus armed, the two groups started moving steadily towards each other. The Germans in the middle looked worried, wondering how the situation would develop. They were only left in doubt for a moment. As soon as the men were within hurling distance of each other, the frozen missiles began to fly. In the ensuing mêlée the Americans in both groups came together, overtook each other, changed sides and generally mixed themselves up so thoroughly that the meticulous work carried out by the Germans over the past hours became a meaningless waste of time. The Germans by then were only concerned with extricating themselves, their precious cards and table and legging it to safety, away from the battering effect of thousands of snowballs.

Realizing that they had won a remarkable victory, the men aimed enthusiastic punches at each other, rolling in the snow, laughing and shouting in an ecstasy of rare joy. This was a day they would remember for ever. And somewhere among these two thousand near-hysterical men were twenty-four entirely bewildered but equally happy Russians. Months later at least a couple of those Russians were still with Odell's group when it was finally liberated.

The Russian armies had started their big push westwards from Warsaw. They were rolling across Poland carrying all before them, not only the German armies, but many other nationalities who had found themselves caught up in the maelstrom of war, all fleeing to the West in a desperate resolve to avoid falling under the terrifying shadow of Stalinist domination. They gave little thought to what would eventually happen when they met the British and American troops moving in from the other direction. All they knew was that they would far rather take their chances with the Western Allies than with the Communists.

On 5 February, 1945, the kriegies in Stalag Luft IV could hear the sound of exploding shells as the Russian artillery opened up on the nearby railway depot at Keifheide. The 'Man of Confidence' told them the German Camp Commandant was negotiating with the Russian Army Commander and offering to hand over his American and British prisoners. This information brought general excitement and a great deal of speculation among the flyers – could this really mean they were to be free at last? Odell heard the news with mixed feelings. He thought he detected a note of reservation in the way the message was announced. Also, putting himself in the position of the Russian general, he could see that 10,000 extra mouths to feed would be an embarrassment to a commander whose primary job was to sweep through Germany to Berlin, achieving a crushing victory as quickly as possible.

Thinking that tomorrow might be an important day, Odell went to bed early. At daylight the PoWs were paraded in the compound. They were told they were to move to Stargard, 150 kilometres to the west and they must be ready to march at once. It took Odell no time at all to collect his possessions – a toothbrush and a deck of cards. For good measure he also grabbed two Red Cross food parcels, each weighing eleven pounds, and slung them round his neck. Hurriedly the men were marched out of the camp under heavy guard. Odell was near the front of his particular column of 300 men. They were escorted by 150 German soldiers accompanied by ten vicious guard dogs, whose viciousness increased as their stomachs became emptier. So, in near-arctic conditions, Odell and his companions became part of the mass trek westwards – the 'Death March' as it became known. It involved a significant portion of the population of Central Europe, to which PoWs added a considerable number. Odell never discovered the outcome of the negotiations with the Russian commander, but he did learn later that a directive had been issued by the German High Command that all Allied aircrew were to be carefully guarded and their lives used as a bargaining counter in the event of Germany's defeat.

Odell's first reaction was a feeling of exhilaration at being free once again from the confines of the camp. Although it was bitterly cold, the kriegies were walking at a brisk pace which generated bodily warmth and a feeling of well-being. They had parcels of food containing more than enough to last them until they reached their destination in about four days' time. It was as well they were able to enjoy those first few hours as their column moved steadily through the forest. If they had known what lay ahead of them, their good spirits would have drained away like melting snow. They would have found it inconceivable that eighty days later they would still be trudging wearily on.

As the days passed it began to dawn on them that Stargard could no longer be their destination, if it ever had been. From their calculations the prisoners estimated that they had walked well to the west of that point and were now heading in a more south-westerly direction. Some of the men were already beginning to feel the strain. Believing that new food parcels would have been distributed on reaching Stargard, they had not made any effort to conserve the supplies they had brought with them. By the fifth day most of them had nothing left.

Trying to extract information as to their real destination brought no useful response from the guards. Their captors tried to give an impression of being in complete control of the situation, but the prisoners felt that the soldiers knew little more than they did about where they were actually going. One thing was certain, they could not survive for long in that climate on the official rations. The Germans gave them three potatoes per day and a 'klim can' of boiling water into which the kriegies mashed their potatoes (the 'klim can' was a condensed milk can, the name 'klim' being derived from the word milk, reversed). They also received one-third of a loaf of black bread per week. Odell disciplined himself to keep one potato overnight in order to have something for breakfast each morning.

He and some of his friends kept a careful eye on a few of the others who showed signs of faltering. 'Keep with it, old buddy,' he encouraged a nineteen-year-old tail gunner who was hobbling painfully along the hard-packed snow track. The youngster was suffering from frostbite. 'Sure, Dobby,' whispered the boy through purple lips. 'I'm just playing for sympathy!' 'OK', grinned Odell. 'In that case we'll pretend we've fallen for your game and treat you like you're some kinda poor helpless cripple.' With that he and the Texan eased him off the ground and more or less carried him between them for the rest of the day.

Odell was determined to keep himself as fit as the appalling circumstances would allow so that he would be in reasonable shape to escape when the chance came. He often worried about the reaction of the more trigger-happy guards should any of their prisoners drop behind the column. It was fortunate that *Feldwebel* 'Big Stoop' was not in charge of his particular party. Odell offered up a silent prayer for the group who had the misfortune to fall under his administration.

It was a few days later and the column had been called to a halt. The flyers were sheltering as best they could from the icy wind which cut through their scant clothing and froze their undernourished bodies. They crouched in the lee of a barn, while the Germans stationed themselves inside the building having coffee. Odell and two of his companions had moved round to the back and were studying the interior through the large open doorway: a tractor stood just inside the entrance, raised on wooden blocks for the winter; the Germans were at the other end of the barn; large bales of hay formed a barrier that masked the three prisoners from their captors. 'Quick!' whispered Odell. 'We'll skip under that tractor and cover ourselves with hay. Come on, right away.' The three men crawled into the barn on hands and knees, slipped quietly under the tractor and lay down. They dragged large armfuls of hay over their bodies until they were completely hidden. 'We'll just lie doggo until they move on,' breathed Odell, 'None of the goons will miss us. Then, after everybody has gone, we'll slip quietly away and set course for the Allied lines. Until then, don't even breathe!' It was a good plan, straightforward and uncomplicated – it might even have worked. Unfortunately one of the other prisoners had been watching their disappearing act. Within a moment twelve to fifteen kriegies had crept furtively into the barn and concealed themselves inside the inviting wall of hay in the middle of the floor. Odell cursed them softly, knowing that such large numbers were bound to be missed. He was right of course. When the time came to get back on the road, there was an all too evident gap in the ranks. On the vast flat expanse of snow-covered ground there was only one place that would-be escapers could hide. The Germans cocked their rifles and moved back into the barn, surrounding the prominent mound of hay. Odell risked tunnelling a small eyehole with his forefinger and was in time to see several guards level their weapons and fire into the stack. The effect on the kriegies was dramatic. They came swarming out of the hayrick with hands held high. By good luck, not one was hit by the flying bullets and they were quickly driven outside by the soldiers.

Meanwhile, Odell and the other two men froze rigid, wondering if they might still get away with it. A guard leaning against the tractor prodded idly at the straw with his bayonet. Suddenly, the sharp point made contact with the man lying next to Odell. With a scream the man sat up, smashing his face into the metal protrusions on the underside of the tractor. His torn face streamed with blood. The guard, who was no youngster, was visibly shaken by his unexpected discovery. Odell noticed that the German's hands were trembling as he scuffed the remaining straw aside with his foot, revealing the other two men.

'*Raus! Raus!*' he croaked, as he gestured them to their feet with his rifle. '*Gehen sie auf!*' He marched them out of the barn and started prodding them in a direction away from their own group. Odell, whose German had steadily improved since he was first captured, asked the guard where he was taking them. 'You are going to join our "special squad". This is for the "Incorrigibles". You will be in good company there, my friends. It is especially for the "bad boys". I do not think you are going to enjoy yourself.'

Odell was sure he wasn't going to enjoy himself. He was well aware that all those men who had shown initiative in baiting the goons, or in trying to escape, had to survive on even thinner rations than the rest. At all costs he must keep out of this group. His life might well depend on it. There could be other opportunities to escape later, but once placed among the 'Incorrigibles' he would be a marked man, watched day and night.

Odell turned to the guard. 'Have you heard from your son lately?' he inquired, with genuine interest. 'I remember you telling me back at the camp that he's a PoW in America – Mississippi, I think you said?'

'That is so', said the German. 'I had a letter from him just before we started this march. He tells me he is very well.'

'I hope my people are looking after him properly. No bad treatment, eh?' asked Odell, pointedly.

'No, I think the Americans are very good to my son.' He grinned ruefully. 'I think he is having a better life than his father, no?'

'Right,' said Odell. 'Damned right! Now listen, Dad. If I was your son, would you want some lousy armed guard to go shoving me in a special group where I would most likely die of starvation? Would you, eh?'

The German stopped in his tracks. He wasn't a bad old Kraut and Odell's words had gone home. He had reacted in the first place more from fright than any basic inhumanity. In fact in the past he had spoken in quite a friendly way to Odell, had even shared his coffee with him on one occasion. Glancing timidly from side to side the old soldier whispered: 'All right, my friend. This once I will do it. I will take you back to your own group – but this one time only. Never again. It is understood?'

'Understood,' said Odell, '. . . and my friends?'

'Your friends also. This one time only.'

Odell looked at him in gratitude for a moment. 'We appreciate what you are doing for us. Thank you very much.'

Within a week, the same three had tried again. Once more escape seemed within their grasp, but they were spotted by some children who gave their position away to the guards. That night Odell and his two companions were locked up in a cramped storeroom in a barn. The following day, to their intense relief, they were again allowed to join their own column. As Odell was leaving the barn, a Polish slave labourer working on the farm handed him a bulky brown paper sack without saying a word. He examined the contents as soon as they were on the march but to his disappointment, instead of something to eat, he found it contained a large quantity of crumbly tobacco. Yet over a period of time he began to appreciate what a valuable gift he had been given. He was able to swap carefully rationed portions of it for food. Odell breathed many a word of thanks to that unknown Pole. By an impulsive act of kindness, the man had bestowed on him so much more than a package of tobacco.

Although their efforts to escape met with failure, they did get some consolation from their sabotage activities. On several occasions Odell and his friends devoted a fair part of the night to dismantling any piece of farming equipment they could get their hands on. Then an assortment of gears, cogs, nuts and bolts were thrown into the ditch while on the march the following day. At first they made the mistake of taking more obvious components, but these were missed as soon as anyone glanced at the machinery. Because the Lager Officer threatened to shoot offending PoWs if it ever happened again, they had to change their methods. From then on they removed small but vital items from inside the machines and later, when they 'obtained' some valuable wrenches and pliers, their work became remarkably professional. In addition they always hedged their bets by pouring sand and dirt into gas tanks and oil sumps. Yet when, in every barn they visited, hundreds of kriegies deliberately relieved themselves over the stocks of seed grain, this was perhaps the most effective mischief they were able to inflict on German food output at the time.

It was 14 February, 1945, St Valentine's Day. At 4 o'clock in the morning the prisoners were roused by the guards and the day's march began. Slowly they trudged on, their heads bowed against a biting blizzard. Human communication was forgotten, as every man shrank within himself. For much of the time Odell was oblivious to his physical forward movement, aware only of the warm comfort of his private thoughts – somewhere at the end of all this they would come to a signpost displaying one word, the most important word the world could ever know – FREEDOM. Beyond that sign, men, women and children lived by a code of human rights, exercised their own wills, trod their own paths and spoke their own thoughts without fear. No guards strutted there, prison camps were unknown, threats were never made – it was a world without hunger or suffering.

On and on they went, shrouded like medieval monks bound on a secret pilgrimage. By 3 o'clock in the afternoon the flakes of snow began to turn to rain, washing the white covering from the prisoners' bodies. As darkness came, the temperature dropped even lower and the men's sodden clothing froze upon them. They became like corpses, preserved in shells of ice and moved by some external force.

It was a little before 9 o'clock that same night and Odell's column was *still* moving. The track was barely discernible, yet the group followed it almost instinctively, like a snail breaking new ground. The flyers were painfully jerked into consciousness by the harsh shouting of their guards. They were being ordered off the road and up the side of a hill. Struggling upwards, they skirted the side of a wood, stumbling in an area where all the trees had been chopped down. The muddy, sloping ground was running with rivulets of water under a covering of fallen pine boughs. They had walked for nearly seventeen hours in near-arctic conditions, sustained only by a small helping of potato mash and a mouthful of black bread. It was almost incredible, but during that time they had covered more than thirty-six miles. They knew this was so because a radio operator, more alert than the rest, had counted fifty-eight kilometre posts. Now, without apparent reason, they were climbing this desolate, eroded hill. Word was passing from prisoner to prisoner: 'They are going to shoot us'. Odell, while still keeping in the column, edged his way over until he was in the rank nearest the edge of the woods. He figured that if firing started he would run for the cover of the trees, hoping to find a place to hide. It was a dark night; he might just make it. Anything was better than standing in the open, waiting to be mowed down. In the event nothing happened. Mercifully, it was a rumour without foundation, born of tired minds and feelings of despair. They were ordered to bed down for the night as best they could. Odell attempted to light a fire without success. Expending his small stock of a dozen matches, he burnt most of his playing cards in an effort to kindle a flame from the wet green branches. He and his two companions had only two blankets between them – the third they had traded with some refugees for a loaf of bread. Spreading one blanket on the saturated ground, they lay there two at a time using the second blanket as a cover, while the other man waited his turn for a little rest and warmth.

Dawn broke, revealing a heavy frost encrusting all the prisoners as they lay motionless on the frozen ground. The scene was like a battlefield after the tide of war had ebbed, leaving many bodies, rigid and impersonal, waiting to be gathered up. Yet these bodies still lived and breathed. These were the men who, when recruited back in the States, had been carefully selected for their fitness to withstand the rigours of combat flying. Lesser men could not have survived these conditions. Even the lives of these once-healthy young flyers hung by a thread. But the spirit of hope was not easily extinguished, and it was this more than anything else that kept them going day after day. Odell was pleased to see a clear sky above them; it would make the day's journey easier. Better to be on the move anyway – cramped muscles and frozen limbs reacted well to exercise. Movement came hardest to those who were suffering from frostbite or the miseries of dysentery brought on by eating dirty potatoes.

The men helped each other as best they could, sharing what little food they had.

That morning Odell felt ill himself, a condition which annoyed and worried him. He took a pride in his fitness even under these circumstances. Often he would add to his total distance covered each day by darting into the fields to forage for extra vegetables. The guards, who at first forbade these sorties, finally came to accept that his raids could do no harm and even went some way towards keeping the other prisoners happy, because he would return, his arms laden with produce and distribute the food among his companions. Today it was different. Odell lacked the energy to do more than plod along. His body was shaking uncontrollably, he could barely lift his head to see where he was going. The guard whose son was in America gave him two large tablets and a sip of coffee from his canteen, telling Odell that within an hour he would feel much better. The German was right. By midday Odell had ceased to tremble and a little of his old vigour began to return.

His mind lapsed into warm memories of the Christmas Concert back in the camp – a smash hit if ever there was one. The hut that served as theatre only held two hundred patrons at a time. The show played to one full house after another until every PoW and most of the Germans had seen the perform-ance. It really was a fantastic presentation, put on by T.J. Edwards, a professional Broadway producer, who stood front of stage and announced with a wry smile: 'A number dedicated to the day I was shot down – "I Surrender Dear."

Later, in an unashamedly sentimental finale, Edwards changed the mood: 'Fellas, it's Christmas Eve at home and there's an extra place set at the table. That place is empty because it's just for you. Wives and mothers and loved ones are all there waiting and longing for the day when you come home. In the meantime, fellas, there's something I want you to remember and never, never forget – it's the title of this next song – "There's a Great Day Coming".' There was many a moist eye in that audience as two hundred homesick young Americans released their pent-up emotions in song. The significance of the words seemed to be lost on the guards who flanked the small auditorium.

By now the sky had clouded over, again threatening rain. Odell was softly humming to himself the tune of 'There's a Great Day Coming' when he heard the sound of machine-gun fire directly above them. A few seconds later an American A26 attack bomber dropped out of the cloud cover, leaving a thick black smoke trail as it plunged earthwards out of control. A Luftwaffe JU88 was following in close pursuit. 'Come on! Come on!' muttered Odell to himself, willing the crew to jump. 'For God's sake get out while you can.' He was aware that an A26 only had a crew of two – a pilot and a gunner. Odell stood stock still, waiting for the two chutes to appear. Just when it looked too late, a small dark object fell from the plane, the canopy billowed open, supporting the flyer beneath it. No second chute appeared and the aircraft hit the ground several miles away, exploding immediately. The parachutist was wafted away by the northerly wind and disappeared from view over the brow of a nearby hill. Some months later Odell was to meet and become firm friends with the gunner who, unlike his unfortunate pilot, escaped death that day. It was Staff Sergeant Edward Von Kasselburg who leapt to safety. Kasselburg had previously been a window dresser at Bloomingdales in New York – a prime example of how dramatically war can change a man's way of life.

Fifty-six days after leaving Stalag Luft IV Odell's group arrived at a prison camp on the outskirts of Hanover – the city that he and his crew had set out to bomb nearly seven months earlier. The PoWs had completed the final three days of the journey by rail. They were crushed into commandeered French box cars known as '40 and 8s' – designed to carry 40 men and 8 horses. On this occasion the horses were missing, but more than twice the stipulated number of men were jammed into each wagon, making it an excruciatingly uncomfortable journey. With no room to lie down, it was impossible to snatch any rest. Sanitary arrangements had been overlooked – klim cans were awkwardly emptied through small grilled windows high up at the ends of the box cars.

While on the march the men had put together makeshift 'Stars and Stripes', displaying them whenever British Typhoons or American P51s flew near. They were sure the Allied air forces were keeping tabs on them and had an accurate idea of their whereabouts at all times. This had been a great encouragement. But now, with no means of signalling from inside the locked railway wagons, they feared their own fighters might strafe their slow-moving train at any moment.

In the event they arrived safely at their destination and found the camp inmates a mixed lot. It was designated originally for the internment of French PoWs, and there were many Frenchmen living in comparative comfort in substantial brick-built barracks. Each of them appeared to possess limitless supplies of food and cigarettes hoarded from an abundance of Red Cross parcels sent from America, England, Australia and Canada. Yet later, when Odell went to see them on behalf of his sick companions, hoping to obtain some powdered milk, cheese and sugar, the Frenchmen refused to give him anything. He tried to explain that the men badly needed some nourishing food to overcome the ill-effects of eating dirty potatoes and drinking stagnant water. All his pleas were met with haughty indifference.

Captives from the American 105th Infantry Division had recently been brought to the camp. These men were far from typical of those American forces who had tenaciously resisted and finally repulsed Rundstedt's armour in the Ardennes. The 105th had been badly chewed up during the 'Battle of the Bulge' when the Germans had mounted their desperate counter-offensive in mid-December. Poorly officered and badly disciplined, their morale, never good at any time, was now at a low ebb. They were no longer recognizable as soldiers in the accepted sense, being nothing better than a disorganized rabble.

Then there was a small group of British Paratroopers. These were survivors from the ill-fated Battle of Arnhem which began six days after Odell had been shot down the previous September. The 'Red Devils' had fought with incomparable valour to hold the vital road bridge at Arnhem. Lacking supplies and denied promised reinforcements, equipped only with light weapons, they defied the enemy's heavy armour for days until their last round of ammunition was spent. By this time all but a few of their courageous company had either been killed or wounded. They were complimented by the troops of the crack SS armoured divisions who had opposed them. The Germans rated them the toughest combat troops in the world, tougher than anything they had encountered on the Russian front. Odell learned they had marched all the way to this camp in parade-ground order, heads held proudly, carrying their wounded and led by their magnificent Sergeant-Major. The shambling German guards had great difficulty keeping up with them. In prison they maintained the same high standard of conduct for which they had become famous throughout the free world.

In a week Odell and his companions were on the move again. The British armies under Field-Marshal Montgomery had moved forward to within twenty-five miles of Hanover. So the Germans decided to shift their air force prisoners – their pawns – further from the Allies' reach. The men had benefited from their short stay at the camp. A week under cover had given them a chance to thaw out frozen bodies and rest aching limbs. But they were still in a state of near-starvation. Suffering from malnutrition, their stomachs had distended into a condition known among PoWs as 'kartoffel gut'.

Just after they had resumed their march, this time in a north-easterly direction, an Allied fighter flew over them and strafed some horses in a nearby field. Every piece of horse-flesh was ravenously devoured by the 'kriegies'. Odell was unsure if the pilot had slain the animals for the prisoners' sake or not. Whatever the flyer's motive, they hugely enjoyed the large lumps of half-cooked meat. Not long after, their digestive systems suffered terribly from the unaccustomed intake.

One companion whom the flyers greatly admired was Padre Morgan. This 'feisty little devil', as Odell called him, did a great deal to bolster the prisoners' morale. As an Anglican monk, he had demanded that the Germans deport him from his native Channel Islands so he could minister to the needs of PoWs in the camps. From that time on he had shared their hardships and suffered the same privations. During the long march Padre Morgan carried the kriegies' radio on his back and regularly listened to the news bulletins. Every morning when the men were paraded before moving off, he would stand in front of the assembly and openly read out the latest information on the Allied advances. Such was the quiet strength of his personality that the Germans never tried to stop him. Odell was convinced the guards were more than a little afraid of this diminutive monk. Whenever anyone needed help, Padre Morgan was first to lend a hand or offer a word of encouragement. Morgan celebrated Eastertide in a service at the camp they had just left. The size of the congregation was a tribute to the man who had earned the respect of all those who marched with him.

It was during one of the Padre's newsreading sessions that Odell learned of the death of President Roosevelt – a sad announcement that left him with a sense of personal loss. Roosevelt had been an outstanding President – as Winston Churchill said, 'The greatest American friend we have ever known and the greatest champion of freedom who has ever brought help and comfort from the New World to the Old'.

Odell racked his brains trying to recall the name of the Vice President who would now take his place. For the life of him he could not remember who he was. None of his friends had a clue either. This was odd, considering the impact later made on national and international affairs by Harry S. Truman.

Eventually they reached the River Elbe at Bleckede and were ferried across on barges propelled by a motor boat grappled to the side. During the crossing an RAF Spitfire flew low over the vessels. Foolishly, the guards fired at the plane with their rifles, but Odell and the others vigorously waved their makeshift flags to let the pilot know they were prisoners of war. To their delight, after circling a couple of times, the fighter gave a friendly waggle of its wings and flew away. It was comforting to know that their position had again been pinpointed by the Allies. About that time 12,000 Royal Air Force PoWs were congregated on the roads round the town of Geese, also north of the Elbe and not far from Odell's group. The British were elated. The half-starved men had just received their first quota of Red Cross food parcels in a long time. Under the eyes of their German guards they sat at the roadside hungrily feasting on corned beef, biscuits and chocolate. Suddenly disaster struck. They were shot up by eight British Typhoons of the 2nd Tactical Air Force and suffered close on 100 casualties, of whom sixty were killed. Among the victims were RAF men who had previously survived up to five years of captivity and had many escape attempts to their credit. It was a cruel fate indeed.

Odell's group had walked north for some miles along the banks of the Elbe–Lübeck canal towards the little town of Büchen. Before reaching the town they moved into a large farm and remained there for several days. It was 2 May when the guards ordered their prisoners to be ready to leave. This was the day that Odell decided he would not walk another step, whatever the consequences. He had in his possession four or five cigarettes, two of which he traded to a farm worker for a klim can of fresh milk. Lying on a pile of straw in the barn, he ate what little scraps of food he still had left and sipped the milk. Then, one after the other, he smoked his remaining cigarettes. 'If they shoot me now,' mused Odell, 'then at least I've had my breakfast!'

After a while he realized something unusual was happening outside. He had expected to hear the usual sounds of PoWs being assembled, shouted orders and the crunch of boots. Any moment the guards would come stomping into the barn to check for missing kriegies. He tried to visualize the Germans' reaction when he told them he was not going to budge another inch. But no guards came. Instead he could hear the prisoners shouting and there was the sound of running feet. Some excited-looking kriegies charged into the barn and he asked what was going on. Acting as if they were demented, they took no notice of Odell, but jumped up and down, bumped into each other and rushed out again. Odell got up and went outside to investigate. People were running in every direction and prisoners and guards were so intermingled that it was difficult to distinguish one from the other. Men crowded near a huge manure heap on the outskirts of the farm. As Odell walked over, he noticed PoWs gesticulating and staring towards something hidden from his view. Climbing to the top of the mound to get a better view of what was going on, he saw that a Jeep had halted on the road beyond the farm boundary. A British lieutenant was standing in the vehicle beside his driver. Odell could see quite clearly that he was very nattily dressed in a beret, battle-dress jacket and immaculately pressed trousers. A sparkling white shoulder lanyard was attached to the butt of his revolver. He was even wearing a necktie.

'Gentlemen,' the lieutenant called, 'you are officially LIBERATED. Disarm your guards and then please proceed to the town of Büchen.'

For a few seconds Odell was too surprised to act. Then, sliding down the pile of dung, he looked around for the nearest guard. Several were in the vicinity, but none of the Germans seemed particularly anxious to cooperate in this unexpected disarmament programme. It was a ticklish situation. Odell dodged behind a nearby oak tree, ready for the worst. Yet, wherever he moved, he was unable to get out of sight of at least one German. There was one old guard for whom the kriegies had quite an affection. They had long ago nicknamed him 'Grossvater'. The Nazi creed held no appeal for him – he was sick of the war and longed for the day it would end so he could return to his little home in Bavaria. Many times the men had been grateful for his leniency, allowing them to scrounge odd scraps of food while he looked the other way. When the march started he had carried a large automatic weapon, which he obviously found heavy and unwieldy. Later, it was noticed that this had been replaced by a much smaller and lighter carbine. When one of the prisoners asked him what had happened to his original gun, he grinned sheepishly and made a throwing motion with both hands towards the nearest ditch. This was clear evidence of his lack of interest in warlike activities. Odell spotted '*Grossvater*', who had quickly sized up the situation and was offering his weapon to the nearest prisoner. The American, who had not yet adjusted to the new turn of events, nervously refused to accept it. Twice more the old German tried to get rid of his carbine without success. Odell took the weapon, immediately turning it on another guard, who in turn surrendered his rifle. After that it was only a matter of minutes before all the guards were disarmed, leaving the Americans in possession of every weapon.

So, as suddenly and unexpectedly as that, Odell Dobson was set free. Later, as he made his way towards the town as directed, Odell came across the bodies of five German soldiers lying stiffly in a row at the side of the road. They were not the victims of battle, but the subjects of a deliberate and vicious execution. The men's faces had been mutilated beyond recognition, yet Odell saw at once the familiar outline of one corpse – a corpse of enormous proportions dressed in the uniform of a *feldwebel*. The kriegies had had their revenge. As Odell gazed down at the grisly display, he was sure he could never have done such a thing, however overwhelming the provocation. Fighting and killing in a battle was one thing, but cold-blooded slaughter in the name of retribution was not for him. He turned his face back towards Büchen. Pain, hunger, dirt, humiliation – all would now be left behind. As realization dawned, a slow smile of contentment spread across his wasted features.

GEORGE PAINE

BRITISH PARATROOPER

As THE MEN streamed back one officer, who had stood in the rain for hours, searched every face. Captain Eric Mackay, whose little band of stragglers had held out so gallantly in the schoolhouse near the Arnhem bridge, had escaped and reached Nijmegen. Now he looked for members of his squadron. Most of them had not made it to the Arnhem bridge but Mackay, with stubborn hope, looked for them in the airborne lines coming out of Oosterbeek. 'The worst thing of all was their faces,' he says of the troopers. 'They all looked unbelievably drawn and tired. Here and there you could pick out a veteran – a face with an unmistakable "I don't give a damn" look, as if he could never be beaten.' All that night and into the dawn Mackay stayed by the road. 'I didn't see one face I knew. As I continued to watch I hated everyone. I hated whoever was responsible for this and I hated the army for its indecision and I thought of the waste of life and of a fine division dumped down the drain. And for what?' It was full light when Mackay went back to Nijmegen. There he began to check collecting points and billets, determined to find his men. Of the 200 engineers in his squadron, five, including Mackay, had come back.

CORNELIUS RYAN, *A Bridge Too Far*

There was another one, a chirpy little Cockney called George Paine. But he took a little longer to get back. This is his story.

To BE A Cockney you have to be born within the sound of Bow Bells. Baby George must have been nearly deafened by the noise when the wind was in the right direction. Young Paine took his first sniff at the sooty atmosphere of Hackney, in the East End of London, in the next parish to Bow, one dull November day in the second year of the First World War. If he had had a choice, he might have picked a more comfortable time to be born and a different place, but then in retrospect he might not. It was a tough environment and the people were bred to match. A smack on the jaw was the accepted style of argument. Words when used were sharp, with a cutting wit. Survival was a way of life. Yet this hardy clan had warmth, compassion and humour in abundance too – much more than you would ever find in more cushioned communities.

George Paine's father, a regular soldier, suffered wounds on the Western Front in the early days of what they then called the Great War. He had previously served in South Africa and India. Now, after twenty-one years with the Colours, he was invalided out of the army with a pension of 4/11 (not quite 25p) per week – hardly enough to support his wife and four boys. He found himself a job in a munitions factory on the Hackney Marshes where he worked until the end of hostilities. Then the family moved to Leyton and Walthamstow where Paine senior leaned towards private enterprise – an inclination strongly sustained by his son George as he grew older. Father became a 'bucket and brush man', tackling odd jobs of considerable variety and mastering a number of skills in the process.

When he came of age, George showed that he was quick to learn. He could turn his hand to most things and demonstrated particular aptitude in carpentry. After an apprenticeship, he joined a firm specializing in fine veneers. Young George soon persuaded his employers to pay him more than his fellow craftsmen on the grounds that he worked faster and more accurately than they did. His sense of free enterprise was already beginning to show. In fact all members of the Paine family were hard-working and resourceful. They were undaunted by the difficult times in which they lived: the General Strike of the Twenties, the mass unemployment of the Thirties. Undoubtedly Cockney resilience helped them through the bleaker days.

Peace must have seemed as only an interlude to George's father and mother when Britain reluctantly declared war against her old adversary Germany on 3 September, 1939. Soon restrictions and austerity began to affect the people. So-called luxury goods grew scarce as factories reorganized to manufacture essential commodities. In the new scheme of things, fine veneers were not important, so George lost his job. Fortunately his father's services were in great demand and his son pitched in to help him. Together they erected dozens of Anderson air-raid shelters in back-yards throughout Walthamstow. To construct these shelters they dug trenches each large enough to accommodate a family in the sitting position. Over these excavations they erected semi-circular corrugated iron structures, like large dog kennels. They also shored up many of the buildings along Chatsworth Road in readiness for war.

Hard work and long hours, but their labours were well rewarded. Undoubtedly George could have continued this partnership for a long while. This was the time known as the Phoney War. The main combatants, France and Britain versus Germany, were sparring warily, trying to size each other up. No one had really been hit – except, of course, poor Poland – and who could do anything about that? Mass call-up for the armed forces had not got under way in Britain. Men like George, now in his mid-twenties, would not top the priority list in any case. The 18 and 19 year olds would go first when the time came. But at this stage only the regular army and some of the territorials were in France.

George never understood how his father had willingly spent the best years of his life in the army. He was a free spirit, hating all forms of discipline. Yet now he was unaccountably restless and discontented with his present mode of life. Times had changed. The 'lads' were in France and, for reasons he could not explain, George wanted to be with them. Before the year was out he had walked into the nearest recruiting office and volunteered.

After some delay he was eventually called up early in 1940. He had expressed a preference for the Engineers, so was well satisfied when told he would be joining the 696 Artisan Works Company. This outfit included many outstanding tradesmen from all parts of the country. Several prestigious firms, such as Wimpey, had lost a number of their best men to the 696. These men, though raw recruits, were well aware of their worth – skilled workers who had served long apprenticeships in their chosen trades. Mostly older than the average volunteer, they were rugged individualists, ready and willing to get on with the job in hand, whatever that job might be. George had no doubt that they would be in France in a matter of days. Little did he understand the ways of the army.

Posted to Margate, they suffered the same rigorous training that greenhorns have always endured: marching with blistered feet in unbroken boots; drilling with heavy Lee-Enfield rifles; shouted at and abused by unrelenting NCOs. Gradually they were transformed from a shower of shambling civvies into something resembling professional soldiers.

This transformation was not easy. George was always in trouble. Returning 'after hours' to his billet, a peacetime boarding-house, was a regular misdemeanour. Then, when he failed to turn up for early morning parade, the sparks really flew. The army knew well enough how to deal with this particular 'crime'.

Yet even the military were a little shaken by one incident which came perilously close to mutiny. Every morning the recruits were marched along the promenade to 'Dreamland', a huge building echoing with memories of happier days. Here breakfast was served en masse. On this particular morning for some reason the men took exception to the way their eggs and bacon had been cooked. The unfortunate proprietor went down under a barrage of greasy fried eggs hurled in his direction by a horde of angry troops. As George admitted later, 'If only we'd realized it, we were damn' lucky to get bacon and eggs at all in those days, whatever way they were cooked.'

When the Military Police arrived, order was restored and retribution followed swiftly: hourly parades with full pack. Soon the men of 696 became familiar with every inch of Cecil Square as they marched back and forth. Hardest to bear were the stares of onlookers, some amused, some downright mocking. It was easy to interpret the expressions on certain young male faces: 'Suckers! We're too clever to be caught like you' – an attitude particularly galling to volunteers. George, with characteristic initiative, soon managed to lighten his burden. He scrounged two large square biscuit tins, which, when fitted snugly into his main pack, made an excellent substitute for all the heavy kit he was supposed to be carrying.

Eventually the initial training was completed. The men were fighting fit and ready for action. But now there was no chance of a posting to France. The superior might of the Wehrmacht's panzer divisions had forced the British Army back to Dunkirk. Miraculously the troops had escaped destruction by a heroic evacuation. France had capitulated. Britain's fortunes were at a low ebb. As her newly appointed Prime Minister, Winston Churchill, wrote:

Now at last the slowly gathered, long-pent-up fury of the storm broke upon us. Four or five millions of men met each other in the first shock of the most merciless of all the wars of which record has been kept. Within a week the front in France, behind which we had been accustomed to dwell through the hard years of the former war and the opening phase of this, was to be irretrievably broken. Within three weeks the long-famed French Army was to collapse in rout and ruin, and our only British Army to be hurled into the sea with all its equipment lost. Within six weeks we were to find ourselves alone, almost disarmed, with triumphant Germany and Italy at our throats, with the whole of Europe open to Hitler's power, and Japan glowering on the other side of the globe.

George and his fellow Sappers embarked at Greenock on a troopship bound for Norway, but in view of the catastrophic situation the order was cancelled en route. The ship came about and headed back whence it started. They sailed peacefully past the tall white tower of the Cloch Light as their vessel nosed into the Firth of Clyde. To the north the soldiers could see the hills rising above Craigendoran while the ship eased over to the southern bank and docked in the industrial haze enveloping Greenock yards. 696 spent six weeks billeted in the Greenock district. For many of the men, including George, this was their first experience of living in Scotland. The good ladies of Toc H and the WVS canteens kept the lads well fed for mere pennies. On Saturday nights the main centre of celebration was the Town Hall. Beer flowed freely and eightsome reels burnt off the surplus energy generated by healthy young bodies. Soon George was convinced that enthusiastic indulgence in Scottish dancing could produce all the symptoms of drunkenness without the aid of alcohol. To sample both at the same time could produce some devastating results.

During their stay at Greenock the Sappers were astonished to see the *Queen Mary*, the mightiest liner in the world, sail into the Clyde – the river from which she had set forth on her maiden voyage only four years earlier. Drab grey paint and wartime armament detracted little from her magnificence and nothing from her 80,000-ton bulk. When she docked at nearby Gourock to disembark the first five thousand Australian troops to arrive in the United Kingdom, the Sappers were detailed to unload the *Queen*'s prodigious cargo.

As a direct result of this duty George Paine earned the nickname by which he was to be known for the rest of his time in the army. It happened this way. After the happy interlude at Greenock 696 was posted to the Orkney Isles. On the long rail journey north through the Highlands George spent his time profitably marching from one end of the troop-train to the other. On his perambulations he thoughtfully offered his mates whatever creature comforts they needed, provided they could pay for them: socks, gloves, warm vests – all items essential to men about to brave those wind-swept islands.

Nor did he forget the 'inner man' – tins of spam and corned beef found a ready sale among the ever-hungry soldiers.

'Where'd yer get all this bleedin' stuff, George? Fall orf the back of a lorry, did it?' George smiled innocently and shook his head. No, he assured them truthfully, none of it had fallen off the back of a lorry. The plentiful supply of goods had 'fallen out of a ship' – an exceptionally large ship.

'Gor, George, yer ain't arf a bleedin' poacher! Ere 'e comes agin – bloody old Poacher Paine!' – and that was the name that stuck. Throughout his distinguished military career, Private Paine was never found unworthy of his honorary title of 'Poacher'.

The Orkneys were awful. Heavy gales lashed the islands. Some of the coastlines had low sandhills, others towering red cliffs a thousand feet high. When the great seas met such natural barriers, they broke, sending foaming spray hundreds of feet aloft. Scapa Flow, the famous base of the Royal Navy's Grand Fleet in the First World War and the graveyard of the German High Seas Fleet, scuttled by its own crews after surrender, is a large landlocked stretch of water in the southern part of the group, enclosed by several islands. In more recent times, about nine months before George's arrival, U-boat U47, under the command of Kapitan-Leutnant Gunther Prien, stole through a gap in the boom defences and torpedoed the old battleship HMS *Royal Oak* as she rode at anchor. The great veteran sank to the bottom with the loss of 833 lives.

The job of the Sappers was to construct hutment camps for troops under training. Starting with a bare patch of ground, they would build a complex fit for a sizeable community to live in: sleeping quarters, cookhouse, officers' mess, communal buildings, classrooms, HQ and office blocks, guardroom and stores. All these units were connected by an interlinking network of concrete paths and roads. Drains had to be dug, electricity wired in and hot and cold water laid on. Good use was made of one of nature's most constant commodities by erecting windmills to generate power and pump the water. The Sappers themselves were camped in tents surrounded by a sea of mud. They never lived in the accommodation they had worked so hard to build. Still, George gave the army full marks for increasing his knowledge of the building trade, a knowledge that was to stand him in good stead in later life. Although he had been a carpenter in civvy street, the army in its wisdom had classified him as a concreter.

Yet in the Orkneys he had a chance to turn his hand to bricklaying, plumbing, plastering and electrical wiring. In the end though, in spite of all this useful experience, the repetitive nature of the work and the boredom of off-duty hours reduced George to a serious state of frustrated discontent. The unremitting harshness of the climate did nothing to lighten his spirits. The Engineers stomping through the everlasting quagmire of mud were prepared to tell anyone that, in their experience, summer on the islands started on 31 July and ended on 1 August. At least, they said, this was true in a good year. However that might be, poor old Poacher endured not only the remainder of 1940 in the Orkneys but the whole of the year that followed.

In desperation he volunteered for every branch of the armed forces that he thought might give him a chance to escape. He applied for service in submarines, in the jungles of Burma, in the Marines and even in the newly formed brigade of paratroops. It was all to no avail. His sergeant-major blocked every request for posting. 'An Engineer should keep his feet on the ground and get on with his work.' George had given up all hope when miraculously, after eighteen months on those benighted islands, he was suddenly posted to help with a construction job in Wiltshire.

This was an ideal billet – set amid gently undulating hills, with a mild climate, a pleasant market town nearby and, best of all, within easy reach of London. No need to worry about putting his name forward for hazardous operations any more. No one but a fool would want to leave this place.

A few days after his arrival he was called to the orderly office. 'News for you, Poacher,' said the corporal clerk; 'You're posted to Hardwick Hall for parachute training. George spent the rest of the day jumping off the roof of a half-completed tank workshop, landing in a pile of sand, just to get in the mood.

Hardwick Hall, Depot of the Parachute Regiment, was near Chesterfield in Derbyshire. The house itself was a great Renaissance mansion set on rising ground overlooking its own parkland. George had never seen so many enormous windows in one building before. The grounds in the shallow valley below had been scarred by rows of brick huts. What followed was a totally new experience for Poacher. It bore no relation to anything he had so far encountered in the army. The course had been specially designed not only to toughen the volunteers physically, and it certainly did that, but also to prepare them mentally for the wholly unnatural act of jumping out of an aircraft.

Under the watchful eye of Regimental Sergeant-Major Gerry Strachan (ex-Black Watch) the would-be Paras were forced through paces that seemed almost impossible to endure. Marches in full battle kit covering ten miles of rough country in two hours; PT like it had never been known before, in vests and shorts yes, but with heavy boots and rifles as well; assault courses that must have been devised by the Devil himself, encompassing a desperate squirm on the belly through slimy mud with live machine-gun fire directed just above the ground. Needless to say, some volunteers did find it impossible. They literally fell by the wayside. Without fuss or recrimination these men were quietly returned to their units.

Physical hazards were not the only obstacles to be overcome. The tests imposed by the psychologists – the 'trick cyclists' – had to be safely negotiated. Not everyone was considered mentally in tune with the business of falling through the air. As the training progressed, RAF instructors explained the basics of parachuting – safety measures; the right way to exit from an aircraft; the correct landing procedures; how a chute is constructed, and why; the meticulous technique of packing the chute correctly.

Confidence grew with understanding. The whole procedure of falling by parachute now seemed far less of a hit-and-miss affair than George had previously imagined. Like his fellow volunteers, he was relieved to learn that the dreaded 'Roman Candle', when the chute fails to open in its customary umbrella shape but streams in a long line of twisted silk above the paratrooper as he plunges to his death, was a much rarer phenomenon than rumour had suggested. Nevertheless, it did happen from time to time and expert opinion was divided as to the reason. It is unlikely that faulty packing was to blame on any but very few occasions. To suggest otherwise would be a slur on the meticulous work carried out by the conscientious members of the Women's Auxilary Air Force. A more likely explanation was that static electricity, under certain conditions, held the folds of the material together.

Having successfully completed their time at Hardwick Hall, George and his comrades were sent to Ringway, near Manchester, where their parachute training began in earnest. Moments of stark terror inevitably accompanied this unique method of training. Only uncommon amounts of courage and willpower could overcome a natural inclination to panic. Yet, this aside, Poacher revelled in the experience, feeling that his life was indeed taking on a new dimension.

The course was divided into two parts: first, 'Synthetic Training', followed by actual jumping. PT was continued throughout the period of instruction to keep the men at a high peak of physical fitness. The fuselage of a Whitley bomber was mounted on a tall tubular steel structure. Trainee Paras dropped through a hole in the underside of the airframe onto thick mats placed on the ground below. A serious problem was associated with the exercise. It was known as 'ringing the bell'. The trainees entered the fuselage in groups of four and moved towards the aperture in the floor. As the opening was small, it was necessary to jump through while standing to attention. On the command 'Go', the men followed each other in quick succession, 'Go' . . . 'Go' . . . 'Go'. The trouble was that each man had a large parachute pack on his back. If the pack hit the edge of the hole it would throw the man forward so that his nose caught the front ledge. Broken noses were a common sight at Ringway.

George had great sympathy for the heavyweights in his outfit. He realized for the first time that he had a real advantage in being diminutive when it came to parachuting. More broken legs and arms were sustained during Synthetic Training than ever occurred in jumping from aircraft.

The nastiest piece of equipment was the 'fan' – an open tower-like structure with a flimsy platform at the top. The only means of ascent was by a vertical metal ladder. George watched apprehensively as the lad immediately ahead of him literally crapped himself, climbing slowly to what he was convinced was certain death. On reaching the summit a contraption was strapped to the man's back above which were what looked like small helicopter blades. These blades were rotated by the upward pressure of air as the trainee fell at a speed approximating that of a parachute descent. More would-be Paras faltered in awe before this monstrosity than at any other stage in their training. Not infrequently a man would be seen ascending this stairway to the stars, only to pause before reaching the top, look down from a dizzy height, then slowly retrace his steps to the ground. There was no second chance – he was returned to his unit.

The RAF instructors had experimented with this and other apparatus – pioneering the training schedule the hard way. They understood the problems better than anyone and did their best to help. Once a trainee was on the platform the sergeant would give him a penny and instruct him to clamp it between his knees. If he dropped it during the execution of his jump, he would have to pay a forfeit – drinks all round. Poacher never lost his penny. He learnt the vital importance of keeping his legs together, knees slightly bent, as he landed. This distributed the load equally and minimized the danger of broken bones.

Eventually George and his mates were taken to Tatton Park. On arrival they saw a solitary barrage balloon with soft floppy fins. It swayed aimlessly from a cable at eight hundred feet. They noted the rectangular container slung underneath. This 'box without a lid' was designed to hold four trainees and their instructor. Almost as awful as the 'fan', at least the balloon jump was a 'one-off'. On successful completion of this exercise they knew they would thereafter parachute from aircraft.

Nevertheless it was all very unpleasant: the balloon oscillated, the container oscillated and the stomach oscillated most of all. George took up position at the opening. He could see the ground tilting sickeningly as the balloon swayed. Suddenly he was thinking of Roman Candles: the ghastly image of a pathetic little figure plummeting helplessly to earth. He was gripped by momentary panic.

'Action stations, 1,' the sergeant yelled. George cleared his mind of all impeding thoughts. A firm tap on the shoulder, then: 'GO'. With more courage than he ever knew he possessed, he leapt into space.

The descent was over in a disappointingly short time. George hardly had a chance to savour the feeling of relief as the canopy billowed open above him.

He hit the ground, rolled over correctly and stood up again, gathering in the chute as he trotted forward. He had fallen through the sky by parachute and survived. He was alive. By now others had landed. They stood in a small group, laughing and shouting and thumping each other on the back – they had been tested and had proved their quality beyond question. A new élite was being born who would forge a tradition to be followed and loyally sustained by their successors.

A further six jumps were made from obsolete two-engined Armstrong-Whitworth Whitley Bombers. These aircraft, with a cramped narrow fuselage and no side exit doors, were quite unsuitable for the job of dropping paratroops. Yet they were the only planes that the RAF could spare for training at the time. As a compromise the ventral turret had been removed, leaving the hole in the floor through which the trainees jumped. The men flew in sticks of ten and were dropped at an altitude of six hundred feet. As with the balloon, a static line attached to the plane automatically tugged the chute open. Again, the fall was over in moments, disappointing for the paras as individuals, but operationally satisfactory; the sooner they were on the ground, the quicker they could be deployed as highly specialized infantry. George and the other lads agreed that leaping out of aircraft was 'a piece of cake' when compared with the other means of descent endured during training.

At last guts and determination had their reward. During the passing-out parade at Ringway George Paine was awarded his coveted blue paratrooper's wings to be worn on the upper right sleeve, and the blue Pegasus emblems against a maroon background on each arm.

Before and during these training activities dramatic events had been taking place. Over two years previously comparatively few RAF fighter pilots had defeated far superior numbers of Luftwaffe fighters and bombers in the Battle of Britain and so staved off invasion by the Germans. But, apart from that, Britain and the Empire had suffered much and succeeded little. The army had been hurled out of Europe with the loss of nearly all its equipment. Unprecedented numbers of merchant ships had been sunk in the Atlantic by marauding packs of U-boats. Singapore had fallen to the Japanese in what was described as 'the most ignominious capitulation in the history of British arms'. The desert army had been pushed back almost to the gates of Cairo by the German Afrika Korps, under the leadership of General Rommel.

Yet now, in the closing months of 1942, for the first time after so many bitter disappointments the fortunes of war were changing. Montgomery's victorious Eighth Army – an Empire force if ever there was one – had defeated the Germans and Italians at the Battle of Alamein, sweeping them out of Egypt and chasing them across North Africa. To quote Winston Churchill: 'It may almost be said – before Alamein we never had a victory. After Alamein we never had a defeat.'

As a consequence of the Japanese bombing of Pearl Harbor at the end of the previous year, America had entered the war on the side of the Allies. She and Britain were now mounting a second campaign in North Africa. The Anglo-American First Army under General Eisenhower had just landed west of Tunisia – the British at Algiers, the Americans at Oran and in French Morocco.

The political situation there was confused. The Vichy French were in occupation, but very much under the shadow of German authority. Admiral Darlan, commander of the Vichy armed forces, agreed to a ceasefire. However, Hitler began to reinforce his existing forces in Tunisia. He was aided in his efforts by some French commanders who disobeyed Darlan's orders.

So, while Montgomery was pursuing the enemy from the East, the First Army's objective was to take Tunis by approaching from the West through difficult mountain terrain. But it was too late to prevent a massive build-up of Axis forces in Tunisia. Bitter fighting ensued which lasted well into the following year. As George and his fellow Sappers were sewing on their wings, the 1st Parachute Brigade, including the 1st, 2nd and 3rd Battalions, was already in action, fighting as infantry ahead of the First Army in the mountains of Tunisia. For the first time the Paras were wearing the Red Beret and were soon to be dubbed '*Die Rote Teufeln*' – 'The Red Devils' – by a respectful foe. Within weeks George had joined them.

On the night of 23 November British Paratroopers were preparing to attack an area named Gué, a small hill rising from the plains near Souk-el-Arba. Moving ahead of the main assault force was a party of Sappers under Captain Geary. Their task was to move round the hill and mine the road running to it from the east. This was to hamper the retreat of the German garrison and impede the possible arrival of reinforcements. The Sappers crept stealthily over rough ground. Each was carrying a Hawkins anti-tank mine in a sandbag, ready for laying. Suddenly a shattering explosion rent the night. One of the paratroopers had stumbled and his mine had detonated setting off all the others. The entire party of three officers and twenty-four men was wiped out. George and his mates were sent out to replace them.

Travelling by sea from Britain, they landed in Algiers. The battle zone lay deep in the mountains of Tunisia, reached only by moving eastwards along more than four hundred and fifty miles of narrow twisting roads or the single railway track. But at that moment George was not preoccupied with distant conflict. His present surroundings, so unfamiliar and strange, fully held his attention. After the cramped confines of the ship he felt a pleasant sense of freedom. The mild Mediterranean climate, in spite of the time of the year, was a welcome change from the chilling fogs of an English winter. The warm, heavy smells fascinated him. As a natural salesman, he studied with professional interest the approach of the Arab street vendors as they enthusiastically plied their trinkets and fly-whisks. He admired their tenacity if not their technique. Poacher revelled in the bright colours, the stately Algerian cavalrymen mounted on their magnificent horses, the barrows piled high with fruit, the veiled women who went silently by. If this was war, then it wasn't bad. He noted with satisfaction that the town was crammed with well-paid American servicemen. The whole atmosphere encouraged happy thoughts of private enterprise, a good chance to do a little business on the side.

But entrepreneurial plans were soon dashed. Within days of their arrival in Algiers they were on the move by train. The Sappers were crushed into trucks designed to carry forty men. The long journey followed the coast eastwards towards Tunisia. At night, because it was bitterly cold, the paratroopers in Poacher's wagon lit a fire on the floor. It certainly warmed things up. Unfortunately, when a large section of the floor area was burnt away and dropped onto the track, it left even less living space for the men.

Having rapidly built up their strength in and around Tunis, the Germans and Italians had wasted no time in advancing west into the mountains with the object of holding key defensive positions. These positions were being stoutly contested by a comparatively small number of infantry divisions – mostly British foot regiments, notably the Argylls, the Guards, the Lancashire Fusiliers and the Hampshires. They were reinforced by an assortment of French units who had rallied to the cause. Americans were also there, predominantly at the southern end of the line. Then, of course, there was the 1st Parachute Brigade, steadily building a reputation as the toughest and most resolute of fighters, constantly rushing in to plug gaps in the line and strengthen those parts of the front that showed signs of breaking. They lived and fought under appalling conditions. Subsisting mainly on bully beef and biscuits, they survived in holes scraped in the side of mountains. Torrential rain soaked them continuously. At night they froze in the bitter cold of high altitudes. Cut off from First Army HQ, without air support, constantly short of ammunition, often unable to move their wounded to safer areas, still they battled on.

General Eisenhower, the Supreme Commander, had to make a decision. He knew that with the onset of winter it would be unwise, even impossible, to launch a full-scale assault on Tunis. Should he therefore withdraw his

hard-pressed infantry divisions from the mountainous regions for the duration of the winter? Or should he order them to hold fast as best they could,
with little hope of support, until the spring? He ordered them to hold fast.

So, while the vast bulk of the Allied Force dwelt in comparative comfort in
Algeria throughout the winter months, a handful of fighting men held the
line. Thus the task of the First Army, advancing on Tunis several months
later when weather conditions improved, was made that much easier.

The question was asked at the time – why didn't the Allies land in Bizerta
and Tunis in the first place? Surely this would have made sense, taking
advantage of the enemy's slim forces before he had time to reinforce. The
Royal Navy had the answer to that one. They had already taken considerable risks getting the troops as far into the Mediterranean as Oran and
Algiers. To have exposed such large numbers of men to a further day's
steaming, directly towards enemy aircraft and submarines based at Sicily,
would have been foolhardy.

So George and his companions were moved up to where the action was. In
spite of their specialized training, they did not fly into battle. Instead they
clattered and clanked their way up to the front in overcrowded railway
trucks, pulled by a tired old locomotive which seemed intent on maintaining
its role as a reluctant neutral. The front had more or less stabilized on a line
running from the coast at Tabarka through the cork-tree forests to Sedjenane, then south-east to the once attractive but now devastated town of
Medjez-el-Bab (the key of the gate) on the Medjerda River – a key it
certainly was and the nearest Allied jumping-off point to Tunis, less than
forty miles away. Beyond this the line meandered southwards over more
mountain ranges until it reached the no man's land of the Sahara Desert.

Their first introduction to war must have been a shattering experience.
Alan Moorehead gave a vivid description of his visit to the battle zone near
Sedjenane. The road was so often blitzed from the air by German fighters
nipping up from their fields ten minutes away that it was closed to vehicles in
the daytime. He parked his car a couple of miles away and walked under
cover to the forward positions.

> I called on the parachutists one day and all around the bush was heavy
> with the sweet and nauseating smell of bodies that were turning rotten in
> the sun after the rain. In their whole approach to death these young men
> had completely altered. They had killed so many themselves and with the
> bayonet. They had seen so many of their companions die. They had
> become so well acquainted with death they had no fear of it any longer.
> The fact that that body lying over there was Bill or Jack or Jim who had
> eaten breakfast with them this morning was not remarkable or horrible:
> you either lived or you died or you got wounded, and any one of these

conditions was an accepted condition. It was not that pity or grief had
gone out of them, but that they were living in a well of danger and their
lives were sharpened and lifted up to the point of meeting that danger
directly. It was all very largely a technical matter – whether you got your
machine-gun burst in first and with the right direction. These men were
soaked in war. They were grown old to war in a few weeks, and all the
normal uses of peace and the ambitions of peace were entirely drained
out of them. At length they were brought a few miles back for a spell.
Some huts had been prepared for them and a meal. But when the men got
off the trucks they did not want to walk the remaining four hundred yards
for the meal and the shelter. They fell onto the mud beside their trucks
and slept in the streaming rain.

Poacher had had the good sense to ally himself with a huge Scot, a
one-time lumberjack, Jock Middlemas. Jock was a giant who fought with his
fists, while his friend Poacher thoughtfully collected the bets! George
claimed he was the hardest man he had ever known – and the proudest. He
habitually refused First Aid, however badly bruised after a set-to. Now they
were at war Middlemas soon established a reputation as the deepest trench
digger in the business. Trouble was that George, who always shared a hole
with him, couldn't see over the top. A large ammunition box, serving as an
observation platform, solved the problem.

With numbers of men, British and German, ranging back and forth over
the same limited piece of ground, the glutinous mud inevitably became
polluted. With uncanny accuracy Poacher and Jock always seemed to pick a
spot for trench-digging activities that had previously been reserved for basic
human evacuation. The trench would be dug, the tiny pup tent erected over
it as a shield from the rain. Then, with the satisfaction of a job well done,
they would climb inside. After a moment the smell would hit them.
Middlemas's reaction never varied: 'Christ, Poacher, have yer farted?'

Just as the Parachutists, fighting as infantry, were being deployed in North
Africa in a role for which they had never been intended, so the Sappers, also
specialists, were being used largely as infantry, rather than Engineers,
within the Parachute battalions. Combat in the mountains gave less opportunity to use engineering skills than would have been the case in other
terrain. The principal menace that George and his mates had to deal with in
the hills of Tunisia was the German anti-personnel S mine. Its presence was
betrayed by three little prongs, easily mistaken for twigs, sticking out of the
ground. Put a foot on one of the prongs and nothing happened; remove the
foot and immediately the antennae shot up to waist height discharging a
devastating shower of ball-bearings, or sharp, vicious nails. The force
behind these projectiles was sufficient to cause death or injury to any soldier

unfortunate enough to be in the vicinity. George always carried a supply of stout wire. On locating an S mine he would carefully scrape away the earth round its base. Then he would insert the wire in such a way as to render the mine harmless.

George was detailed to look after his officer, Lieutenant Brown. This duty included attention to the lieutenant's welfare during the quieter times, and to keep close to him and protect him as well as possible during combat. No officer could have picked a better man. Although the army rations were so meagre, George had seen how the Arab farmers continued to work their land regardless of shot and shell. He quickly grabbed an opportunity to slip away and make the acquaintance of some who lived nearby. Soon he had arranged a fairly regular supply of eggs and fruit for his officer and other members of his troop. In far-away Algiers troops, paying hugely inflated prices, were being happily exploited by the locals; but out here, beyond so-called civilization, Poacher paid no more than 10 francs for an egg or a whole kilo of oranges. Naturally, as middleman, he felt entitled to take a modest profit for his trouble.

On one occasion preparation was made to take an enemy position. Strategically dug in on a hill, it had been causing the battalion a considerable amount of trouble. When the attack began, George, weighed down with rifle and grenades, crawled forward, closely following Lieutenant Brown. The night air was shattered by the steady thunk, thunk, thunk of their own Bren gun. George hugged the ground closer as the Germans replied with the rapid, tearing brrr of a Spandau LMG, firing many times faster than the Bren, at well over a thousand rounds per minute. Suddenly the order was yelled: 'Fix bayonets'. Raising his head warily, George was horrified to see Lieutenant Brown leap to his feet and charge forward in the direction of the enemy machine-gun post, firing his Sten gun as he went. Slamming his bayonet into position, George raised himself dutifully from the prone position and stumbled after him. Bullets whistled past his head as he ran. A moment later Brown fell, mortally wounded. He died almost immediately, his stomach shot through. George crouched over him, lobbing grenades in the direction of the German machine-gunners. More men arrived and doggedly they fought their way forward until, after suffering many casualties, with bayonets still fixed, they overran the enemy stronghold. George, Jock Middlemas, another mate called Alex and three others took over a German trench. They settled in for the night, preparing for the enemy counterattack which they knew would come at dawn. To call these German dugouts trenches was an injustice to those who constructed them. They were minor works of art. Carefully lined, with wooden floors and protective roofs, they were nearly always free of damp, in strict contrast to the waterlogged holes in the ground inhabited by British infantrymen. Their comparative contentment was sadly shattered when Alex decided to look over the top to get his bearings. He was killed at once with a bullet through the head.

All that long night George and his mates shared the confined space of the dugout with the dead body of their unlucky comrade. In that small dark world the night held a concentration of horror, anger and sadness. For a long time afterwards George had nightmares, and he knew he was not alone in this. Beneath that hard protective shell men remained bewildered, bruised and hurt.

At one time the Paras were particularly hard-pressed, facing heavy opposition from a force far greater than themselves. They were hanging onto the hill by the skin of their teeth, but the Germans, part of the formidable Witzig Regiment, were slowly gaining ground. Then a most unexpected message was received at Battalion HQ. An American mobile artillery battery was on its way to give assistance and should arrive at approximately 1100 hours. Scouts were sent back down the road to meet their welcome guests and guide them to pre-arranged positions. Well ahead of time a business-like roar of engines was heard approaching from the west. As the sound increased it was identified as belonging to a substantial column of vehicles packed with determined-looking GIs and towing a variety of large-calibre guns.

To the amazement of the British, the trucks did not pause in their forward rush, although one driver stuck his head out of the window and shouted: 'Where in hell's this goddamn' shootin' match?' He had passed long before anyone could reply. On up the hill they went, skirting round the Paras entrenched near the summit. To the amazement of the onlookers, this unorthodox convoy mounted the top of the hill and disappeared from sight. For a short period there was a stunned silence while men tried to envisage the reaction of the Germans.

Then all hell was let loose; the sound of heavy gunfire rent the morning air. As quickly as possible the Paras scrambled up to the crest to see what was going on and to render what help they could. The sight that met their eyes was not the one they expected. The US artillery was lined up on a ridge, almost in parade ground order, firing off in all directions. 'What are you firing at?' a British officer enquired. 'That tower way over there,' an American captain replied, pointing to a building down in the valley. 'Why?' asked the puzzled Para. 'Well, when it falls down, we'll sure as hell know we've hit it!'

It transpired that this unit had never before fired a shot in anger. They were indulging in competition among themselves to be the first to shoot at Germans. They had raced along the winding mountain passes, recklessly overtaking each other, in their determination to claim the privilege of being the first to lob a shell at the enemy. By all the rules of war they should have been wiped out – if not when they appeared over the crest, then certainly during the delay while they were setting up their artillery. During interrogation of prisoners later it was learned that the Germans were as astonished as anyone else by this extraordinary manoeuvre. Suspecting an elaborate trick, they had retired off the hill to think things over!

Poacher, and most of his comrades, liked the Yanks. Their antics were a constant source of conversation. If the Doughboys had descended by spaceship from Mars they could hardly have appeared more strange in their approach to life and the war. For the Paras, subsisting on the bare necessities of life, it was staggering to see the lorry-loads of provisions constantly available for the welfare and comfort of American troops. They dined on well-cooked meals as a matter of course. Tinned meats, fruit and vegetables abounded. Cigarettes and chewing gum were there for the asking. Poacher gazed in open-mouthed wonder at a wagon dispensing hot flapjacks. He had never seen a contraption like this, let alone tasted such delicacies. The GIs always showed great generosity in sharing what they had with their comrades-in-arms. Their clothing and equipment was superior in nearly all respects to that of either the British or German armies in North Africa. The Garand rifle and the officer's carbine were excellent. From Sherman tanks to Willis Jeeps, from rubber-soled boots to heavy artillery pieces, everything was brand new – unlike the battle-torn gear of the British and German armies, patched and repaired beyond belief.

The Paras lived in battle-dress worn threadbare in combat. Their boots were scuffed and broken on the rocks of the *jebels* (hills). They wore parachutists' smocks that had a flap designed to fold forward between the legs and fasten in front with press-studs. The studs had long since broken and so the flap hung down behind. The Arabs nicknamed the paratroopers 'the men with tails'. Yet the American troops had to learn the arts of war from these scarecrows. At night they learned the value of stealth and silence, just as their own Indian scouts had done a century before. At dawn, they soon understood that vigilance meant survival. They learned to rely on themselves more than on mechanical aids – for, if they had a fault, it was too great an abundance of everything and often the matériel got in the way of the action. Yet with remarkable speed, they absorbed the lessons of war.

Towards the end of March, 1943, weather conditions showed signs of improving. Torrential rains, which had lasted for an unusually long period that year, abated. Slowly the chocolate-coloured mud on the valley floor began to harden, allowing the tanks to move forward. The victorious Eighth Army, after pausing for breath following its westward dash, had at last arrived in the south of Tunisia. It was obvious that the Allied First Army, now commanded by General Alexander, would also soon advance through the mountain passes and eastward out onto the plains to link up with their comrades in the desert army. The Germans and Italians, in order to avoid being squeezed between these two great forces, would be pressed back to the shore around Tunis and Bizerta. But for them there would be no 'Dunkirk', not with the Royal Navy constantly patrolling the coast, and the RAF at last commanding the skies. The work of the infantry, including the paratroopers would soon be over. The day of the big mechanized battalions was near. Yet before that one last effort by the Parachute Brigade was called for.

It was once more in the area of Sedjenane. Two key peaks, known as Green Hill and Bold Hill, had to be retaken. Whoever commanded these heights held Mateur and whoever held Mateur could take Bizerta. As before, their toughest opponents were the men of the Witzig Regiment, paratroopers like themselves. The attack started on the evening of 27 March, 1943. A warm tribute was paid to the Sappers as, yet again, they took their places in the front-line positions. It was given by Lieutenant Colonel John Frost (later Major-General Frost CB DSO MC): 'On this day we were strengthened by the arrival of a troop of our Parachute Engineer Squadron. These staunch old friends took up positions on our left flank, just where we had been most vulnerable before and we nicknamed their position the Citadel.'

After hours of bloody battle, matters had reached a crucial stage. The German parachutists were firmly entrenched in a forest of cork trees. Poacher and his comrades, having lobbed everything available into the woods in an attempt to dislodge the enemy, were running short of grenades. George, by now an old hand at moving about under fire, dodged to a point some way down the hill; he had remembered seeing a pile of captured Italian hand-grenades stacked neatly near some rocks. He loaded as many as he could carry into a wooden ammunition box. Placing the carrying rope round his neck, he supported the precious cargo on his chest and struggled back up the hill. The Paras spotted him walking through their positions, distributing grenades and calmly calling out: 'Chocolates, cigarettes!' Against his better principles, he didn't charge anyone a penny.

George seemed to lead a charmed life, but many were not so lucky. Yet the injured were not left for long in their agony. Stretcher-bearers bore them away to an advanced dressing-station, just beyond the immediate range of enemy small-arms fire, but still constantly bombarded by shells. The doctors and surgeons worked steadily on. Oblivious to their own danger, they too were forging a tradition. From this time on the medical teams attached to the parachute battalions would always operate as closely as possible to their fighting men.

All through the following day and into the second night the battle raged, but with the British paratroops gradually gaining ground as they fought their way up the slopes. Colonel Frost's ranks were so depleted that the weight of the attack could not be sustained for much longer. He called for one last supreme effort and then, not for the first time in that North African war, he ordered 'Fix bayonets'. He blew a note on his hunting horn. 'Here we go again,' muttered George. 'Let's get this bloody thing over and done with.' Shouting their now famous war-cry, 'Whoa, Mohammed!' The paratroops first heard this cry when they arrived among the hills of Tunisia. It was uttered by Arabs calling to each other across intervening valleys and also as an exhortation to their mules and donkeys to get a move on. Soon the men had adopted it for their own. The Paras charged up the hill. It was too much for the enemy, who broke and scattered down the opposite slopes. The last key battle of the Tunisian hills had been won.

At the time no credit was given to the Paratroops for their efforts. Apart from themselves and their respected enemy, hardly anyone knew what had taken place during that final mountain conflict. Nothing was reported in the press. People back home in England were later to ask 'What did you do in North Africa?' Perhaps even more hurtful, the Paras were not included in the great thrust forward into Tunis itself.

During the first half of April the battalion had taken up positions to the north of Sedjenane. After a couple of weeks they were relieved by an American division primed for the final advance on Tunis. During those last few days, George was involved in a strange experience. It happened when he was engaged in one of his solo recces for food. On a narrow mountain pass he was suddenly confronted by an Italian major in a resplendent green and white uniform. With a disarming smile the major held out his glittering sword in both hands. It was a symbolic gesture of surrender. A little embarrassed, Private Paine tried to explain that he didn't think he was entitled to accept such a privilege. On the other hand he would be glad to take him to one of his officers, who would surely be happy to meet his wishes. With an elaborate gesture the Italian officer motioned Poacher to lead the way. As they moved off, hundreds upon hundreds of Bersaglieri (infantry soldiers) rose up from behind rocks and, forming into single file, followed their leader along the stony track. Poacher could feel the hairs rising on the back of his neck as he realized his footsteps were being dogged by close on a thousand of his recent enemies. He was mightily relieved to hand over his wards to someone of higher rank.

From this time on similar mass surrenders both of Germans and Italians became commonplace. On the coastal plains round Tunis and Bizerta the enemy soldiers throwing down their arms were numbered in tens of thousands. Left virtually leaderless, with their backs to the sea and with no chance of escape, they saw no reason to fight on. Ironically, the Allies' failure to secure Tunisia in the autumn, when Axis strength was light, meant that the victory now was much greater. By the second week in May all conflict in North Africa had ceased. Whole German divisions, flown in during those intervening months, plus the Afrika Korps, forced west by Montgomery, were effectively removed from the war.

In the meantime the 1st Parachute Brigade had moved in easy stages hundreds of miles west to a hot, dry, dusty camp surrounded by airfields near the town of Mascara, south of Oran. There they joined up with the 1st Airborne Division, recently arrived from Britain. The men of the Brigade were to be re-equipped and trained for the impending invasion of Sicily. On their long train journey west George and his comrades slowly chugged past a vast prisoner-of-war compound. As their former enemies spotted the red berets, they rushed in their hundreds to the perimeter wire and cheered the British Paras with all the enthusiasm they could muster. No higher tribute could be paid. The legend was secure.

The Brigade had taken 3600 prisoners in four months – all captured in small numbers during bitter fighting. Based on enemy reports, at least 5000 of their troops had been killed or wounded by the Paratroops. This had been achieved while fighting the best the Axis could throw into the line against them: the Hermann Goering Jaeger Regiment, the Barenthin Regiment, the Witzig Regiment, the Austrian Mountain Division and the 10th Panzer Grenadiers. In addition the Italians disposed their Alpini and Bersaglieri. During this campaign the Brigade suffered 1700 casualties (killed and wounded). (These grisly statistics probably give only a hazy idea of the almost unbelievable achievements of the three battalions of the 1st Parachute Brigade. We get a clearer perspective if we realize, for instance, that the 2nd Battalion under Lieutenant Colonel Frost was reduced to no more than 160 officers and men during a crucial period of their final struggle with the enemy. This does away with any preconceived ideas of massed armies locked in battle.) According to battalion commanders, practically the only recorded 'military crimes' were – desertion from hospitals. A steady trickle of wounded Paras struggled from their sick-beds and found their way back to the fighting front. Some came from as far away as Algiers, more than 450 miles to the west.

Once more in training, George and his mates resented being placed under the command of a 19-year-old officer, freshly arrived from the UK as a replacement for Lieutenant Brown. The contempt was mutual. Matters came to a head when this new lieutenant ordered A Troop on a forced march with full kit across the hot, sandy plateau – 'as a toughening-up exercise'. The men agreed among themselves that this was a heaven-sent opportunity to adjust this unsatisfactory situation. On and on they marched, with the fierce sun beating down on their heads. Not a man touched his water-bottle. Their eyes never left their inexperienced leader. In the end, gasping with thirst, the officer was forced to reach for his supply of water and drink deeply. The contempt was now one-sided. Out in the Algerian wilderness a young man was told truths and learned lessons few people of his age are privileged to experience. After that the lads had no more trouble from Lieutenant——

At the beginning of July the Brigade was flown back to Tunisia, a country now at peace, and landed near Sousse on the east coast. They encamped in a pleasantly shady area surrounded by olive trees. After a quick recce, Poacher decided that this set-up was much to his liking. He convened an urgent business meeting with one of his closest allies, Gus Woods. Although a Sapper, like the rest of the troop, Gus was a university graduate and the son of a regular army major. Yet, most important from Poacher's point of view, Gus acted as driver to Captain Mackay (an officer later to win fame for his valiant resistance in the schoolhouse at Arnhem). This meant that a very useful Jeep was at their disposal. Having met the transport requirement at a stroke, the partners, without irksome formality, floated a company; they called it the Woo-Pay (Woods & Paine) Wine Company.

The marketing strategy was refreshingly simple. They established sources of supply in Sousse, paying hard cash in francs for local wine, Black Dog Whisky and White Cat Gin. A short drive brought them to the American airfields where they sold their hooch at double the price to the grateful GIs. With huge profits in their pockets, Poacher and Gus returned to Sousse for even greater quantities of liquor. Had they had time to draw a daily sales chart, it would have looked astronomically successful. Every 100 francs doubled and then doubled again as the daily transactions proceeded. Occasionally, for a limited period, the precious jeep had to be returned to the British Army for official duties – sometimes to undergo a necessary service. The only other limitation on the activities of the Woo-Pay Wine Co was the physical state of its clients. Once the Americans had consumed the goods, the resulting hangovers made it advisable for the British wine salesmen to allow a decent period for recovery, say two weeks, before offering further supplies. The firm's directors overcame this problem by working out a system of well-spaced visits to a number of US bases.

Not unexpectedly, business activities were occasionally interrupted by further bouts of training. For the first time since leaving England, George did some parachute jumping. He flew in twin-engined Albemarles accompanied by nine other paratroopers, exiting through a sort of cupola built into the underside of the aircraft. They carried out some experimental drops with weapons attached to their bodies, rather than parachuted in separate containers which had to be recovered later. By and large this new idea worked well and it enabled the men to get away from the DZ (dropping zone) much more quickly, especially at night.

On one occasion George had a memorable weekend leave. He was granted permission to visit his younger brother, Bert, a sergeant with the Royal Artillery stationed at Bougie, a town on the coast some miles east of Algiers. Poacher hitched a lift from a friendly RAF pilot and arrived in time to watch Bert playing football for his battery. They had an enjoyable couple of days, swapping news and doing the high spots of Bougie. The war years must have been an anxious time for George's parents with three out of four sons in the army. Another of George's brothers served in India and Burma. Yet they all came through without a scratch.

At another time the Sappers went off to a coastal rest centre, bathing and generally taking life easy. Poacher, being guilty of some minor misdemeanour, missed this trip and was confined to barracks. But then it is an ill wind that does not blow away the sand, revealing something of interest. With only a skeleton staff left in charge of the camp, he had no difficulty in raiding the quartermaster's store. Many a bottle of rum destined for the officers' mess was considerably watered down during that period of Poacher's punishment. When the Battalion returned, George learned that the cook had been taken ill. To his amazement he was ordered to take over all culinary duties and found himself catering (and no doubt poaching) for hundreds of men. Because his mother had brought him up properly, he had no real difficulty in coping well. His roast beef and Yorkshire pudding became a byword. The full-time cook, fearing a threat to his professional standing, made a remarkably swift recovery.

On 9 July, 1943, the invasion of Sicily began with an assault by glider-borne troops and parachutists. 'A' Troop did not take part in this campaign because their numbers were still depleted. As events turned out, they may have had a lucky escape. Flown in by inexperienced American pilots, gliders were released over the sea and ditched. In trying to avoid enemy flak, many Paras were dropped miles from their DZ. Some even landed on the slopes of Mount Etna twenty or thirty miles away. In one or two cases determined Paratroopers forced the pilots to go through to their destinations at gunpoint. To add to the confusion, the Royal Navy fired at some of the approaching aircraft that were far off course. Many lives were lost and only a fraction of the intended airborne force arrived to hold the planned positions. Needless to say, those who did get through, gave a superb account of themselves. They were eventually relieved by the Eighth Army which had arrived by sea. Sicily fell to Allied arms on 17 August.

Back in North Africa an inquiry was held into the airborne fiasco. George was present when Montgomery spoke to the 1st Parachute Brigade. He pledged that in all future operations only RAF aircrew would fly British paratroops to their DZs. Relief was evident on every face. (Just over a year later, well-trained and experienced American crews flew their paratroop compatriots straight and steady through fierce enemy fire to DZs near Eindhoven and Nijmegen in Holland.)

Two months after the start of the campaign in Sicily George was involved in the invasion of Italy. On 8 September the Paras sailed from Bizerta. The following day, while still at sea, it was announced that an armistice had been signed between the Allies and the Italians. George watched as units of the Italian Navy sailed westwards, making good their escape from the Germans. Battleships, cruisers and destroyers were heading for safety in Malta. Later that day their own ship arrived at Taranto, in the heel of Italy. As they disembarked, George was horrified to see the bodies of scores of British Paratroopers floating in the docks. The exceptionally fast minelayer, HMS *Abdiel*, a ship without protective armour, had arrived from Malta. She came into Taranto harbour carrying 400 men from the 6th Royal Welch Battalion of the 2nd Parachute Brigade. Around midnight she had dropped anchor immediately over a German magnetic mine. A gigantic explosion rent the air and the *Abdiel* was blown asunder. 156 men died in this tragedy and many more were seriously wounded. The surviving Paras, kitted out in naval uniforms, were ready for action ashore within hours.

Fortunately, little resistance was encountered, the bulk of the German forces having retreated further north. Yet a few isolated snipers took their toll. Major-General 'Hoppy' Hopkinson, the Divisional Commander, was killed by a German rifleman. During the next four days George and the others dug defensive positions around Taranto in case the enemy retaliated. Nothing happened.

The Eighth Army was moving steadily northwards up the toe of Italy, having crossed the Strait of Messina from its new bases in Sicily. Meanwhile, the US Fifth Army, which included the British X Corps, was fighting desperately to establish a beachhead at Salerno, on the west coast of Italy about a hundred and fifty miles south of Rome.

Eventually the Paras moved up to Bari on the Adriatic coast. Poacher and his fellow Sappers enjoyed their brief stay in Italy. When they sailed for England in November, they took with them pleasant memories of tranquil days in olive groves, drinking good Italian wine and singing to the accompaniment of an out-of-tune piano in the open air. They also remembered the friendly rivalry that existed between their patrols, each claiming to have penetrated further north than the others. Gus Woods and Poacher were adamant that they held the mileage record in their attempts to find the invisible enemy. Indeed the exploits of these 'intrepid heroes' somehow received a mention in the UK press at the time.

Back in England, George spent a cheerful leave with his family. He went up to the West End with his girl friend, Marjorie. Poor old bruised and battered London, under grey skies, looked even shabbier than he remembered. It was an extraordinary contrast to the Mediterranean places that he had got to know so well. The people were obviously tired and strained – but still resolute. Cockney humour, unlike fags and decent beer, remained in good supply; there were plenty of shows to enjoy and the theatres were packed with audiences determined to defy the bombing. Christmas was celebrated in the usual festive manner – or almost – in spite of rationing.

In March, 1944, George and Marjorie were married and after a brief honeymoon the happy groom returned to base. The men were being prepared for action in Europe. Route marches of thirty miles per day, carrying half-hundredweight loads on their backs, became regular routine. Although many of them were old campaigners, they were obliged to put in a great deal of practice on the firing range.

At last, on 6 June, the great Allied invasion of Europe was launched. D Day came and went, but the men of the 1st Parachute Brigade, unlike other parachute units, were not called on to play their part. Later, after the British and Americans were established ashore, George and the lads were briefed to drop near Caen, where the Germans were putting up stiff resistance. This operation was cancelled. Then preparations began for a descent on the outskirts of Paris, ahead of the main army. Again the operation was scrubbed. A series of such standby calls all came to nothing. The Allied armies were now pressing forward so rapidly that the DZs were overrun before the planned missions could be carried out and the 1st Brigade feared the war would be over before it had a chance to take a swipe at Hitler on his own ground. All the skill and highly specialized training of this finely tuned fighting unit would then be wasted.

It was a time of difficulty for the CO and his officers. Morale was in danger of slipping. Commanding a group of such independently-minded men, under these frustrating conditions, was no easy matter. Some of the men, including Poacher, adopted the attitude that they had volunteered to jump from the skies to fight the enemy. When that time came they would be ready. Meanwhile, there was no point hanging around in camps when they could be enjoying themselves in better places. It is recorded that when the call eventually came, some paratroopers arrived by taxi on the actual morning of take-off!

By 7 September an operation called Comet was planned and ready. It was a bold scheme assigned to the 1st Parachute Brigade and the Polish 1st Parachute Brigade. The main objective was the huge road bridge at Arnhem, in Holland, spanning the Lower Rhine. The nature of this objective meant Sappers would play a key role in defusing explosives on the bridge before it could be blown up by the German defenders and then, paradoxically, re-wiring it with British explosives.

George was given an exciting duty. Reconnaissance photos established that an armed patrol boat was anchored in mid-river. Poacher was to seize a speedboat known to be moored on the northern bank and dash a platoon of Paras out to capture the larger vessel. At the same time gliders would land on and around the bridge, with supplies of guns, jeeps and ammunition. The Paras themselves, some two thousand men in all, would be dropped on *both* sides of the Rhine.

When the briefing was completed, George and his mates were each issued with some Dutch money and, after being warned not to say a word about the operation, were sent on thirty-six hours' leave. (It was during this brief visit home that George and Marjorie's first child Tony was conceived.)

As soon as they re-assembled at the camp, the lads were told that Comet was off. Cynical jeers greeted this latest disappointment. Then, within days, they were being briefed for a new mission, codenamed Market Garden. This latest plan retained many of the elements of Comet, but was on a much larger scale. Arnhem was the gateway to Germany itself. Field-Marshal Montgomery's tanks were poised on the Dutch border sixty-four miles to the south. The task of the British paratroops, reinforced by the Poles to be dropped on D Day + 2 on the south bank, was to seize the Arnhem bridge and keep it open until the army arrived in an estimated two days. A 'carpet' of American Paras and airborne troops was to be laid along this route to Arnhem – principally near Eindhoven and Nijmegen – to take and hold the other vital bridges over which Monty's tanks would rumble on their dash north to reach that final bridge. This was to be the largest airborne operation the world had ever witnessed. 10,000 troops would be dropped at Arnhem alone. It was no longer just a 1st Battalion and Polish effort, but now also included the 1st Airborne Brigade (Gliders) and the 4th Parachute Brigade as well – all to be known as the 1st British Airborne Division, commanded by Major-General Robert Urquhart.

On a fine Sunday morning, 17 September, they were driven out to their C47 Dakotas waiting on the tarmac at Saltby, in Lincolnshire. As they flew over the North Sea, they looked out in astonishment at the vast armada of planes, planes towing gliders and protecting fighters all heading east, as far as the eye could see. Down below scores of rescue vessels dotted the sea ready for any emergency.

Whatever qualms the Paras may have had were largely dispelled by the sheer magnitude of this force. Whoever organized this lot in such a short time knew what they were doing. When they got to Arnhem they would do the job without any bother. Monty and his tanks would be with them in no time at all. They felt sure the direction of this operation was in good hands and there was nothing much to worry about. As for Poacher, he was quite looking forward to doing his bit in the scheme of things. A pair of bulging socks hung on a piece of string slung round his neck. He had thoughtfully filled them with tea.

They flew without meeting opposition, over the enemy coast and across Holland. The DZ was eight miles from their objective. The RAF had felt that suspected opposition from anti-aircraft batteries in the vicinity of the bridge made it unwise to land too close to the target. Instead it was planned to drop near the district of Oosterbeek, north-west of the town and make their way to Arnhem as fast as possible. Each of the three battalions had been given a specific route. Lieutenant-Colonel Frost's 2nd Battalion, to which George and the other Sappers under Captain Mackay were attached, had the primary task of taking and holding the road bridge. They were to approach along a minor road skirting the northern bank of the Lower Rhine.

They were also briefed to secure the railway bridge and a pontoon bridge. Both these crossings would be encountered before reaching their main objective. The 3rd Battalion was to take another route coming in to the bridge from the north and reinforcing George's battalion. Meanwhile, after this operation had been successfully launched, the 1st Battalion was to advance along the main Ede/Arnhem highway and occupy the high ground north of the city. George and his mates had been told that a special reconnaissance squadron would dash ahead in jeeps and hold the bridge until the 2nd Battalion arrived. (In the event this never happened. The jeeps, coming in on the central route, were halted by Germans in armoured cars and by 20mm guns.)

The red light glowed. The Paras lined up ready to jump through the comfortable wide side-exit of the C47. Poacher glanced at his watch. It was 2.20pm. Over his standard issue battledress he was wearing his Denison smock, a loose-fitting camouflage garment in green and brown. It was lined in warm blanket material, which was good for keeping out the wind, but not altogether rainproof. It had a front-fastening zip and four large patch-pockets. The tailpiece was held securely by the press-studs in front. Over this he wore normal webbing equipment – waist-belt, pouches, straps and small pack. On his head he had a rimless helmet with a green string-net camouflage cover and a softer, loosely-woven camouflage face veil, which he was wearing as a scarf. In addition his equipment included a respirator, water bottle, bayonet, entrenching tool, toggle rope and bandolier of small-arms ammunition. A knife was strapped to his right leg. This was for cutting himself free from his harness and was also useful in hand-to-hand fighting. A simple sleeveless gabardine garment, known as a jumpjacket, enveloped all else. The purpose of the jumpjacket was to prevent any of the many bits of equipment fouling the parachute harness which, in turn, was strapped over this jacket. The harness, chute and jacket would, of course, all be discarded on landing. Finally, he carried his Mark V Sten gun, and two

No 4 (T) Lee-Enfield rifles fitted with superb No 32 telescopic sights. Some of his mates, instead of two rifles, were lumbered with large kitbags full of explosive.

He turned and grinned at Gus standing in the queue behind him. Then the men were on the move. The stick was leaving the aircraft. Suddenly, as Poacher neared the open doorway, the man in front of him tried to break away from his position in the line. His eyes stared wildly, his white face worked convulsively in panic. George was thunderstruck. 'Look, mate, 'he yelled in the terrified youngster's ear, 'For Christ's sake, jump. You're on active service, you silly bugger – if you don't jump, you'll be bloody shot!' The lad continued to kick and struggle as he was bundled unceremoniously through the doorway. (Much later, when George checked on the youngster's fate, he learned that he had made a heavy landing, broken an arm and a leg, and taken no part in the subsequent battle.)

George followed him without delay. Buoyed away in the slipstream, he felt the comforting jerk on his harness as the canopy billowed open above him. In the approved fashion he lowered the two rifles on cord lines. Dropping from only 800 feet, he was soon down. One of the rifles pierced the ground like a javelin. George landed on top of it, bending it beyond use. Retaining the Sten, he gave the remaining rifle to another trooper. There was a flurry of activity all over the drop zone as the Battalion sorted itself out. He soon located the clearly numbered canister which had floated down on its own chute. Inside was a most important piece of equipment – a collapsible canvas wheelbarrow with a strong metal frame. Quickly he assembled it and packed it full of explosives. Not the most enviable of assignments, his task was to steer this load over eight miles of enemy-held territory, all the way to Arnhem bridge.

The familiar sound of Lieutenant-Colonel Frost's hunting horn brought the men scurrying to the assembly point. Shortly after landing, George had heard shots coming from the direction of nearby woods, but now there was no sound of conflict. The 2nd Battalion wasted no time in setting off at a fast trot, following their designated route to the bridge. As they approached the outskirts of Oosterbeek there was an incongruous air of tranquility. The mood was reinforced by crowds of Dutch civilians, all anxious to show the British 'Tommies' how happy they were at their sudden and unexpected arrival. They seemed convinced that the war was over. Captain Mackay went out of his way to warn George and the others not to relax their vigilance. He was anxious lest the presence of these people might give their position away to the Germans. He was sure the situation could change without warning. Begging the civilians to stay away from them, the men pressed on along the north bank of the river.

Before long they were encountering machine-gun fire from the Germans.

A company was detailed to secure the railway bridge that spanned the Lower Rhine between Oosterbeek and Arnhem. Firing was now also coming from the opposite bank. Throwing bakelite smoke canisters to obscure their movements, the Paras charged onto the bridge, covered by their own Bren guns sited on the north bank. It seemed certain that in a matter of moments their first objective would be taken. Suddenly a thunderous explosion rent the air, sending sheets of yellow flame high above their heads. The Germans had completely demolished a section at the southern end. The bridge was no longer a viable crossing and casualties had been incurred without anything being achieved.

Enemy opposition increased as the day wore on. Poacher, trundling his wheelbarrow, timed his forward movement to coincide with lulls in German machine-gun fire. At each road junction he waited until the firing subsided; then, taking a deep breath, galloped across the intervening space making for the shelter of the houses on the far side. By some miracle both he and his explosives survived each crossing intact. As darkness fell, enemy activity died down, just as it had done so often in North Africa. The Paras increased their pace, determined to reach the main bridge as speedily as possible.

Drawing level with the pontoon bridge, they quickly discovered that the centre section had been removed – another crossing made useless. Two down and one to go; it had to be the main highway bridge now – there was no other. Less than a mile further along the river George and his mates arrived at their principal objective. They stared at the massive edifice towering above them in the gloom. A great concrete ramp led up to the bridge itself, giving an impression of impregnable strength and permanency. Poacher, viewing his cartload of explosives, concluded that, if the need arose, his little contribution would barely dent such an awe-inspiring structure.

German tracer bullets hosed down a side street, exploding a Paras wheelbarrow similar to George's. Standing in a small square, the Sappers were lit up in stark relief. Led by Mackay, they dashed onto the ramp itself. They saw that the roofs of several houses rose level with the road leading onto the bridge. Whoever occupied those buildings would hold the bridge. Spotting a schoolhouse on the east side of the bridge, Captain Mackay ordered his men to make a dash for it. Every man reached the building in safety.

George was struck by the immaculate standard of the school's interior – highly polished floor, gleaming desks, floral curtains at the windows and children's paintings brightening the walls – far more inviting than what he remembered of his own shabby council school in the East End of London. Captain Mackay addressed his men: 'Look after this place – be careful not to cause any damage.' One of their first tasks was to refill their water-bottles and canteens in preparation for a siege. It was as well they took this precaution, as the Germans later cut off the supply.

Lieutenant-Colonel Frost had set up his HQ opposite in a house on the other side of the ramp from which he could overlook the bridge. Unknown to them at the time, both the 1st and 3rd Battalions had been halted by heavy opposition on their respective routes. Apart from a couple of hundred stragglers, they would remain cut off from their comrades at the bridge for the rest of the battle. Yet all in all Frost did not think the situation was too bad: 'We had come eight miles through close, difficult country to capture our objective within seven hours of landing in Holland . . . a very fine feat of arms indeed.' He had a force numbering about 500 men, including Mackay's fifty Sappers in the schoolhouse opposite. In any case he would have to hold, at most, for another 48 hours – until the tanks of General Horrocks's XXX Corps arrived.

That night Frost sent A Company platoons on to the bridge. The men were raked with fire from a pillbox sited at their end of the bridge and also by an armoured car parked at the southern extremity. Helped by Mackay's Sappers using flame-throwers, they succeeded in silencing the enemy in the pillbox. The northern end was now firmly in their hands. Burning fires and explosions made it impossible to mount an attack on the rest of the bridge at that time. Nevertheless, apart from a lull around midnight, the battle raged all through the night.

On two occasions the British paratroopers attempted to rush the other end of the bridge, but were driven back. Similarly, truckloads of German infantry came roaring across, determined to re-take the northern end. Their reception was devastating. Halted by the intensity of British fire, lorries slewed across the road, some toppling over the parapet. Few of the attacking troops survived this holocaust.

As dawn broke, silence settled for a short while over the battle area. Captain Mackay made a recce around the buildings in the immediate vicinity of the schoolhouse. During the night the Sappers and a few others who had drifted in to join them had managed to hang onto their building in addition to one other. The Germans occupying the surrounding houses had infiltrated the British positions. Hand-to-hand fighting had ensued in which the Paras drove the enemy back with bayonets and knives. Mackay had been hit in the legs and several men wounded. The defenders had no medical supplies other than morphia and some bandages. Poacher, and a friend called 'Pinky' White, who had had some brief instruction in first aid before leaving England, did their best for the injured. They carried the wounded men down to the cellar, applied dressings, injected them and gave them mugs of tea.

During the early part of that morning, enraged by the activities of a German sniper hidden in a clock tower, a paratroop corporal climbed on to the roof of the schoolhouse to get a better shot at him. As he stood up to take aim, he was cut down by automatic fire. Poacher and Pinky went up to rescue him. As they lifted him down the stairs, they saw that his guts were hanging out of his stomach. 'What in Christ's name do we do, Poacher?' asked Pinky. 'Nothing we can do, Pinky. Just push 'em back in, and bind 'im up tight.' And that is what they did.

Mackay's orders to keep things tidy had been forgotten. Desks had been upended and shoved against windows to form barricades. The floors were deep in broken glass and fallen plaster. The curtains had been torn down and the material tied round their boots to muffle the sound of movement.

The enemy, mostly crack SS troops, were intent on crushing the tiny force by sheer weight of numbers. At 9.30 am a line of German armoured cars came over the bridge towards the paratroopers, taking them completely by surprise. The drivers skirted round the debris of burnt-out vehicles. Even a row of Teller mines laid across the road by the Sappers during the night failed to stop them. Only one of the armoured cars touched off a mine, but the damage was too slight to stop it. Behind them came half-tracks, more armoured vehicles, personnel carriers and a few truck-loads of infantry. They were reinforced by German foot soldiers shooting from sheltered positions behind the vehicles.

The Paras let off with everything they had. Withering fire came from Frost's anti-tank guns sited on the west side of the ramp. The British repulsed every effort by the Germans to batter their way across the bridge in strength. After two hours what was left of the armoured column was forced to retreat to the southern bank. Behind they left a mass of charred and twisted debris, stretching almost to the centre span. From slit trenches at the edge of the ramp itself, from buildings reduced to rubble, came a great shout of 'Whoa Mohammed' as exultant Red Devils gave voice to their battle-cry. So the day wore on and still the battle raged.

Not a single German had reached the northern end of the bridge. Instead they changed their tactics. They began shelling the buildings occupied by the British with a huge 150mm gun. The shells were phosphorous; the intention, to burn the paratroopers out. Instead the paratroopers, using well-aimed mortars, destroyed the gun and killed its crew. Morale among the men of the 2nd Battalion was high. They still believed that the tanks of XXX Corps would come to their relief within hours. George, when not helping Pinky with the wounded, spent long periods on the wireless transmitter trying to contact the main army, without success.

That night the Germans attacked the schoolhouse with anti-tank *panzerfausts*. They blew away one end of the building and Mackay ordered his men, the twenty-one who were still fit to fight, into two upstairs rooms. Previously the Germans had set fire to the roof with flame-throwers and the lads had spent three exhausting hours on the wooden roof subduing the flames with their smocks and the school fire-extinguishers. Ammunition was growing scarce and there was no hope of fresh supplies. The diminution in the Paras' activity must have convinced the Germans that they had finally finished them off.

A paratrooper signalled Mackay over to the window. Looking cautiously out, he was amazed to see crowds of Germans surrounding the house on three sides. Oddly, they were standing on the grass below just chatting. Mackay quietly told his engineers to take up grenades and wait for his order. As he shouted 'Now!' the men hurled the grenades through the windows onto the heads of the enemy below. Then they opened up with every weapon they had left – six Bren guns and fourteen Stens. George felt the whole school shake. In the silence that followed nothing moved outside. A carpet of grey uniforms covered the ground.

Early the following day a German was seen standing on a heap of fallen masonry, waving a not very white handkerchief on the end of a rifle. 'Surrender!' came the cry. Captain Mackay chose to misinterpret the invitation. 'Go away', he shouted back. 'We have no room for prisoners!'

Soon after this the enemy began a methodical destruction of all the houses on either side of the bridge. Their object was to level every building to the ground. Tanks slammed in shells from east and west, while from the north their artillery pounded the same targets. To the Germans watching the collapsing houses it seemed impossible that any paratroopers could survive. It was estimated that high-explosive shells were ripping through the school-house at the rate of one every ten seconds. George noticed that with every explosion the building seemed to spring apart. He could see daylight between each course of bricks. Then the bricks would come together again until the next explosion.

Towards evening it began to rain. Mackay contacted his CO on the other side of the bridge. He told him he could not hold out for another night if the attack continued with the same intensity. Colonel Frost said that he could not help him, but told him to hold on at all costs.

At 7pm two enormous 60-ton Tiger tanks were seen heading for the bridge. Shells burst through the walls, filling what was left with choking dust. It seemed as though the end had come. Looking at their small stock of explosives, Mackay had an idea. He called for a volunteer to go out and try to blow these monsters up. For a moment no one spoke, the mission was certain suicide; then Tam, who had been with George all through the African campaign, stepped forward. The others gave a ragged cheer. In the event no further action was necessary; the two tanks pulled back and went away.

Tiredness and hunger were the worst enemies. The lulls between times of intense activity proved hardest to combat. The sheer physical problem of keeping awake became more acute as the hours dragged on. The men were issued with benzedrine tablets. These produced strange effects in some cases, including double vision. A man who had crouched in his firing position for hours turned to George and asked him if he would take over for a while, until his eyes got back into focus. Poacher grabbed the rifle and peered through the sights. After a time he became aware of a grey-clad figure ambling along among the ruins, about four hundred yards away. He was an ordinary German soldier. From his stumbling gait he too looked tired out and rather pathetic. Poacher's finger tightened on the trigger. Then, instead of firing, he eased off and slowly lowered the rifle. 'Poor bastard,' he thought.

Mackay and his men did hold on throughout that night. They had been reduced to only thirteen able-bodied men, yet they fought off three enemy attacks in two hours, leaving four times their number in enemy dead. The schoolhouse looked like a sieve. All the surrounding houses had been burned down, except for one which was occupied by the Germans.

About 11am on Wednesday morning George listened with Captain Mackay to a conversation on the radio between Lieutenant-Colonel Frost and a Captain Briggs: Captain Briggs: 'The position is untenable. Can I have permission to withdraw?' Colonel Frost: 'If it is untenable, you may withdraw to your own positions.' Captain Briggs: 'Everything is comfortable. I am now going in with bayonets and grenades.'

Shortly after this their wireless was hit by a shell and destroyed. From the schoolhouse they could hear that a tremendous battle had erupted on the other side of the ramp.

The main concern now was for the wounded and dying. Time and again George slithered his way down the cellar steps, slippery with blood, to see what help he could give Pinky White. It was little enough. His stock of tea had long since gone and water was rationed to one cup a day. The cellar itself was like a charnel-house. The broken bodies of his mates lay all over the floor, swathed in dirty, blood-stained bandages. Poacher longed with all his being for this carnage to end. By this stage he knew the British tanks would never come and that their efforts had been for nothing. He was sure that it was only a matter of hours before he and the few who remained would be killed too.

They stayed in position until the afternoon; then the Germans brought up another Tiger, which blew what remained of the schoolhouse to smithereens. Eric Mackay ordered George and the others to bring their injured comrades up from the unbearably hot basement and put them in a nearby garden. As they did so, they were attacked by a barrage of intense mortar fire.

For the sake of the wounded, before they became casualties twice over, a surrender had to be concluded. Meanwhile, Mackay with five Paratroopers all carrying Bren guns, each with one last round in the breech, marched off. George never forgot his Captain's final words as he departed: 'Remember lads, when you are taken prisoner, it is your duty to escape.' The more pressing problem at that moment was how to act for the best. George's small group of still uninjured Paras, with no ammunition left, was lying on open ground surrounded by their wounded mates. Poacher was sheltering behind a substantial paving-stone as the bullets whined perilously close. A man crouching nearby raised a bloodstained towel knotted to the end of a stick and waved it furiously. The stick was shot out of his hand. The man crawled over and retrieved the once-white towel. Then, standing up, he moved in the direction of the Germans waving the towel above his head. He was instantly shot down. The next moment they were surrounded by Germans pointing guns at them. The Paratroopers were ordered to stand and raise their hands above their heads. Their captors then made signs that the few who were fit enough to do so must start marching. Poacher and three others went over to their injured comrade. They knew that it was his bravery that had saved their lives. They lifted him gently onto a broken door; then, carrying him shoulder high, they marched off.

Under heavy guard the little group was escorted to the grounds of a large country house on the outskirts of Arnhem. Here, worn out and hungry, they were ordered to wait their turn for interrogation. The officer who interviewed George was a friendly man who, in perfect English, asked a lot of seemingly innocuous questions about London restaurants and various places of entertainment in the capital. Almost imperceptibly, as the confrontation continued, the queries demanded answers of a more military nature. George, tired though he was, cottoned onto the ruse at once. He shut up like a clam. Realizing he was getting nowhere, the interrogator discarded his show of good nature, dismissed Poacher and called impatiently for the next British soldier in line.

By now a large number of PoWs had been gathered in from the other parachute and airborne battalions. That night the Germans herded all their captives into an enormous Dutch barn. It was so crowded that George and the others had difficulty in finding room to lie down and sleep – the overwhelming need of every man who had fought at Arnhem from Sunday until the following Wednesday without respite. A few individuals, possessed of remarkable spirit, did suggest that this was an ideal opportunity to escape. Indeed, two or three actually got away at this time. But for the majority weariness had taken such a hold on their minds and bodies that any further activity which called for initiative or physical exertion was out of the question. George was unconscious within seconds of hitting the ground.

After a few days in this uncomfortable billet, the paratroopers were marched to the railway station where they were loaded into cattle trucks and the train moved off in a south-easterly direction over the border into Germany. The conditions on the train were appalling. The wounded had received little or no attention. They lay in acute discomfort on the filthy floor. With fifty men in each wagon the air soon became stale and difficult to breathe. Toilet facilities did not exist. A Paratrooper who had managed to retain his knife laboriously cut a hole in the planking large enough to dispose of human waste. Hunger and thirst added to their misery.

After some hours the train pulled into a bomb-damaged railway station looking as desolate as the few people who stood on the platform.

'Water! For Christ's sake, give us some water!' the cry went up from the wagons. The shouting reached a crescendo and was accompanied by hundreds of boots kicking viciously at the timber sides of the trucks. 'Give us water, or we'll tear this bloody train to pieces!' The German civilians waiting at the station looked alarmed. Someone with responsibility for this unruly British mob decided that it was probably wise to comply with their request. A ration of water was distributed along the length of the train. In Poacher's wagon two or three particularly tough characters tried to grab the can for themselves. Others moved in to prevent them. A near-riot seemed imminent. In such an event the precious liquid would have been spilled and lost to everyone. A corporal, known to George as Len, had been sitting quietly in a corner. He rose to his feet and, in a voice that carried undeniable authority, demanded that the can be given to him. After a moment's grumbling the water was handed over. 'Now,' he said, 'each man will get his fair share – no more, no less. The wounded will be served first.' Order was restored.

Eventually the train reached its destination. The men found themselves in a vast and unpleasant transit camp, Stammlager XIIA, on the outskirts of Limburg – about twenty miles east of Coblenz.

The men were stripped naked and relieved of all their possessions. Poacher's watch and the ring that Marjorie had given him were taken, never to be seen again. Then the men were herded through a form of steam bath that left them clean, but breathless. Their uniforms must have received similar treatment, being returned to them in a much more wholesome condition. Lined up in a vast compound, they were harangued by a Jäger officer on their duties as prisoners, read rules and regulations, and told of dire punishments that would be the fate of miscreants. It was a degrading experience for troops who had recently fought so valiantly. Finally they queued endlessly for a meal which seemed to consist of tepid water and bits of blackened potato. Not surprisingly, dysentery plagued many of the inmates who had been there any time at all. Morale was far from high that first night at Stammlager XIIA.

Much to Poacher's relief, it was only a matter of days before he was sent to another camp near Mertzburg. The place gave the impression of being efficiently run by British prisoners of war under a reasonable German commandant.

Soon after his arrival, an offer was made to all Paratroopers below the rank of sergeant. The men were given the opportunity to work, for nominal pay, at various tasks to be allocated to them in the town. The 'nominal pay' bit appealed to Poacher, as did the chance to get out of the camp. So he volunteered his services as a carpenter. Around seventy other men agreed to take part in the scheme. It was explained to them that they would be living in an old beer hall that had been converted to accommodate PoWs. Because they would operate as a separate unit, they were obliged to elect a committee to run their affairs. The key figure would be the Confidence Man, a position of considerable trust and importance in the affairs of wartime prison life. George mentioned one man he thought was suitable for the job. Both for strength of character and natural authority he proposed Len, the corporal who had averted serious trouble in the railway wagon, and Len was elected. A German-speaking Australian joined the corporal on the committee as an interpreter. The third man was a veteran 'kriegy' who knew all about the workings of prison life.

An inspection of the beer hall satisfied its new inmates that it was adequate for their living and sleeping purposes. Even though surrounded by a barbed-wire barrier, it was preferable to being in a camp. Wooden bunks had been built in tiers against the walls and trestle tables stood in the middle of the room.

They had been told that they would be marched every day to work at the Mertzburg chemical factory. However, their arrival coincided with a series of Allied air raids in the district and they were employed on more grisly tasks. Early each morning they were escorted to the scene of devastation and ordered to dig out the bodies lying beneath the rubble. On the way they were often stoned by hysterical women.

In spite of Red Cross parcels which supplemented the prisoners' rations, they were always hungry. Poacher, as a non-smoker, managed to augment his supply of food by swapping his small allowance of cigarettes for the occasional bar of chocolate. Unfortunately, a minority of the others did not deal so fairly. During meal-breaks a table, sometimes even with a tablecloth, borrowed from a bombed building, would be set up at a convenient spot. With some ceremony, loaves of black bread were then cut into as nearly equal portions as possible – one portion per man. If the recipient failed to keep his piece of bread in his hand, but unwisely put it down for a moment and turned to talk to his neighbour, it would be gone. This was a serious crime, when food was so scarce, made even more serious because it was committed by their own mates. It bitterly angered the paratroopers who resolved to seek out and punish the perpetrators. When the guilty men were caught, justice was dealt out swiftly and very roughly. The 'criminals' were tied to wooden posts while nearly seventy hardened shock troops landed blows on their unprotected bodies. The German guards made no attempt to interfere, realizing that this was essentially a 'family' matter. From that day on a man's bread was held sacred by all.

Around this time Poacher saw his first real chance to escape. While the others were taken in fatigue parties to the centre of the town, George was detailed to stay in the beer hall to repair windows shattered during recent air raids. Unsupervised for long periods and with a handy set of carpenter's tools, he was able to cut a hole through the back wall of the stage. The newly formed exit was conveniently hidden by the backdrop curtain. Through a stroke of luck, a wall ran at right-angles from this escape-hole until it reached the pavement. George carefully snipped through the barbed-wire strands that covered the top, ready for a quick getaway when the time came. He confided in Gus Woods and Tam, who agreed to join him. In order to keep the scheme 'official', they reported the details to the committee, which, after due consideration, gave the escapers its blessing. The Confidence Man, however, asked if others could escape with them. The three originators were not happy about this. They felt that larger numbers of people, all leaving at the same time, would surely give the game away. In the end a compromise was reached; it was agreed that two other men could go with Poacher, Gus and Tam; but as soon as they were clear of the beer hall, those two would set off in another direction. Meanwhile, the committee was helpful in drawing up maps of the district and pinpointing the railway marshalling yards. The participants made whatever preparations were necessary. These included hoarding scraps of food, sufficient to keep them going – they hoped – for about ten days.

On the night chosen for the escape *appel* (roll call) was called as usual at 7pm and lights-out followed shortly after. For once, George and his friends were praying for a visit from the RAF to create a useful diversion. On that score they were not disappointed. Just after 8pm the 'heavies' arrived and set about plastering the town. At one moment bombs rained down so close to the beer hall that they were convinced that they would not live to escape. In fact, Poacher dived under his bunk and got his head stuck. When the time came to leave, Gus and Tam had to lever up the wooden structure to enable him to wriggle free. They had a little trouble dissuading 'unofficial' would-be escapers from joining the party, but eventually the five men, bulbous with bread, chocolate and cheese concealed under parasmocks, forced their way through the hole.

Crawling along the wall, they were soon made aware of their first mistake. The metal canteens tied to their waists clanged and clattered against the brickwork. The noise sounded like a steelworks blasting at peak capacity. It could only have been the RAF overhead that had distracted the attention of the German guards. Anyway they reached the cobbled road outside the improvised prison undetected. After a hasty farewell to the other two men, George, Gus and Tam set off in the direction of the railway track indicated on the map.

They reached it without difficulty and were surprised at the number of trains shunting back and forth into and out of Mertzburg. As they lay concealed at the side of the embankment, they realized the trains were travelling too fast to be jumped successfully. Following the line into town, they were obliged to move up on to the road as they approached the more built-up area. Crossing a bridge running over the railway, they heard the sound of approaching vehicles. Without hesitation the three vaulted the stone parapet and hung above the tracks. Soon they heard, but could not see, a column of heavy traffic rumbling across the road bridge. Simultaneously, a train clanked by beneath them, the locomotive enveloping them in smoke. Poacher was suddenly overcome by a sense of the ridiculous. It was as though they were taking part in one of those far-fetched B movies. He burst out laughing and shook so uncontrollably he was in danger of losing his grip and plunging onto the rails below.

As the sound of vehicles died away they climbed back on to the road. In buoyant mood they arrived at the vast marshalling yards indicated on the map. The first signs of dawn were showing in the eastern sky. The plan was to travel by night and rest up during the day. Seeing a stationary goods train parked in a siding, they hauled themselves into an open truck and settled down to spend the hours of daylight as comfortably as possible. They allowed themselves a small portion of breakfast – dry bread and a sliver of cheese. As day came, sleep overtook them.

They had no idea how long they slept but they each woke at the same moment, aware of imminent danger. A troop-train full of soldiers had pulled up alongside them. Through a crack in the side of the truck George and his companions observed the enemy at alarmingly close quarters. Some of the German troops had jumped down from the carriages and were stretching their legs beside the track or answering calls of nature. An alert-looking *oberfeldwebel*, however, seemed more interested in the goods train. He was strolling from truck to truck, hauling himself up and glancing inside each one in turn. 'Pretend to be asleep,' whispered George: 'Perhaps he'll think we're off-duty railway workers having a bit of a kip.' Of course it did not work. They heard the click of jackboots on the metal step. Next moment: '*Raus! Raus! Verdammt Gefangener!*' Not wishing to be shot where they lay, they struggled to their feet and gave every sign that they wished to cooperate. At bayonet point they were marched off to the police station. On the way, ignoring orders to keep their hands above their heads, they did their best to eat the remaining nine days' rations before being put back in prison. Stale bread, cheese and Mars bars from Red Cross parcels soon disappeared. They were lined up in front of an enormously fat police inspector, who obviously took a poor view of their attitude. He shouted at them in German, accompanying his speech by thumping his desk. The men understood not a word.

Poacher's eyes wandered to the picture hanging on the wall behind the inspector's head. It was a portrait of Hitler. George grinned at his captors. Then he pointed at the portrait of their Leader. 'Do you silly bastards realize that if it wasn't for that stupid bugger hanging up there, we could all go home?' Whether the Germans understood is uncertain, but the meaning behind his message was unmistakeable – especially when he reinforced that meaning with an upward thrust of his two fingers in a vigorous Churchillian gesture. In an instant a Mauser pistol, held by the *oberfeldwebel*, was pressed behind his left ear.

Gus hissed at George through clenched teeth: 'Shut your trap, you silly sod. You'll get us all shot.' The pressure of the weapon against his skull convinced Poacher that his mate was probably right. At least his outburst had the effect of bringing their interview with the inspector to an end. Without another word they were marched off to prison.

It was lucky they had eaten all their rations before submitting to the customary search. For the next seven days they had to make do on a diet of bread and water. This time they were incarcerated in a real bricks-and-mortar criminals' gaol, surrounded by a high wall. 'Not an easy one to crack,' thought George. His depression deepened when they were led down stone steps to cells below ground level. He and Gus were thrust into one of these dungeons, while Tam was led further along the corridor. Within moments they had stripped to their underpants – big-bore hot-water pipes ran along the entire length of the cell, producing a temperature rarely found outside the tropics.

It was now mid-December. Each day they were let out into the prison courtyard for twenty minutes for exercise. They needed no encouragement to run round and round the courtyard at top speed to avoid being frozen to death. Then they would be returned to their oven-like cells to roast for the rest of the day. It was a miserable existence. During the days a little light filtered through a grille high up near the ceiling, but in the afternoon this faded and, with no artificial lighting, they remained in total darkness until the following morning. During the day Gus and George tried to relieve the tedium by playing a form of chess with bits of cardboard.

After about a week they were surprised when one of their gaolers announced that it was Christmas. 'Today,' he said expansively, 'will be a good day for you.' He beckoned them into the corridor, where Tam was already waiting. 'Come with me,' ordered the German as he led them upstairs. After walking along several passages, they came to a massive iron-studded oak door which led into a long dormitory, lined with two rows of comfortable-looking beds. 'Here live your companions from France,' explained the guard. With them you will have the privilege of spending Christmas. I wish you a good time.' With that he left and the door clanged shut behind him.

Since volunteering for service in the army, George and his mates had seen many unusual sights and witnessed many strange events. But what they saw now reached well beyond even their realms of imagination. The Frenchmen were all civilians. Because of the heating most of them were lying on rather than in their beds. Each man was naked and, with few exceptions, each man shared his bed with a companion.

'Christ, Poacher,' breathed Tam, 'they're all bloody screwing each other!' They stared in amazement, astonished as much as anything by the air of normality with which the Frenchmen were conducting their affairs. They certainly made no attempt at concealment, nor did they acknowledge the presence of the Englishmen.

British and American ex-PoWs nearly always affirm that in captivity the sexual urge quickly becomes sublimated – it hardly ever featured as a significant topic of day-to-day conversation. Dreams about wives and girlfriends become part of a deeply private world, rarely discussed between even closest companions. Yet here was a community of men indulging in an orgy of lust in a way that, under other circumstances, would surely have seemed bizarre to most of them. It is unlikely that they could all have been homosexuals before coming to this place.

'Well,' said Poacher, 'it's a funny way to celebrate Christmas!' Already his eyes had wandered to the centre of the room. The one topic that *did* overshadow all others whenever PoWs talked together was FOOD. Here, piled high on a large trestle table was a veritable mountain of Red Cross food parcels. Poacher approached one of the few solo occupants of a nearby bed. He made it clear by gestures that he and his companions were very hungry and pointed at the parcels. The Frenchman gave a non-committal shrug and then grunted something unintelligible. George decided to interpret this as an invitation to go ahead and help themselves. The three set to without delay and soon demolished the contents of several packages. No one attempted to stop them.

Later, when their strange hosts tired of their amorous activities, Poacher and his mates encouraged the Frenchmen to join in a sing-song. It seemed appropriate to the occasion. When the time came for them to be escorted back to their cells, they gathered up a further parcel apiece. After all, it *was* Christmas.

A few days after this event they were posted to a new billet. This time it was an old bakehouse on the outskirts of the small town of Douben, not far from Mertzburg. Their new companions were a friendly bunch of about thirty veteran British and Australian kriegies who had been captured at Benghazi three years previously. They had long ago worked out a strict code of conduct to which they all adhered. This had helped to make their long incarceration endurable. None of them had seen a Paratrooper before and they were eager to be brought up to date with all the latest military developments. George and the others carefully played down the damage inflicted on London and the Home counties by the V1 and V2 rockets. It seemed pointless to add to these men's anxieties when they were powerless to do anything about it.

Gus and George were sent to work in a neighbouring sugar factory, Gus in the office, and George once more as a carpenter. Tam was found occupation in the local sausage factory. So, not for the first time, they ate well. Sugar was plentiful, and Tam never failed to return without cuts of beef or pork concealed in the sleeves of his parasmock. With a little judicious trading they were able to wash it down with a powerful concoction of 'near-beer' laced with schnapps, made from potatoes by Russian workers. In some ways the atmosphere created by this comparatively good living was similar to that which George remembered in far-off Greenock during his early days in the army.

The onetime bakehouse resounded most evenings to the sounds of laughter, singing and the thump of dancing feet. Rarely can such a congenial style of living have been conjured from such adverse circumstances. This made it all the more difficult for the long-term kriegies to understand when the three gave notice that they intended to make another escape attempt. It was incomprehensible that anyone should want to run away from such a comfortable billet. Anyway, what was the point? The war would be over before long.

George and his mates took the opposite attitude – it was their duty to escape and to cause Jerry as much trouble as possible. Besides they wanted to get home under their own steam. Having fought at Arnhem, they had too much experience of waiting in vain for advancing armies to put much faith in early liberation. One of the old brigade who thought as they did was George Endsworth, an infantryman still walking with a limp from a wound sustained in the battle for Crete. He begged them to let him come with them. Impressed with his enthusiasm, they agreed. Maps were again drawn up from details freely available in the office where Gus worked. Food was stored in readiness – a much easier task this time. Bread was avoided because of its comparatively short life. As before, Poacher prepared the ground for the breakout. This time he sawed through the bolts on the main door of the bakery until he reached a point where a sharp push from the inside would snap them completely. He disguised the fresh saw-cuts with grease and dirt. He pocketed a pair of pliers to deal with the barbed-wire surround on the actual night of the escape. The barrier was too exposed to risk tackling it in daylight before the event.

On the evening of the escape, the guards bolted the doors as usual and detected nothing amiss. Now that the time had arrived, several kriegies expressed regrets that they were not sharing in the adventure. Almost everyone pressed letters on the four men to post to relatives and girlfriends at home. The moment arrived. Everyone enthusiastically leaned against the large front door. There was a satisfying click as the bolts snapped and the door swung open. A freezing blast of night air stung their faces.

In absolute silence, their boots wrapped in sound-deadening rags, Gus, Tam and the two Georges moved outside. The door was pulled shut behind them. This was the worst stage of the escape. At any moment they could be shot by a trigger-happy guard. They had learned a lot from their previous attempt, however, and were confident of getting away. This time they rationed themselves to one billycan apiece so that embarrassing clanks would not give them away. They reached the barbed-wire barrier. Poacher snipped through the strands. The resulting twangs sounded deafening in the still night air – the men froze in anticipation of a volley of shots, but nothing happened.

Within seconds they were crawling through the entanglement and were within feet of freedom. Suddenly Gus hissed: 'Freeze! Keep quiet!' The other three followed his gaze. He was staring in the direction of a wooden hut. In the small porch it was possible to make out two figures gently swaying back and forth.

'Bloody hell!' whispered George, 'it's the soddin' guard, and he's doing a bleedin' bird!'

For what seemed an eternity the escapers lay motionless while the German soldier took his pleasure. The man seemed insatiable and the girl was obviously content with his company. Poacher and his comrades thought they would be frozen to the ground, but the amorous couple finally assuaged their passion and walked away.

The four men forced their way through the remaining wire and bolted for the cover of some nearby trees. The plan was to put the greatest manageable distance between themselves and the scene of the breakout. During the day they intended resting up in hiding. The objective on the second night was the River Elbe. Once across this barrier it was more than likely they would be able to make contact with the Allies. A spot on their maps marked a disused ferry; what state it was in, or whether it still existed, they had no means of knowing.

Their route lay through a dense pine forest whose natural cover gave them an increasing sense of security as the night wore on. It was as though no person had reason to enter this gloomy place. This illusion was shattered alarmingly in the small hours of the morning. First an unwholesome smell assailed their nostrils. Then, as the sickly stench grew even stronger, they heard the sound of barking dogs – not the playful domestic variety, but the full-throated howling of bloodthirsty hounds. Almost before they realized it, they came to a large wooden structure that loomed above them in the darkness. It consisted of a high platform on which was mounted what looked like an outsize football goal. Half a dozen ropes were suspended from the top bar – each one knotted in a noose. The escapers had inadvertently stumbled onto the very edge of a death camp.

In spite of the cold, they were all sweating freely when they eventually paused for a breather. They had run hard for over half an hour. 'What a terrible place,' murmured Poacher. 'Who'd have thought it?'

For the remainder of the night the men walked on in silence. At last they reached the far side of the forest. Descending a gentle grass slope on open ground, they came to a minor road marked on their map. For some time they headed south towards the Elbe until the sky began to lighten, then decided to hide for the rest of the day. They chose a bracken-covered hollow some hundred yards from the road. Apart from providing natural concealment, it gave them a good view of the surrounding countryside.

The following night, by keeping to the road they made speedy progress. On the few occasions that vehicles were heard approaching, they dived for cover. Within hours they had reached the river and it was only a short time before they discovered an old wooden rowing boat partly concealed in some rushes. The men succeeded in sliding the boat into the river where it immediately started to fill with water. The extra weight made the craft extremely difficult to pull back onto the bank and they lay wet and exhausted after their exertions. Gus cheered them up by explaining that this was a perfectly normal state of affairs. The boat had obviously not been used for a long time and so the seams had opened. Now they must fill it up with water and leave it for a while until the planks expanded and sealed up the cracks. Laboriously, with their four canteens, they kept the boat topped up. It was a freezingly cold and frustrating vigil.

It seemed an age before the vessel showed signs of retaining the water, but at last it was considered fit to re-launch. During the wait, George Emsworth had cut a stout pole. On the strength of his father being a Thames lighterman, Emsworth took charge of the operation to cross the river. This time the boat remained afloat and the four men were swept downstream at a furious rate. In the darkness it had been impossible to estimate the width of the Elbe. Now for the first time, as they reached mid-river, it became apparent just how wide it was. Whether Emsworth senior would have been proud of his son as he struggled to handle his craft will never be known, but certainly luck played a remarkable part in at last depositing the adventurers safe, but soaked on the southern bank several miles below their planned landing place.

They estimated it was between 5 and 6 o'clock. Each man was shaking violently: it was a bitterly cold morning and they had all been up to their waists in the freezing water. If they were to survive they had to have warmth. They gathered rushes and undergrowth and lit a fire. After a while their spirits revived, the flames were damped down and they moved away from the river towards some woods. There they went into hiding for their second day of freedom. The hours dragged by with painful slowness. No one could sleep – it was too cold.

By early evening the temptation to move on became irresistible. This was their first mistake. Within minutes they ran into a group of workers returning from a nearby factory. There was no time to hide, so they decided to bluff it out by walking straight past them. Poacher hoped these people were unfamiliar with a British Paratrooper's uniform! Not a word was spoken by either party as they drew level. The workers appeared indifferent to the strangers and when, ten minutes later, nearly a mile separated the two groups, the four escapers felt confident that they had got away with it. Their relief lasted only a moment. Without warning, as they rounded a corner, they were surrounded by seven or eight German soldiers all levelling rifles at them. Caught again!

That night was spent under guard in a barracks. It was warm and comfortable accommodation and the food was good. Many of the soldiers turned out not to be Germans, but Poles and Czechs in Wehrmacht uniforms. Next morning the prisoners were given shovels and marched out to do a day's ditch-digging. Far from being depressed the four quite enjoyed themselves.

Then they were sent back to prison, this time to serve fourteen days' bread and water for their misdemeanours. In this gaol each man was allocated a separate cell – lonely and depressing, yet they soon found the solution. They observed that the guards were extraordinarily slack in attending to their duties. They also noticed that the cells, rather than having locks, were fitted with handles that opened the doors from the outside only. A bellpush was provided in each cell for the use of prisoners who wanted to visit the lavatory, situated down the corridor. Poacher soon decided to make use of this facility. When he had finished, he saw that the escorting gaoler had gone back to the guardroom, obviously thinking his prisoner would return whence he had come. But Poacher had other ideas. First he let Tam and George Emsworth out of their respective cells. Then the three of them joined Gus who was delighted to receive such unexpected company. It was not until the evening that the Germans discovered three cells were empty. After a crescendo of Teutonic oaths, accommodation arrangements were restored at the point of a bayonet.

During the time they had been together, the conversation had revolved round the pressing subject of food. Poacher, the arch provider of good things, felt that his reputation was at stake. Requesting an interview with the authorities, he volunteered to clean up the toilets, many of which were in a less than healthy condition. The Germans were only too happy to accept this strange offer. Working on the principle that all drainage is inter-connected, Poacher soon traced his way to the kitchen. By prison standards food lay about in plenty. He gained the sympathy of the French staff, who felt sorry for the man with the filthiest job in the building. Each evening, when he had finished his work in the shithouses, Poacher returned to his cell via the kitchen and received an abundance of supplies which kept his companions and himself content until the following day.

On the completion of their 'sentence' the four were returned to their bakehouse prison in Douben. They were greeted warmly by their old friends who were eager for details of their exploits. Sadly, the water-stained letters were handed back to their writers unposted.

After about three weeks the thirty occupants of the bakehouse were ordered out of their home for the last time. For four days they were marched under guard in a southerly direction, roughly following the Elbe. By the end of the journey, their ranks had been swollen by many hundreds of other prisoners. On several occasions they saw stragglers, too weary or sick to continue, fall by the wayside. They were immediately shot by the guards. On the fourth day their section reached a massive camp near Torgau, with hutments all round the shores of a lake. (Torgau was later to go down in history as the place where the Russian and American armies first linked hands.)

To George, it looked as if the much-vaunted German skills of organization had finally broken down. The camp was in chaos. Sanitation, medical care, feeding arrangements were non-existent. Human beings from all parts of Europe were gathered here. Their physical condition varied, from the reasonably fit such as Poacher and most of his companions, to the totally emaciated who, by all appearances, should have been already dead. In fact, Poacher and Tam, taking pity on a couple of barely living skeletons, fed them from the contents of a Red Cross parcel. To their distress, the unaccustomed intake of food later killed them. Many of these poor creatures had been existing, God knows for how long, in structures that were no more than wooden boxes – too small to lie down in.

Among the British PoWs assembled here were a number who had fought at Arnhem, but none as far as George could see who had been with him at the bridge. He made contact with a Scots medical orderly who spoke good German. George explained that his friend Gus had suffered terribly on the march, being afflicted by piles. On the final day his mates had to support him as he was unable to walk for the pain. The orderly told him of a schoolhouse not far away that had been set up as a medical centre. Utilizing bandages, Poacher, Tam and George Emsworth made homemade Red Cross armbands. Then, placing Gus on a stretcher, with the help of the Scotsman, the four marched straight through the camp gates with their patient and passed the German guards without being challenged. About a quarter of a mile along the road they had a severe fright when a single-engined fighter came straight at them. The men dived into ditches on either side, leaving poor Gus lying on his stretcher in the middle of the road. Fortunately, the aircraft was American. It waggled its wings and flew away. 'Silly bastard!' grumbled George angrily.

At the school they found three doctors hard at work. Most of the severe casualties were German soldiers being moved back from the front. While Poacher was doing his best to assist the medical staff, he was approached by an elderly German woman who explained that she was the schoolmistress. She told George that she was terrified by the thought of the approaching Russians – she had heard they cut off people's fingers to steal their rings. What was worse, she had a daughter and God alone knew what would happen to her if they got their hands on her. Would he and his friends accompany them to the west? Of course he would!

In the shortest possible time, having regretfully said goodbye to Gus who was now under medical care, Poacher, Tam and Emsworth set off along the road with their two women companions, taking it in turn to push a pram loaded with domestic chattels.

The route was thronged with hordes of refugees all fleeing from the Russian menace. The ages of their travelling companions ranged from babes in arms to old men and women. It was the saddest sight that George had ever seen. They came to a checkpoint where grim-faced SS troops were inspecting people's papers. 'Here we go again,' muttered Poacher. It might be supposed that under the circumstances three men dressed in British paratroop uniforms, accompanied by two women with a pram, would arouse some interest on the part of the German soldiers. On the contrary, the group passed through the checkpoint without a word being said. 'Phew!' breathed Tam. 'For God's sake don't look back!'

They walked on for perhaps a mile, hardly daring to believe their luck. Here the countryside again became wooded. Over by a line of trees they were staggered to see hundreds of German soldiers lying on the grass or standing about in groups. They showed no interest in the shambling wretches passing in their hundreds immediately below them.

'Looks as though they've had this war,' said Poacher. 'Can't say I blame them.'

On they trudged for several more miles, the elderly schoolmistress making no complaint. All of a sudden they were surrounded by GIs from an advance American force. These men were tall and clean and business-like. They stood out in the midst of all the human flotsam like creatures from another world. Poacher explained about his group and gave a brief description of how they had escaped. Then he told them of the German soldiers back along the road. 'I'm almost sure they're waiting to give themselves up.' This obviously aroused the GIs' interest and they prepared to leave at once. 'Wanna come with us?' they called to Poacher and the other two. Tam, who remarked rather icily that he'd seen German soldiers before, opted to stay with the schoolmistress and her daughter.

Poacher and Emsworth were given a superbly equipped Jeep with a forward-mounted machine gun. The convoy roared down the road and soon came to the spot where the Germans were waiting. Fortunately George's hunch was correct; these members of the Wehrmacht were only too glad to surrender. They had no desire to move east into the arms of the advancing Russians.

Poacher helped himself to a selection of wrist watches in compensation for the one that had been taken from him at Limburg. He also lifted half-a-dozen Luger pistols as souvenirs. Remembering how hurt he had been at losing the precious ring from Marjorie, he refrained from taking anything so personal from any of his captives.

Later in the day he rejoined his friends. After snapping a group photograph with a 'commandeered' camera, George, Tam and Emsworth said goodbye to their women companions who had arranged to stay with relatives in a nearby town.

That night the three ate and slept in near luxury in a small hotel. The following morning they were wakened by sounds like wailing banshees. Stepping onto the bedroom balcony, they were amazed to see hundreds of wild females thronging the street below. The gates of a prison camp full of women had just been thrown open. Shops were being looted, skirts, shoes and blouses tried on in a frenzy of haste, as though, at any moment, these precious goods might disappear for ever. Any men caught up in this stampede were being molested by these liberated women in a way that made their eyes pop.

'Now I've seen everything,' said Poacher.

The three British soldiers waited until the street had cleared, then drove a small Opel tourer out of the hotel garage. Their generous American hosts had presented the vehicle to them the previous night. After raiding the cellar, they loaded the Opel with bottles of wine and enough food to last them for the rest of the day. All the German staff had disappeared, so no one waved them goodbye.

The route they followed to the west was strangely deserted. Nothing moved. It was as if the surrounding country might be drawing breath in readiness for some dramatic event.

'Don't like this,' admitted Poacher, sitting beside Emsworth who was driving the open car. 'Too bleedin' quiet.' From the back seat Tam was about to reply. As he leaned forward, there was a sharp crack of rifle fire and he slumped to the floor of the car. 'Christ, Tam's been shot in the head,' yelled Poacher. Emsworth brought the Opel to a skidding stop. The two Georges wasted no time in carrying their wounded comrade to the nearest ditch. Poacher applied a First Aid dressing to Tam's injured head, which was bleeding alarmingly. It was a mercy that the bullet had only grazed the top of his skull, leaving a deep furrow. Being unarmed, except for half-a-dozen Lugers without ammunition. Poacher removed his shirt and waved it vigorously above his head.

There was no reaction from the unknown assailant and no more firing. After a while Poacher and George Emsworth, carefully supporting Tam, moved cautiously back to the car, started it up and set off down the road again. Poacher sat up high on the back of the front seat and waved his shirt continuously. Still no one fired at them.

After a short while they came to a large dam, over which military traffic was passing. An American major came towards them apologizing profusely: 'Gee! I'm sorry, you guys. Word's just come down the line what happened. Some of my men up the road there are a mite trigger-happy.' He looked at Tam, covered in blood. 'We'll get your pal over to the medics right away.' The American officer called some stretcher bearers and Tam was borne away to receive proper treatment. 'Poor old bastard,' thought Poacher, 'All the things he's been through, then to finish up like this right at the end.'

A little wearily he told their story once again, and explained how they met a US advance party and later helped to take the surrender of nearly a battalion of German soldiers. Full of good will and sincere regrets for their hasty action, the Americans offered the two Georges a beautiful Mercedes. They promised to look after Tam and get him safely back to England as soon as he was well enough to travel. As they drove away, Poacher turned to George Emsworth with a mischievous grin: 'We'll ride all the way to Paris in this one – then we'll flog it to the Frogs!' But they never did. It was not long before they found themselves in the efficient hands of the British Army of Occupation.

They were soon embarked on a plane bound for Britain. As Poacher settled back into his seat, he knew his days of soldiering were nearly over.

And he was glad. The Russians were at the gates of Berlin. He and his mates had long since cleared the enemy out of North Africa. Italy was out of the war. In the Pacific the Japanese were in retreat everywhere. Soon it would be time to rebuild and raise a family – and this was exactly what he was going to do: build all those houses that people were going to need in run-down Britain. He would make some money in the process too. What he did not know, as he flew contentedly over the English Channel, was that his first-born was almost due. That was the surprise which Marjorie would have in store for George when he reached home.

HELMUT STEINER

PANZER DRIVER

I AM CERTAINLY NOT inclined to underestimate the German soldier. He was outstanding and he repeatedly attacked and defeated enemy forces with a superiority of five to one. The individual qualities of the German soldier, when well-led, more than compensated for such numerical inferiority. But now, after five years of intensive fighting, with ever-diminishing supplies, weapons, and above all with decreasing hope of victory, the burden put upon him was indescribably heavy. The Supreme Command, and above all Hitler himself, should have done everything in their power to lighten the stupendous burden or at least to ensure that the soldiers were capable of bearing it. I was faced with the problem of whether in fact what was now demanded of our soldiers was humanly feasible.

GENERAL HEINZ GUDERIAN

Helmut Steiner was a German soldier.

To ERICH AND Hildegarde Steiner the year 1926 must have seemed like the dawn of a new era, not only in their private lives, but in the affairs of their country as well. Germany had not had an easy time since her defeat in the First World War, or even for two years before that defeat. Now at last, after a decade of instability and internal unrest, there were signs that a more settled way of life was beginning to emerge. The purchasing power of the mark had been restored after years of runaway inflation. In 1914, at the beginning of the war, the mark was valued at 4.2 to the dollar. Nine years later the rate had exploded to an unbelievable 4.2 million to the dollar! In a society where it took two days to earn enough to buy a pound of butter, the German workers were close to despair. The middle classes too had seen their savings blown away before the winds of this raging inflation.

Erich Steiner had suffered as much as any of his neighbours. As a skilled shoemaker living in the normally prosperous city of Cologne, he had struggled to survive under a system that paid its workers in almost worthless paper. How much trade could he expect when it took the average wage-earner six weeks' wages to pay for an ordinary pair of boots? Only the state and big business benefited from the situation, being able to pay off enormous internal debts at little real cost. Yet by 1924 the mark, renamed the rentenmark, had regained stability. Goods reappeared in the shops and food once more became plentiful. The following year Field-Marshal von Hindenburg had been elected President. The political allegiances of this venerable Junker were certainly not in accord with the ardent socialist convictions of Erich and Hildegarde. On the other hand, his solid presence seemed to guarantee the continuation of the Republic – the only bulwark against the numerous disruptive factions rife in Germany at that time. In 1923, for instance, one Adolf Hitler had staged a beerhall putsch, supported by his own stormtroopers. The plan was to seize power in Munich, after which he intended to extend his influence throughout the entire country. Starting from his Bavarian base, his dream was to clear up what he called the whole 'Jewish Traitor Republic'. Naturally, he was arrested and put in prison where he belonged. True, he was free again now, but presumably he had learnt his lesson.

1926 was a good year. Erich and his friends saw a much brighter future stretching ahead for them and their country. On 1 February British occupying troops withdrew from Cologne which, as the principal city in the Rhineland, had been their HQ since the war. Germany achieved new international respectability in September when she took her seat in the League of Nations.

But for Erich and his wife one event that year outshone all others. On 14 August their first son, Helmut, was born. They already had a daughter, Marlene. The happy young parents truly believed their children would now grow up in a peaceful, increasingly prosperous Germany, free from all the turmoils that had plagued the years following the war.

Erich had always taken an interest in politics and as a Social Democrat played an active role in the affairs of the city. Konrad Adenauer, the Oberburgermeister of Cologne, was described as one of the three most powerful men in Germany. In 1921 he came close to becoming Chancellor. Policy disagreements within the proposed coalition, however, thwarted his chances of ruling Germany at that time.

The people of Cologne admired Adenauer as a superb administrator. It was as part of this administration that Erich Steiner achieved some prominence himself. Putting his shoemaking to one side, he became a full-time civil servant. At thirty he was Deputy Oberburgermeister. Then a second son, Kurt, followed Helmut into the world. Life indeed seemed full of promise for the Steiner family.

But sadly, not only for Germany, but for all civilization, the storm clouds were gathering again. In a few years, a regime more foul than man had so far dreamed of was about to suffocate Germany. After a number of earlier setbacks, the National Socialists under Adolf Hitler had achieved remarkable results at the polls. By the beginning of 1933 the Nazis became by far the biggest party in the Reichstag. Germany was now ruled by a coalition government with Hitler as Chancellor. Hitler himself was flying round the country hypnotizing the crowds with his highly individual style of dramatic oratory, demanding that the people confirm him in power at the next elections, which were fixed for 8 March, 'so that he might wipe out the Marxist traitors once and for all.'

When his campaign trail took him to Cologne, the future Führer of the Third Reich was enraged to find that the Oberburgermeister of that great city had deliberately snubbed him by failing to turn up at the airport to greet him. Instead Adenauer had added insult to injury by sending a junior

Odell Dobson at the Overseas Training Unit, Casper, Wyoming, in March, 1944.

'Ford's Folly': the first B24 to be built by the Ford Motor Company of America.

The crew of Ford's Folly: *back row L to R*: Clairborne R. Maynard, Upper Turret Gunner & Engineer; Richard E. Modlin, Nose Turret Gunner; Harvey G. Hoganson, Right Waist Gunner; Odell F. Dobson, Left Waist Gunner; Roger E.E. Clapp Jnr, Radio Operator; Robert K. Place, Tail Gunner: *front row L to R*: William A. Spencer, Bombadier; Robert J. Benson, Co Pilot; Charles R. Rudd, Pilot; William J.A. Dawson, Navigator. Dobson and Clapp were the only two to survive.

The author with George Paine, Marbella, 1985.

George Paine's 'partner', Sapper Gus Woods, with 'Pinky' White leaning on jeep.

George Paine (*left*) after his escape, with (*centre*) George Emsworth and the schoolmistress and her daughter who 'escaped' with them.

Helmut Steiner: a portrait painted towards the end of his military career when he was 18 years old.

Helmut Steiner with Margot on their wedding day in 1950.

Antonio Benetti 'riding the recruits'.

The Fanfara (band) of Benetti's Alpini Battalion.

Benetti's Alpini carrying timber up the mountain to build a *rifugio* as a punishment after their performance of The Sheik of Araby.

Antonio and his batman, Pepe, going into exile.

The Alpini in the mountains.

Steiner, Paine and Benetti together in Spain.

George Paine

Helmut Steiner

Antonio Benetti

Odell Dobson

representative in his place. Erich Steiner was fully in accord with his chief's decision and relieved that he had not been chosen for this particular 'honour'. Erich loathed Hitler, despised his associates and detested his policies. He prayed fervently that the socialists would have an overwhelming victory at the next general election, but in his heart he was afraid this might be a forlorn hope. The Nazi propaganda machine had reached a peak of professionalism, unmatched by any rival faction. A fuming Hitler was driven off at high speed to stay at his favourite Dreeson Hotel at Bad Godesberg.

The following Sunday morning the police rang Adenauer to tell him that Nazi banners had been prominently hung from the flagpoles along the length of the giant Deutz bridge, opposite the cathedral. The Oberburgermeister gave orders for their removal. 'They have no authority to hang their swastikas on civic property.' (He had previously ignored a demand to fly the Nazi flag over the City Hall.) When Adenauer's deputy arrived at the bridge, accompanied by a gang of workmen supported by the city police, he was met by Nazi stormtroopers. Ordered to remove the flags, the storm-troop leader, after fierce protestations, strode off to telephone higher party authority for instructions. When he returned, he said: 'All right. Go on. Take them down. But this is not the end of it.' Time was to prove him right. A sizeable crowd had gathered to watch this confrontation and people visably relaxed as the matter was temporarily resolved. The basically Catholic population of Cologne, like that of the rest of the Rhineland, were not amoung Hitler's more fervent supporters. Yet virtually everyone was convinced that their courageous Oberburgermeister had, by his anti-Nazi stance, signed his own death warrant.

Many former colleagues and friends moved away from Erich during the weeks that followed. His wife found that life-long acquaintances looked the other way when passing her in the street. Paradoxically, an 'opportunist Nazi' turned out to be a genuine friend when he sidled up to Adenauer while attending a memorial service to the dead of the previous war. In a whisper he begged Adenauer to get out of Cologne at once, as he knew stormtroopers had been ordered to murder him in his office the following morning. So Konrad Adenauer fled his much-loved city and spent the rest of the war avoiding Hitler's vengeance, only to replace him eventually as leader of Germany.

Erich Steiner, with his strong socialist principles and as a close associate of Adenauer, was a marked man too. The Nazis presented him with a document, declaring that he had been mistaken in his political views and affirming that from now on he would toe the party line. On signing this paper his future would be secure, they said. Bravely he refused. Without warning, a posse of SA men arrived at the Steiner home and Erich was carted away into the night, not to be seen again by his wife or children for five years.

Helmut, aged six at the time, could not even recall the incident in later years.

Within moments all the plans and hopes for the family's future had been shattered. A young mother, suddenly deprived of her husband, without income, had now to struggle to bring up three children and fight to survive in a hostile world, where even confiding in a close friend could be fraught with danger. She had no idea, nor could she find out where Erich had been taken. It was only years later that she learned he had been incarcerated in Oranienburg concentration camp, fifteen miles north of Berlin. At the time she had no knowledge that such places existed. Erich endured unimaginable horrors for no greater crime than that he believed in a free society and had not been afraid to say so.

Sometimes, as the years rolled slowly by, her children would look at Hildegarde and see her silently weeping. Helmut and his young brother, at least, did not know why she wept. Within days of Erich's arrest, the family had been given notice to quit their home. The landlord was not taking any chances of offending the local Nazi party officials. She moved with her children from the pleasant tree-lined suburb to a small cramped apartment near her place of work. Fortunately, she had managed to find employment as a secretary with a large paper manufacturing company, whose offices were near the centre of Cologne.

Helmut's recollections of these days were hazy, but certain incidents did remain in his mind. He remembered the sadness with which they said goodbye to the friendly Jewish family who had been their neighbours since before he was born. The children of the two households were of a similar age, and they had all played happily together. Later, when his young mind was assailed with repetitive clichés about the foulness of the Jew, Germany's eternal enemy, his thoughts were for a while clouded in confusion. He remembered too, although the significance escaped him at the time, how his mother furtively hid socialist pamphlets under her skirts and distributed them in great secrecy after dark. In spite of regular exhortations at school for 'loyal children of the Third Reich to tell tales' concerning their parents, it never occurred to Helmut to utter a word about his mother's activities.

Nevertheless, like all the other unfortunate youngsters who fell under Nazi indoctrination during that period, Helmut began to develop an admiration, even adoration, for the Führer. Hitler was always presented as a strong but benign, godlike figure who loved children and embodied all that was perfect in the New Germany. Day after day Helmut and his classmates were shown photographs of a smiling man accepting flowers from a loving population. In the classroom their little voices shrilled out in songs of praise for their almost divine saviour. Their lives were his to do with as he wished. They heard only those opinions and doctrines doled out ceaselessly by party-inspired teachers. Any dissenters on the school staff had long since been silenced. They had either been 'persuaded' to see the error of their ways, or been dismissed, or simply disappeared. Views contrary to the 'Great Nazi Ideals' rarely, if ever, reached the ears of young Germans. Parents either kept their own council through fear, or actively supported the ideas being poured into the receptive heads of their offspring.

Apart from the normal school activities, children were dragooned from an early age into attending 'special functions' two or three times a week. These were for instruction in duty to the Fatherland and participation in physical activities, including group games calculated to inspire a sense of nationhood. From kindergarten level up to the age of nine, they wore a simple uniform of white shirt, black shorts or skirts, white socks and black shoes. From ten to fourteen years children were 'taken care of' in an organization known as the *Deutsche Jugend* (German Young Folk). The emphasis was now on biology lessons based on 'racial purity'. History lessons underlined national heritage. Great stress was placed on physical prowess – pupils with physical disabilities were at a severe disadvantage in this new régime where 'Strength through Joy' was the prevailing theme. The constant message was 'to labour for Germany's future and the beloved Führer to whom we belong, today, tomorrow and for ever.'

It became compulsory for every fit boy and girl to join the *Hitler Jugend* (Hitler Youth) under the national leadership of Reichsjugendführer Arthur Axmann, an ardent Nazi of extraordinary vitality. In this organization preparation for future service to the Reich, with a strong military bias, really began in earnest. The youngsters wore shorts and stout leather boots with ankle straps. A smart bearing had to be maintained at all times, with the hair cut short in soldierly fashion. Evening assemblies, regular excursions and a three-week camping session each year took care of most of the young people's free time.

Even in the *Wehrertüchtigungslager* (military fitness camp) the schedule was arranged to keep the Hitler Youth occupied for twelve hours each day. Carefully planned indoctrination of Nazi ideology continued without remittance throughout these activities. Thus during his most formative years, a youngster was brainwashed with ritual chants: 'Führer and allegiance, courage and obedience, honour and blood, national loyalty and racial superiority.' All this was reinforced with popular radio programmes and films specially produced for the young.

No wonder that, in Helmut's case, his hard-working mother, tired, worried, bowed down with everyday problems and grieving for a lost husband, had few resources to combat the waves of propoganda that flooded over her son. It was enough, under the circumstances, that Helmut, like her other children, showed kindness and respect for his mother and helped her in many ways.

Helmut enjoyed his Hitler Youth activities very much. He revelled in his growing athletic prowess, the abundant opportunities for sport and the cheerful camaraderie of his companions. Above all, by the time he was ten years old he believed Hitler was a fantastic man who had saved the German workers from the evil machinations of the wicked communists, world Jewry and other non-Aryan devils. Never once did it occur to Helmut that Hitler or his régime had anything to do with his father's disappearance. For obvious reasons it was a subject that his mother never discussed with her children.

The family survived financially because Hildegarde was able to remain at her job. Fortunately, too, her husband's father and mother lived in Cologne and they did what they could to help. Then, without warning, such security as they had was swept away in a single night – a night that was to become a milestone in the black history of Nazi atrocity.

Early in November, 1938, Herschel Grynszpan, a young German Jew of Polish origin living in Paris, learned that his family had been expelled by the Nazis from their home in Germany and, with thousands of other Polish-born Jews (including a number from Cologne), deported to Poland. Moved by anguish at the plight of his family and race, Grynszpan walked into the German Embassy on 7 November and shot the Third Secretary, Ernst vom Rath, who died two days later. Using the murder as a pretext, Hitler ordered the SS and SA, with the connivance of the police and fire service, to launch the first nationwide pogrom against the Jews in Germany on the night of 9/10 November. Synagogues were burned down, Jewish shops, offices and factories were wrecked and looted. Many Jews were beaten up, others murdered and some 30,000 men (aged between sixteen and eighty) were sent to concentration camps. The morning after this nationwide hysteria, city streets all over Germany were littered in shattered glass and henceforth this night of infamy was known as 'Crystal Night'. For Hildegarde this was the end of her employment. The office where she had worked for nearly five years had been burnt to the ground. The paper manufacturers were Jews.

Determined not to become a burden on her relations, Hildegarde took her three children and found accommodation on a farm in the countryside near Cologne. In return for living quarters and food for the family she laboured long hours, carrying out the most menial tasks. Helmut remembers how weary his mother looked during this time and how she wept to herself when she thought she was alone. He and his young brother did their best to help. Whenever they had the opportunity, they pushed a small handcart to the nearest forest to gather firewood. This they sold around the neighbourhood, giving what little money they made to their mother.

Before long Hildegarde sent the two boys to live with an uncle and aunt in Beuel, a small town about twenty-five miles to the south of Cologne and just east of Bonn. Here they remained until, one day towards the end of 1939, they were summoned to their grandfather's house in Cologne. Helmut greeted his grandfather and looked with interest at the stranger standing beside him.

'This is your father, Helmut,' said his mother. 'He has been away such a long time – do you remember him?' Helmut shook his head. This gaunt figure with sunken cheeks meant nothing to him.

'Hello, Helmut.' The man's voice was so quiet, as if it came from a great distance, that Helmut could barely make out the two words he spoke. His father held out his hand. Helmut shook it formally, bowed his head politely, turned and walked stiffly out of the room. A father was something he had not taken into account as part of his daily life. He was not at all sure he approved. After all, Germany had provided a 'father-figure' more perfect than any ordinary man could ever hope to be.

During the weeks that followed Erich tried hard to build a relationship between himself and his elder son. Helmut felt vaguely uneasy whenever he was alone with his father. They had so little experience in common. The past was never mentioned. It was only many years later that Helmut's mother told him how his father had been forced by the Nazi authorities to sign a paper. In it he had sworn that he would never mention to a living soul one word of the terrible ordeals he had endured at Oranienburg concentration camp. Failure to keep his word would have meant immediate return to that awful place – for ever. Helmut knew enough by now to realize his father was totally opposed to Nazism.

One day Helmut returned home from a youth parade proudly wearing his uniform. As he entered the living room his father was sitting by the large tiled stove, warming his hands. When he saw his son dressed as a young Hitlerite, Erich, now normally subdued and introverted, flew into a paroxysm of rage. In one bound he was out of his chair and standing, shaking with anger, in front of a very frightened Helmut. Without uttering a word he grabbed his son's brown uniform shirt and tore it from the boy's body. In a voice choking with emotion his father said, 'Don't ever let me see you in a Nazi uniform again!'

Some time later Helmut was walking with his father along a quiet street in Cologne when they were suddenly confronted by a group of rough-looking men. They started pushing his father about and calling him 'Traitor' and 'Socialist swine'. The situation looked really serious as Erich did his best to dodge several vicious blows. 'Run for it, Helmut!' shouted his father. 'Go on, get off home as quick as you can! I'll be all right.' The next moment the sound of firm footsteps on the pavement brought the incident to a close. A huge, stern-faced man in a black uniform, shiny jack-boots and a high-fronted peaked cap, which made him look even taller, placed himself between Helmut's father and his assailants. Never had Helmut heard grown men so stingingly reprimanded. The man in black dominated those thugs. By the end of the tirade they were cringing in terror. Helmut always remembered the final warning thundered out by their saviour: '. . . and remember this, you bastards. Erich Steiner is a good man. He's worth any ten of you cretinous pigs. Get out of my sight, before I have you all shot for disturbing the peace!' The powerful officer in black accompanied Helmut and his father as far as their home and then bade them farewell. 'Try to play it cool, Erich,' the man advised Helmut's father; 'I can't promise I will always be around when you need me!' When they were safely indoors, Helmut asked his father who it was who had rescued them. 'That was your Uncle Hermann, your mother's cousin. A very important man in Cologne's *politische leiter*.' As far as Helmut could remember, that was the first time he had met that particular uncle. He certainly never saw him again.

Incidents such as this awakened a strange mixture of tender feelings towards his father. He began to see him as a man of courage and conviction. Although Helmut was certain his father was wrong and inexplicably misguided in his political ideas, nonetheless he admired him for the way he refused to compromise in his beliefs. As the weeks passed, a deepening affection flowered between father and son, filling the void created by so many years of enforced separation. They talked little. Concerning the past the father was gagged. As for the present, there was nothing Helmut could say about his Hitler Youth activities without risking hurt and distress. On one rare occasion they did touch on the future. Helmut's father, with momentary enthusiasm, spoke of plans to restart his shoemaking business and how between them they would make it grow until prosperity returned. Helmut said how keen he was to play his part in any scheme that might benefit them all as a family. But within minutes his father's words began to falter, to lose conviction. All too soon he lapsed into silence, his head buried in his hands – a man without hope.

Before the year was out Hitler's patience was once again exhausted and he ordered the Wehrmacht to march into Poland. Britain and France at last honoured their treaty obligations, declaring war on Germany on 3 September, 1939. The Second World War had begun. Within days Erich Steiner (now 37) was called up for service in the army. He was conscripted into the notorious Brandenburg Battalion, BB 505, reserved for political undesirables. Principal duties included moving ahead of the main force, clearing pathways through minefields for the benefit of the more valuable combat troops who followed them. Erich Steiner had never had any illusions about the depths of degradation to which German society had sunk under the weight of political corruption and the Nazis' reign of terror. Now he saw at close quarters the utter futility of an evil war unleashed by his country's depraved rulers. Far from home and family he existed day by day in a mood of hopeless despair.

Helmut, on the other hand, was excited by the war. He knew that Germany was in the right. Her leaders had shown almost superhuman restraint in dealing with the devious machinations of wicked statesmen from the decadent democracies. Now those countries who had foolishly tormented poor Germany for so long were going to get what they deserved – a damn good hiding from a new, strong, pure and powerful Fatherland. He thrilled to the sight of glamorous uniforms. It did not escape his notice that, while on leave, the heroes wearing these dashing outfits had first pick of the girls. He saw too how these women looked at their escorts with undisguised admiration. If it had not been for his Hitler Youth activities, Helmut would have found it almost impossible to contain himself until his sixteenth birthday. At that age, with certain qualifications, a boy could join the armed forces. Helmut lived for that moment.

During the infrequent times that his father came on leave, Helmut tactfully hid his Hitler Youth uniform in a cupboard. Less tactfully, he once begged his father to sign a document giving him permission to join the services when he was sixteen. (A parent's signature was one of the necessary qualifications.) Not unexpectedly, his father refused. He counselled him to avoid being drawn into the war for as long as possible and concentrate instead on obtaining the best education he could manage under the circumstances. Helmut felt that life was totally unjust. He longed to go and fight for his country but was denied this privilege. On the other hand, his father, who was in the army, hated every moment of it and should have been back home looking after his family.

On 14 August, 1942, a little over a year after Germany had invaded Russia, Helmut celebrated his sixteenth birthday by taking matters into his own hands. Forging his father's signature, he filled in the appropriate forms to join the Waffen SS. In due time he was summoned to SS Headquarters in Düsseldorf. Here he underwent a variety of physical and mental tests, none of which taxed him beyond his capacity. To his bitter disappointment disqualification came because of something beyond his control – he was 3 cm (an inch) too short.

Nothing daunted, back home he filled in another document, forged his father's signature again and applied for flying duties. Within days he was undergoing the most rigorous grilling in the Luftwaffe's selection centre in Münster. At one stage, strapped inside a kind of carousel, whirled up and down, back and forth, and over and over, he felt sicker and more giddy than he had ever believed possible. The instant this torture ended, he was ordered to read some letters and figures placed in front of him. Fighting back an overwhelming sense of nausea he tried his best to make sense of the blur that swam before his eyes. He failed conclusively.

Once more kicking his heels back in Cologne, he sought advice from an old army officer with whom his family had been acquainted for a number of years. The old warrior looked Helmut up and down for some moments before giving his opinion. Then he said: 'You tell me you want to see action. Well, you're only a little lad and you'd find life very hard in the infantry. There's only one thing suitable for you – tanks.' Helmut was rather pleased with the old man's decision. He had seen tank men on leave. They certainly looked rather special in their black uniforms – abbreviated jackets, short leather boots and distinctive headgear. As for their machines, he had once stared in wonder at a long row of Panzer Kpfw IVs mounted on flat trucks in the Cologne railway marshalling yards. He would be happy to charge into battle in one of those. Preparing yet a third forged application, Helmut set out for the army recruiting depot. This time acceptance was swift and the formalities simple. Almost at once he was posted on initial military training – Reichsarbeitsdienst, Course 1/328 – at Saarlouis, fifteen miles north-west of Saarbrücken.

The course lasted for three months and included combat training, lectures, sports and drilling, but not – in spite of a popular misconception – the goose step. It was the basic licking into shape experienced by army recruits anywhere in the world. However, this was preparation for the German army, so naturally discipline was stricter, instruction more thorough and routine more rigorous. Punishment, when warranted, was harsh but just. Helmut kept his record clean. This was not surprising, for when he had finished his long hours of training, like his companions, he collapsed and slept.

By the end of the course Helmut was left in no doubt that he had embarked on a serious business – not quite what he had envisaged before enrolment. He was now a tiny part of the deadly German war machine. For the first time he realized that being a soldier meant a severe curtailment of personal liberty. Therefore, it seemed to him, he might as well make a proper career of professional soldiering. He would try to win as much promotion as he could. Since Hitler had come to power Helmut knew that all men in the armed forces, according to their merits, had an equal chance of rising to the top. Gone were the days when only sons of wealthy Prussian families stood much chance of becoming officers. Now there were opportunities to be grasped Helmut reasoned that, when he became a senior officer, he would be in a strong position to arrange his father's discharge from the army. He filled in an application to be admitted to officers' school. He was tested and interviewed. After a surprisingly short delay he learned that he had been accepted. Documents were completed and signed, Helmut pledging himself to the service of Hitler and the German Army for an intial term of twelve years.

Officer-training in Germany at that time was spread over a period of sixteen to twenty months. The instruction was intensely practical and divided into three main phases. First there was an officer applicant course lasting ten months, including four months in a basic training unit. Then the trainee was transferred to a field unit to test his qualities of leadership in action. In three or four months, provided he proved himself, he was made a *fahnenjunker*, an officer candidate, and sent on an officer cadet course. Finally an advanced officer candidate course lasted for another three months. On successful graduation the *fahnenjunker* was promoted to *leutnant*.

Certain arms of the Wehrmacht had their own specialized courses and Helmut attended panzer schools for potential tank officers. Unfortunately, because of the pressure of war, he never had the opportunity to complete the third phase of his course. He rose to the rank of *oberfähnrich* by the end of his days in action (*fähnrich* is equivalent to the obsolete rank of ensign in the British Army).

He found the training tough, but well within his mental and physical capabilities. He scored high on leadership and initiative, but his instructors noted that he sometimes displayed an unfortunate independence of mind. This occasionally led to a disregard for the rules and a thinly concealed contempt for discipline. One NCO, *Obergefreiter* Ueffing, was incensed by Helmut's attitude and never missed a chance to put him in his place. On one occasion he ordered Helmut to climb a tree. Helmut responded with a display of agility that took him to the upper branches in record time. The instructor yelled up at him: 'Who the hell do you think you are? You're more like a bloody monkey than a man!' Helmut slowly descended the tree and faced his tormentor. 'Do you mean to say that the German Army is now training monkeys to become officers, rather than recruiting men?'

For a moment the *obergefreiter* was speechless. Angrily he yelled: 'The enemy is attacking!' Pointing to a muddy puddle immediately in front of Helmut, he roared: 'Down on your bloody face. Quick!' Helmut, who believed potential officers should think before acting, took two steps sideways before falling on to a dry patch of ground. As he lay there the explosion came: 'You've done it this time, you little sod! Oh yes! You've really done it this time! By the time we've finished with you, you won't be fit to clean out the pissing shit-house, let alone become a farting officer!' The *obergefreiter* stomped off to make his report, leaving Helmut to wonder if, for once, he *had* gone too far.

Later that day he was summoned to his section OC's office. The OC, a quiet-spoken *oberleutnant* with considerable combat experience, asked

Helmut for his version of the morning's incident. When he had finished, the *oberleutnant* lectured him briefly but firmly on the importance of iron discipline at all times, pointing out that, if as an officer he expected obedience from others, then he himself must conduct himself in a manner that was beyond reproach. Then he was dismissed and *Obergefreiter* Ueffing was called into the OC's presence.

Helmut paused outside the door and was able to overhear the *obergefreiter* having a far hotter roasting than he himself had received. Monkeys and shithouses were mentioned several times, '. . . and in future, Ueffing, if you wish to remain an instructor you will treat potential officers of the German Army with more respect and understanding.'

Helmut had reason to be grateful to the officers at that basic training establishment. Most of them were young men who, having seen active service, had learned to look beyond a man's documents when assessing his worth to the army. This was just as well, because, all through one section of his papers, ran a thick red printed band. Alongside, in minute detail, were listed the facts of his father's political 'deviation'. In respect of 'political purity', Helmut was under closer surveillance than many of his companions. So his period of probation was crucial to his future military career. From time to time he was called upon to reaffirm his loyalty to Hitler. However, his own enthusiasm and transparent admiration for the Führer were enough, in the end, to satisfy his superiors that his convictions ran along correct party lines. Eventually the situation probably worked in Helmut's favour – 'all credit to a boy who showed such singleness of mind in spite of his adverse background.'

Later, he and his fellow pupils were transferred to Podebrad in Czechoslovakia, about thirty miles east of Prague. Here tank training began in earnest. It was a long and thorough course, which included road and cross-country driving exercises, and lectures on tank warfare. There was no question of jumping straight into a panzer and roaring off across the plains. The instruction was carefully graduated, beginning with humble four-wheeled vehicles such as the Kubelwagen scout car, a light army four-seater. (It was developed from the 'People's Car' – the Volkswagen – of the mid-thirties, a domestic vehicle promised to – and paid for by – many, but never delivered! An excellent scheme for swelling the Nazi Party coffers. It was in every way inferior to the American Army Jeep, but a good vehicle on which to learn, having a corrugated metal body!

From this Helmut progressed to larger vehicles including the general-purpose Opel 'Blitz' three-ton truck. Not until he had passed his driving test and been awarded his licence was he allowed near anything even vaguely resembling a tank. Helmut never forgot what happened the day before taking this test.

The NCO driving instructor, a gentleman with a dry sense of humour, had thought up a plan to guarantee himself a steady flow of beer money by levying forfeits from pupils who were foolish enough to commit driving errors. The trainees, having little cash, were obliged to relinquish an item of clothing for each mistake. They could only recover these on payment of a fine. Helmut was unable to do anything right on this occasion; he finished up dressed in nothing more than his underpants! Happily, wearing a borrowed uniform, he drove flawlessly on the following day, and passed his test with flying colours.

Now qualified drivers, they moved on to a variety of armoured cars – the four-wheeled Leichter Panzerspähwagen, the eight-wheeled Schwerer and an ungainly Sdkfz 251, the German Army half-track; controlling this thing was a test of any man's skill. At last the long-awaited day arrived and instruction began on a genuine tank. It was an obsolete version of the Panzer Kampfwagen IV – armed with the short 75mm gun and only recently, in April, 1943, withdrawn from active service on the Russian front. It had the basic characteristics of the updated, and much more heavily armoured Panzer Kpfw IV currently bearing the brunt of the war in Russia.

Driving a tank was like nothing Helmut had ever imagined. The restricted view from the driver's position was something he had not expected. Sitting in the driver's seat, behind the three-quarter four-spoke wheel, was rather like being crushed into a metal dustbin, while viewing the outside world through a narrow slit no wider than that in a letter box. Anyone suffering from claustrophobia could never go to war in a tank.

The layout conformed to the usual design of German tanks, with the driving and transmission cockpit forward, the fighting compartment and turret in the centre, and the engine at the rear. The driver sat on the left-hand side with the wireless operator, who was also the hull machine-gunner, on his right. The radio equipment was mounted between them above the gear box. The other three members of the crew, the tank commander, the turret gunner and the loader, were situated behind them in the turret.

Training from now on was of the highest professional and technical standard. The excellence of this instruction was a crucial factor contributing to the German army's outstanding performance in the field. Helmut became proficient not only in driving, but in gunnery and signals as well. In addition the cadets were given a thorough grounding in all aspects of commanding panzers in action.

For some reason the teaching schedule had been speeded up. It was now the end of July, 1943, and extra tank-driving exercises were carried out in the evenings, while additional lectures took place before breakfast. In consequence, Helmut's course was passed out in double-quick time. Several weeks before he expected, he was sent off on his first spell of active service. By a matter of days Helmut had missed the greatest tank battle the world had ever known.

Earlier that year the panzer armies had faced a crisis that threatened their very existence. Since the terrible winter of 1941, the failure to take Moscow, the débâcle at Stalingrad and the shattering defeat in the Ukraine, Germany had lost close on 7,800 tanks. A thin grey line of no more than 495 panzers remained along the entire Russian front. *Generaloberst* Heinz Guderian, who could rightly be called the father of the German armoured force, had been sent into semi-retirement by Hitler at the end of 1941. Although Guderian had directed his panzers with singular brilliance, he had spoken out with characteristic bluntness about what he conceived to be misguided orders from the Army High Command, of which, of course, his Führer was the chief! In the circumstances he was lucky only to be shunted into the shadows.

Now, however, in the spring of 1943 panic overcame prejudice and Hitler recalled Germany's most illustrious tank general. Guderian became Inspector-General of Panzer Troops, with unprecedented freedom and power. Naturally this roused considerable resentment among some established members of the General Staff who, even in their country's hour of peril, did their best to impede Guderian's efforts to rebuild his panzer force. In spite of 'the enemies at his back', he set about his new task with remarkable energy. In order that his planned reconstruction should have at least a chance of success, Guderian made it clear that 'The task for 1943 is to provide a certain number of panzer divisions with complete combat efficiency capable of making limited-objective attacks. For 1944 we must prepare to launch large-scale attacks.'

Under the able leadership of Albert Speer, Reich Minister for Armaments and War Production, armoured fighting vehicles began to pour off the production lines. The time taken to build a tank was reduced from six weeks to a week and a half. Stocks of the mighty Tiger tank, introduced the previous year as the PzKpfw VI, were beginning to build up. The first of many new Panther PzKpfw Vs appeared. At the same time the up-gunned and more heavily armoured PzKw IV, the much more powerful version of the tank on which Helmut had trained, was arriving in considerable quantities.

Guderian was satisfied that, although he could never equal the Russians' prodigious output of tanks, he would achieve ascendancy over his enemy with a combination of better trained crews, superior tactics and, for the first time since the war began, more powerful equipment. All he needed was time to organize and develop his armoured divisions until they were ready to strike back in strength. Sadly, and not surprisingly, Hitler and the High Command insisted on instant, dramatic and decisive action. So, only four months after his appointment, he was ordered to engage in an offensive operation, codenamed Citadel, for which his armoured units were totally unprepared. Thus began the last German initiative of the war in Russia.

Supported by a Luftwaffe armada of almost a thousand planes, the battle began on 5 July with an assault on Soviet positions in the Kursk salient. As expected, Russian tanks far outnumbered those of the Germans and, although the panzers inflicted losses at a ratio of 2:1, their enemies could afford to sustain those casualties. During the first week more than 3000 tanks were involved, until, in order to avoid total destruction, the Wehrmacht was forced to retreat. Yet the two sides slogged away at each other through the rest of July, August and September. At last, what had long turned into a Soviet offensive halted in October. Some 2500 German fighting vehicles had been destroyed and only a little over a third of the panzers were still fit for battle. As Guderian said: 'By the failure of Citadel we had suffered a decisive defeat. The armoured formations, reformed and re-equipped with so much effort, had lost heavily both in men and in equipment and would now be unemployable for a long time to come.'

In August Helmut had arrived at Poltava, only a few miles from the front. He had come close on a thousand miles by train from Prague. A dozen of his companions from Podebrad were with him. Apart from the wagons, the train had a number of flat trucks on which were loaded some artillery pieces, a variety of lorries and nine tanks, including two Tiger Is. In the course of their training, they had learned that the entrainment of an infantry division required thirty-five to forty trains, while an armoured division needed twice that number. It had been a long time since panzer divisions had called for rail transport of those proportions, even including their artillery, anti-tank equipment, infantry, engineers and all else. Such figures had been derived from textbooks written years before, in the days when the complement of tanks in an armoured division was conceived in hundreds. How different it all was now.

When their train steamed into the Poltava marshalling yards, the 9th Panzar Division, some thirty-five miles to the north-east, was trying to stem the Russian onslaught in its sector with only seven remaining tanks.

Naturally, Helmut and his comrades knew nothing of the perilous situation into which they were about to be plunged. They had no idea that the Wehrmacht was in real danger of annihilation. They believed that they were about to witness the start of a new offensive which would drive the Russians far back to the East.

They knew equally little of the war in other theatres. After the news about Rommel's successes with the Afrika Korps in North Africa, information had dried up. They were quite unaware that the German armies had been totally annihilated in Tunisia by the British and Americans earlier that year. However, letters from home and evidence of their own eyes when on leave made them only too conscious of the effects of Allied bombing on their towns and cities. Yet they knew the brave German women and children would only have to endure these attacks a little longer. Soon the new German terror weapons would be ready. Then England could consider herself wiped out in a matter of hours; Adolf Hitler had said so himself.

A tough-looking *feldwebel* was waiting to escort Helmut and his small party to a large hut on the edge of the railway sidings. 'Come on my lucky lads,' he roared, as they stumbled after him through the darkness. 'We'll soon get you lot sorted out.'

As they moved into their temporary billet, the senior NCO studied the little group more closely. 'My Christ!' he grunted. 'Look at you! Nothing but a bunch of school kids. They'll be posting babies out here next!' Helmut and the others settled down for the night to sleep on straw palliasses.

Around 1.30am the sound of gunfire woke them. Simultaneously, shuddering explosions rocked the hut in which they lay. They thought that a Russian armoured unit had broken through and was about to smash them. The door crashed open and they saw the *feldwebel* silhouetted against the gun flashes. Then he stepped forward and swung the door shut behind him. 'Don't worry, my little heroes – it's only old Ivan trying to prove he's still got an air force! It'll be a bunch of clapped-out DB111s and one or two P2s – that's all. If he hits anything, he'll be bloody lucky. His one idea will be to drop his load as quickly as he can and then piss off out of it! He doesn't like our flak one little bit, I can tell you!' The *feldwebel* was right. Within a few minutes it was all over and Helmut and the others rested undisturbed for the remainder of the night.

In the morning they looked round for the damage but, apart from a handful of craters, nothing seemed to have been disturbed. They stared across the marshalling yards to where their train still stood in the sidings. The tanks had already been unloaded onto road transporters which were on the point of moving off. Tank engineers swarmed everywhere, carrying out adjustments and making all secure. To Helmut these massive war machines seemed invincible. The two great slab-sided Tigers, with their enormously long 88mm guns, could hurl an armour-piercing shell through 140mm of steel plating at a thousand metres, while the latest Mark IVs, equipped with new high-velocity 75mm KwK 40s, had been transformed from close-support vehicles into hunters. With this increased armament, the Mark IVs looked much more formidable than the earlier models on which Helmut had trained.

He heard the *feldwebel* call his name. The NCO stood over by the hut, accompanied by a *leutnant* in his late twenties. Helmut saw the officer's uniform – worn almost threadbare, yet still conveying an impression of soldierly smartness. He noted that the *leutnant* was wearing the Knight's Cross, awarded for outstanding service in the field of battle.

Helmut drew himself stiffly to attention, saluted and announced his name and rank.

'This is *Leutnant* Thiemann,' said the *feldwebel*. 'He wishes to speak to you.'

Thiemann looked him up and down. After a moment, he said: 'There is a vacancy in my crew for a driver. Having read your progress report from Podebrad, I have decided to give you a try.'

Helmut was flattered: 'Thank you, Sir. Thank you very much!'

'Don't thank me, Steiner,' said the *leutnant*. 'I'm not inviting you to join a picnic. Collect your gear and meet me in ten minutes at the dispersal point.'

Helmut saluted again and made for the hut. Inside the time he was standing beside a battered Kubelwagen, his kit stored under the back seat. A few minutes later Leutnant Thiemann strode up carrying a large parcel. He swung himself over the side of the vehicle and settled onto the front passenger seat.

'Right you are, Steiner. You're the driver – let's go!'

Helmut slipped into gear, and they sped eastwards. As soon as they were away from the built-up area of Poltava, the road deteriorated into a dusty pot-holed track. Sometimes they left the track altogether when overtaking a slow-moving convoy of heavy vehicles grinding its way towards the front, or dodging round other columns heading back to Poltava.

The surrounding countryside was flat and featureless – a vast expanse of steppe stretching into infinity.

'Good tank country here in this south sector,' remarked Thiemann, 'easier than the terrain farther north.'

'Have you always served in this sector, sir?' asked Helmut. For the next two hours, Thiemann talked of his experiences in the Wehrmacht since the war began. It was in fact a close-up commentary of the fighting in Europe, the drama as seen through the eyes of a soldier who had served with the 17th Panzer Division throughout. Originally, they had been an infantry division and fought as such in Poland and France. In the autumn of 1940 they were reorganized into a panzer division later to be commanded by Major-General Karl Friedrich von der Meden, a skilled and dynamic tank expert, who had earned the respect and devotion of his troops. His personal courage was legendary. At forty-seven Meden was one of Germany's youngest generals and, said the *leutnant*, 'a great inspiration to those who are just starting out on their own army career'.

Thiemann said that, after serving in the infantry, he had transferred to tanks and had had the good fortune to remain with the 17th. While a trainee officer, like Helmut, he had taken part as a panzer driver in Operation Barbarossa, the invasion of Russia, at the end of June, 1941. The division had been deployed on the Centre Section, so their path lay due east, in a direct line to Moscow. In those early days of the war against Russia the Wehrmacht was unstoppable. Hundreds of miles were covered in record time, while Russian troops fell into their hands in hundreds of thousands, together with countless tons of war matériel of all kinds. They kept advancing and encircling, advancing and encircling, drawing more and more of the enemy into the bag. By the time winter came, the Russians had lost five or six million men.

'And all this,' said Thiemann, was achieved with tanks that were just about obsolete. Nearly half our panzer strength was made up of the poor old PzKw Is and IIs.' During the rapid advance the light under-armoured tanks did well enough. They were at least reasonably nippy and manoeuvrable. It was when winter set in that the trouble started. Apart from getting bogged down in the mud, they were attacked by the fearsome T34 Russian tanks. With their long 76.2mm guns they stayed out of range and blew the panzers to pieces. Having much wider tracks, the T34s could move more easily over soft ground. Thiemann continued: 'In every way they were superior to our tanks. The panzers were dead ducks. Even before that, in August, when the weather was still on our side, things started to go wrong. The panzers could have swept on and entered Moscow. Nothing could have prevented a complete victory. Instead, we were ordered by the High Command to halt our advance. In the case of the 17th Division we were instructed to proceed south-west to support Army Group South. The idea was to carry out encircling moves in an effort to destroy more large enemy formations between the frontier and the Dnieper. Unfortunately, by then we were down to less than half-strength. Like the other panzer divisions, we had suffered from breakdowns, lack of spares and the effects of enemy action. There had been no replacements of any sort from Germany. When the 3rd Division had completed its massive encirclement round Kiev, it only had ten serviceable tanks left, and six of those were decrepit PzKw IIs! Yet all the divisions did a good job and many thousands more Russians were removed from the war.

'Towards the end of September an order came through to return to the centre and resume the advance on Moscow. For about a week all went well. Then the Russian winter struck. First there was the mud. Then the temperature fell, the mud hardened and more progress was made. But later the temperature dropped further. Tanks had to be chipped free of the ice with pickaxes. They could only be started by lighting fires underneath to thaw out the engines. It was so cold that even the fuel froze at times, while the oil became as thick as tar. Guns wouldn't fire when the lubricant in the recoil mechanism solidified. The men suffered terribly from the appalling conditions. Their inadequate clothing gave them little protection. Many died of the cold during that awful winter. Others were crippled for life by the effects of frostbite. And to think that we were within twenty miles of Moscow – twenty miles! Some troops had even got as far as the outer suburbs. Yet now there was nothing for it but to go on the defensive until the spring.'

At that point, Helmut had to swerve off the track. A seemingly endless column of men in brown uniforms, many with their limbs bound up in dirty blood-stained rags, came stumbling towards them, following a German armoured car. Spread out at wide intervals, German guards trudged alongside the captive Russians looking no less dejected than their prisoners. The numbers were so great that Helmut was convinced the war must have ended in a great victory for the Fatherland. On and on they came, expressionless individuals merging into a single living organism nearly three miles long.

Thiemann shrugged his shoulders and said: 'They keep coming. Every day since the war started in Russia the prisoners have kept coming – thousands upon thousands upon thousands. It's a puzzle to us where the folks back home find room for them. Mind you these are the lucky ones. If you're going to get yourself captured, choose the summer. I don't think many of our winter prisoners survived to tell the tale – nobody's fault, just the freezing cold and shortage of rations. We were all in the same boat.'

Helmut suggested things must be going pretty well up at the front.

'Doesn't follow,' said Thiemann. 'Encircling an isolated bunch of Ivans doesn't mean a thing. There are millions more where they come from. As a substitute for tactics their commanders sacrifice them without a thought. I have seen the Ruskies advancing in row upon row when we were dug in outside Moscow. As they came within range our machine-gunners mowed them down. Then more came clambering over the dead and we mowed them down too; and more and more until great mounds of dead and dying men were piled high in front of our trenches. It only ended when our artillery found the range and made further advance impossible.' Thiemann shook his head. 'No soldier is proud of such fighting, but we have to survive.'

Helmut was silent for a while, then he ventured: 'But we *are* doing well at the moment, aren't we, sir?'

The officer said with a note of irony in his voice, 'It depends what you mean by well. If you mean are we standing up well against overwhelming odds, then the answer is, yes, we are doing very well. We started a massive offensive against the Soviets in the Kursk area about a month ago. It was unbelievable – tanks were fighting tanks in their hundreds. At the same time Ivan was fully prepared for us. He was dug in in such depth that when we overran one anti-tank position at great cost to our panzers, another would be waiting for us and another and another. We were knocking out the Ruskies hand over fist, but he was bashing hell out of us too – our losses were appalling. Their defence system was over a hundred miles wide across the neck of the salient! There were hundreds of groups of five 76.2mm anti-tank guns in mutually supporting batteries backed up by infantry with mortars. Then their engineers had laid thousands of mines to each mile. They had been placed in such a way that, to avoid them, we were forced to move towards their guns. After a week or so we had no choice but to pull back; otherwise we would have been wiped out. Meanwhile, Ivan remained in his thousands – that's the way it always is. Yes, we do well all right, but it's not enough. At best all we do is dent the opposition. We always finish up worse off than when we started – a lot less tanks and a lot less territory. Ever since Stalingrad the story has been the same. Now we are fighting to save Kharkov, or at least to hold it long enough for our men to get out of the city before the Soviets swarm all over it.'

Helmut was thunderstruck. The truth had been laid bare before him for the first time. Thiemann had smashed his rosy picture of an all-conquering German army heroically advancing to victory. His mind was full of confused thoughts – this officer must be brave. He wears the Knight's Cross. Yet, if he had spoken like this back home in Germany, he would have been arrested for defeatist talk. We *must* be winning, Helmut assured himself. We have to be winning. Look at all those prisoners. Think of our fantastic tanks. Remember the support of our unbeatable Luftwaffe.

Then he recalled something else: 'Sir,' he said, 'surely it's only a matter of hanging on for a little while? After all the Führer has promised that all kinds of secret weapons will be ready soon.'

'Very good, Steiner, very good,' Thiemann replied. 'In the meantime it would be nice to have a drop more petrol for our tanks! There's nothing so frustrating or dangerous as grinding to a halt through lack of fuel in the middle of a battle.'

There was no time for further talk. They had reached the advanced depot. It had once been a village. Now those buildings which had remained intact had all been utilized by the German army as a supply dump and tank-repair laager. Thiemann indicated where he wanted Helmut to park. As they climbed out, he said: 'Don't be too depressed by what I have told you. You will learn for yourself soon enough. The important thing is to remember you are a professional soldier – soon to become an officer. We have a job to do and, whatever the situation, good or bad, we will always do it to the best of our ability. As Germans, our spirit can never be broken. We know beyond doubt that we are the best soldiers in the world. Governments may come and governments may go, but the German soldier goes on for ever – so long as there's a Germany to fight for.' Suddenly he grinned. 'And now, young Steiner, come and meet the crew.'

Carrying his large parcel, Thiemann led the way along a dusty path followed by Helmut lugging his kit-bag. They entered what had once been a peasant's crude *izba*. Three tankmen sitting on upturned ammunition boxes were playing cards. One of the players, a thickset *obergefreiter* in his late thirties, looked up momentarily. Seeing them, he jumped up, calling to the other two, 'On your feet, boys, the boss is back.' For a moment all three stood smartly to attention. Then they relaxed, crowding round their leader as though they were all equals.

The other two men were much younger than their companion; one, whom Helmut guessed to be around twenty-one, wearing the single V insignia of a *gefreiter*, was unusually skinny and had a shaven head. His partner, looking little older than Helmut himself, wore denim-type green overalls and the recently issued *einheitsfeldmütze* – a black, peaked ski-cap. In contrast to the *gefreiter* he was well-built and, from the way he hopped from foot to foot, obviously bursting with nervous energy. Yet all three shared the indefinable assurance of men who had seen war at first hand, who knew the worst and had come to terms with it – and each other. They were a team welded by fear, by danger and by trust.

Thiemann introduced Helmut to the men: Manfred, the veteran, was announced as the gunner who had destroyed many more Popov tanks in the last two years than he had had hot dinners; Ludwig, the loader, skilled at keeping up with Manfred's demands for ammunition; and Hans, who, as wireless operator and forward machine-gunner, would share the tank's cramped front compartment with Helmut. The occasion was extraordinarily formal. The men's reserve gave no hint of pleasure on the one hand or resentment on the other. They were suspending judgment until later.

Thiemann quickly restored the mood of bonhomie. He set the heavy parcel down in front of his crew and tore it open. 'Gifts for the righteous and, as it happens, for you lot as well!' He extracted packets of cigarettes, small bars of Italian chocolate, tins of soup, miniature bars of black soap and several pairs of thick woollen socks in a variety of colours – strictly non-regulation, but very practical. As each item came to light, it was greeted with appreciative cheers by the men, who automatically divided the goods into five separate piles.

'Come on, Steiner, collect your share,' urged Thiemann.

'Thank you, Sir,' replied Helmut, grateful to be included.

He studied the small heap of luxuries that had been shoved in his direction. 'Excuse me,' he said hesitantly, 'but I don't smoke. If anyone would like my cigarettes . . .' He got no further. The three tankmen instantly voiced their claim to this unexpected bonus. Eager hands reached out to grab the packets.

'Hold it!' Thiemann's voice cut through the babble. 'Thank you, Steiner. Divide his cigarettes into three lots, Manfred.' Then he looked at Helmut. 'I have two extra bars of chocolate which you can have in compensation. In future, if you still want to part with your cigarettes, the going rate will be a packet of smokes for a small bar of chocolate.'

When this minor, but important, ceremony had been completed the men looked again at their leader. Thiemann knew exactly what they were waiting for. 'I'm sorry,' he said, 'but there's nothing. The supply officer at Poltava told me no mail has come down the line for over a month.' As he noticed his men's crestfallen faces, he added, 'Next time for sure. Now we must get moving. There's a job to do.'

Helmut wondered what job they were about to do and looked at the others for a clue. They were gathering up gear, straightening uniforms and checking watches. Beyond that, their expressions revealed nothing – no more than any other group of men about to go to work.

Leaving the *izba*, Thiemann led the way to a Panzer IV parked nearby. It was a model H equipped with the new 75mm KwK L48/87 gun. Tank tracks had been attached to the front to provide extra protection. Strange-looking cement-clad plates with a ripple surface covered the sides of the turret and hull. These reduced the effectiveness of the enemy's magnetic mines.

'There she is,' said Ludwig. 'It looks as if they've put the old cow back into reasonable shape.'

An *obergefreiter* with a clipboard tucked under his arm marched up to Thiemann and saluted. 'Your machine is satisfactory again now, Sir. All repairs completed. Everything else checked through.'

The NCO handed back the tank's Engine Service Record, the Wireless Logbook and the Gun History Sheets. 'If you will sign the inspection cards, Sir, you can be on your way.'

Thiemann studied the fresh entries in the documents carefully. Then he said, 'We'll do our own running check round the laager area. If I'm satisfied, *then* I'll sign your bits of paper.'

'Sir!' barked the engineer with studied correctness.

Helmut could hear the bumbling sound coming from a number of tank engines as they ticked over. Every now and then there was a resonant clang as an engine hatch was dropped into place or a cupola-lid slammed shut.

'On board!' ordered Thiemann. The crew sprang onto the tank and, while Manfred, Ludwig and the *leutnant* clambered through the turret apertures, Hans and Helmut opened up their hatches and slid into the forward positions. Helmut looked hastily round the driving compartment. To his relief, apart from a few minor details, the controls appeared to be the same as on his training tank. He unhooked his intercom set and settled it over his black sidecap. Adjusting his driving seat until his tank boots rested comfortably on the foot controls, he then raised the visor on his front aperture and checked the overhead periscope. Turning the periscope from left to right, he was pleased to see that it gave him a clear field of vision, both sideways and to the front. It was obvious that the lenses had recently been polished.

Thiemann's voice came clearly over the intercom: 'Everyone hearing me? Right! For Steiner's benefit, because he is new to our crew, a few important points. To avoid confusion when in action, each crew-member will be called by his functional name, that is: driver; wireless operator or front gunner, according to which job Hans is carrying out at the time; loader; and main gunner. There will be no needless chatter over the intercom. I will give all necessary directions. Any remarks by crew members will be confined to those of operational importance – for example, warning of enemy approaching, spotting anti-tank positions, or reporting malfunctioning of equipment within the tank, either of the driving function or any of our armaments. In an emergency, no one will leave the tank until they hear the order: "Bale out!" If I am unable to speak through injury or death, then Manfred, the gunner, will deputize for me and give all necessary instructions. In this crew we make a practice of understanding as much about each other's jobs as possible. We can never know when this might prove useful. As soon as there is more time for training sessions, we will practise exchanging roles. You, Steiner, will have learned gunnery and signals procedure at tank school. We'll make sure you don't forget them. Meanwhile, Hans, you are second driver. Be ready to take over in an emergency. That's enough for now. You've been thrown in at the deep end, Steiner, but you'll learn quick enough, be sure of that. Meanwhile, do only what I tell you.'

For the first time the full magnitude of his responsibility struck Helmut. His life and those of four other men could well depend on his actions. What was he doing here anyway, sitting in a steel box in the middle of Russia with four complete strangers?

Suddenly an order, 'Driver, start up. Prepare to move off,' came over the intercom. He leaned forward, turned the fuel switch, checked the gear lever was in neutral and pushed the starter button. The twelve cylinders of the great 300 bhp Maybach engine burst into life. Helmut eased back the throttle to a fast tick-over. Soon the sharp tang of engine fumes was added to the rich smell of gun oil.

'Driver, advance!' Helmut slammed the lever into gear and felt the massive machine moving forward beneath him. Steadily he climbed through the gears, making each change as smoothly professional as possible. He was acutely aware that his every move was under critical surveillance.

'Left!' came the order. Helmut swung the driving wheel. 'Increase speed!' He opened the throttle steadily. The tank vibrated and clanked like a mobile iron foundry. Only headphones saved the crew from the worst effects of the noise. 'Halt!' Helmut applied the brake hard and knocked the lever out of gear. 'Reverse!'

Achieving reverse efficiently in a Panzer IV was near to impossible. For some reason the gears would not mesh happily in this position without the application of enormous strength. Only all-in wrestlers stood much chance of carrying out this operation smoothly. Helmut whammed the lever across the gate and jiggled it down at an angle. Simultaneously he pumped the clutch pedal twice for good luck. To his amazement, instead of the expected grinding and crunching, the lever slotted sweetly into place and, with a touch on the throttle, the tank started to roll steadily backwards.

Over his headphones, Helmut thought he heard at least one grunt of appreciation. After several other manoeuvres Thiemann asked: 'Is everything working well, driver?'

'Working well, Sir,' Helmut replied proudly.

Attention was then turned elsewhere: checking the forward and turret 7.92mm machine guns, the radio equipment and the main gun. Once Thiemann was certain the panzer was in fighting order, he returned to sign the papers, much to the *obergefreiter's* relief.

Then they headed east. His brief spell at the wheel had done Helmut a power of good. His self-confidence had grown beyond measure. Now he was ready to show anyone that his skill as a panzer-driver was second to none. As they bounded over the steppe country he felt as though he had been handling tanks all his life.

After travelling for about half an hour Thiemann spotted a small dark protrusion on the horizon, slightly to the north of their own route. He told Helmut to edge towards it, maintaining cruising speed. Narrowing the distance rapidly, they soon made out the unmistakable slab-sided shape of a mighty PzKw IV Tiger 1. Its sixteen-foot, 88mm gun barrel was even then swinging round towards them. They were taking no chances in a war where both sides used captured enemy tanks.

Thiemann fired a recognition flare. The answering signal from the Tiger was immediate. Within moments they were alongside their fellow Germans, who turned out to be from the 16th Panzer Division operating in conjunction with their own 17th. The Tiger's *panzerführer* told Thiemann that companies of both divisions were patrolling this area, south-east of Kharkov, ready to prevent a complete Russian encirclement of the city. Soviet armour had been reported moving in from the north and east, heading in their

direction. Thiemann established radio contact with his own company commander, who ordered them to move in a north-westerly direction, closing on
Kharkov itself. 'Keep on that course and you'll meet up with us' was the
message.

Shortly after bidding farewell to the Tiger's crew, they were motoring up
to their company commander's Panzer IV. He had been stationed below the
horizon, just out of sight from their previous position.

'Carry on past panzers C and D and then keep an eye on the gap between
them and Kharkov,' signalled the commander in code. Helmut opened the
throttle and in a short time they had sped past first one panzer of their own
Division and then another.

Now they could see the silhouette of the city in the distance. It looked
remarkably like the outline of a gigantic battleship floating on the plain. Tall
buildings at the centre formed the image of a warship's superstructure. At
the outskirts black palls of smoke reached up into the sky – evidence that
heavy fighting was already taking place in the northern suburbs.

'Slide down into that depression, driver – and switch off,' the command
came over the intercom. 'We'll station ourselves there and save fuel.'
Helmut drove into the hollow, which brought them hull-down below the
level of the surrounding terrain. He switched off immediately.

'We'll open up and keep a close watch for Ivan.' said Thiemann.

Helmut reached up above his head and released his hatch cover. It was
pleasant to push up into the fresh afternoon air. He and Hans sat like
newly-hatched chickens half out of their shells. Thiemann and Manfred
stood on top of the turret, scanning the endless vista through binoculars.
Ludwig jumped down beside the tank and relieved himself with an exagger-
ated sigh of content. Hans lit a cigarette and inhaled deeply: 'If only our
people back home could see us now. Brave German heroes preparing to
throw back the Bolshevik hordes!'

Hoping to hear something encouraging, Helmut asked Hans: 'How long
before the Ruskies come?' Hans shrugged, took another drag at his cigarette
before replying: 'Could be hours, even days. Could be minutes. You never
know with old bastard Ivan.'

As if to emphasize the point, Thiemann suddenly called: 'Action stations!'
Everyone shot into position and lids clanged shut.

'Stand by, gunner – traverse left. Start up, driver. Ivan closing fast – see
him, gunner?'

'See him, Sir!'

'Right. Keep on him. I'll tell you when. Driver, be ready to move off on
my order.'

'Sir!'

Helmut fired the engine but was unable to see a thing through his front aperture because the tank was hull down. He swung his periscope until he caught sight of the Russian – a T34. It was throwing up clouds of dust and seemed to be coming straight for them. Helmut recalled the outline pictures he had seen at tank school – sharply sloping sides, wide tracks, clean lines. It mounted a highly lethal 41.2 calibre, 76.2mm gun. His periscope just topped the depression in which they were partially concealed. So his view was that of a worm hypnotized by a monster approaching at frightening speed.

'Why don't we fire?' Helmut asked himself. 'Why don't we fire. He must have seen us by now!'

'Steady, gunner,' came Thiemann's voice, calm and controlled. 'In a moment he will present his flank – then we'll have him.'

By now the T34 was nearly filling Helmut's lens. Then he realized what Thiemann meant. It had been an optical illusion that the enemy was heading straight for them. Now as he reached the nearest point to their position, he was passing them at an angle, exposing his more vulnerable, less heavily armoured side-plates. His gun was pointing straight ahead. Incredibly, the Ruskies had not seen the panzer in its hide-out.

'Fire!'

Helmut jumped as the panzer's main gun hurled an armour-piercing shell straight into the flank of the T34. The Soviet tank pitched forward on its tracks, hung nose-heavy for a moment, recovered equilibrium, slewed round and ground to a stop. A gaping hole had appeared a foot or so forward of the turret. Meanwhile, in the panzer, Ludwig lifted another 75mm shell, thrust it forward into the breech – then slammed the block shut. He slapped Manfred's arm to indicate the gun was loaded. The gunner's face was pressed against the rubber-mounted eyepiece of his telescopic sight, his finger curled round the electrically controlled trigger.

'Fire!'

Heat, combined with the odour of cordite and hot gun oil, momentarily overcame Helmut in a wave of nausea. He felt his stomach heave and thought he was going to vomit. But the feeling passed. Peering through his periscope he now saw there was a second hole at the base of the T34's turret, while the tank itself had half-heeled over. Thiemann decided not to waste another round – the enemy was completely immobilized. He thought it highly unlikely that any member of the Russian crew could have survived. Calling up his Company Commander he explained what had taken place. The Commander surmised that their victim must have been an advanced scout for strong armoured forces now confirmed as moving in their direction. He ordered Thiemann to race immediately for the town of Chuguyev about fifteen miles to the south-east, on the west bank of the Donetz. This position had been heavily fortified as a jumping-off point for German armour engaged in preventing the encirclement of Kharkov. They would all meet there.

Even as Helmut, engaging low gear, clawed them out of the hole, ominous shapes were appearing on the skyline.

'Full speed for Chuguyev, driver. These T34s are faster than us!'

Helmut needed no second bidding; his throttle was open to the last notch. The Mark IV roared away, kicking up a miniature dust storm that must have been seen for miles. It was an eerie experience – fleeing from a powerful enemy, an enemy invisible to Helmut with his field of vision limited to the front and sides. Because of the self-imposed silence, there was no chatter from the crew to tell him how quickly the Russians were gaining on them. They had covered about ten miles at a creditable 18mph, when Helmut noticed that they were gradually converging on another of their panzer IVs travelling in the same direction. After a short while he spotted the other two German tanks further over to the left.

A snapped instruction came over the radio from the Company Commander out on the far flank: 'Hold this distance from each other. Don't crowd any closer.' The wisdom of this order soon became evident. To Helmut's consternation a great fountain of dirt rose up a few yards to their right. The T34s, firing on the move, had got their range. More shells fell all round them. Suddenly there was a frightening eruption dead ahead. Instinctively, not waiting for an order, Helmut flung the wheel over, barely missing the newly-formed crater that lay directly in their path. Stones and rubble clattered down like hail-stones on the upper surfaces of the tank. Helmut, sweating from every pore, was utterly convinced death was only moments away. This conviction seemed justified when the panzer nearest to them blew up in a sheet of orange flame. Although he was shaking uncontrollably, Helmut kept his foot hard down on the accelerator until the bones in his foot ached under the pressure.

'Eject smoke,' Thiemann ordered calmly. A great blanket of smoke rose from the phosphorous bombs fired to the rear, forming a protective screen between themselves and their pursuers. The two remaining panzers who accompanied them had taken the same precaution. Enemy shells continued to fall, but the aim was now confused and most fell wide.

New instructions came from the Company Commander: 'Reaching Chuguyev is out of the question with this lot breathing down our necks. Close in on me under cover of the smoke.'

When the three panzers had come together, the Commander again spoke over the radio: 'There are twelve T34s behind that smoke. On my order, we'll turn about and charge through them, taking them by surprise. Once past, we'll turn again and attack them from the rear, before they recover their wits. Understood?' Everyone understood only too well

Outnumbered four to one, manning outdated tanks, they were about to go onto the attack.

Strangely, Helmut's mood was no different from other members of the crew: excitement and optimism. Anything was better than being chased by a numerically superior enemy.

The order came: 'Turn about. Follow me. Line ahead. Once through the smoke, you fire to the left, Thiemann, you to the right, Ulrich.' A momentary pause, then: 'Turn now. Follow me.'

The three PzKw IVs charged through their own smokescreen, one behind the other. Surprise was complete. Within seconds each panzer had selected a target and blasted it at short range, reducing the opposition to nine. They had passed right through the ranks of Russian tanks and begun to turn before the startled Soviets realized what had happened. Yet the enemy's recovery was remarkably swift. Even as the panzers swung round to pour fire into the vulnerable engine compartments at the back of the Soviet tanks, the T34s were also changing direction to face their attackers. Manfred was lining up on one of the opposing tanks, when Helmut felt the driving wheel kick in his hand. The machine was refusing to respond to his controls. Although he was unaware what had happened, an armour-piercing shell had penetrated the left-hand track, jamming against a guide wheel, bringing the rotary mechanism to a stop. With only the right-hand track in operation, they slewed round and round in circles, throwing up clouds of dirt. They were sitting ducks. For a fraction of a second Helmut was paralysed with crippling fear. Then training and discipline came to the rescue – it was his duty to report.

'Driver here, Sir. We're out of control.'

Calmly, Thiemann's voice came back over the intercom: 'Try her in reverse.' Helmut banged the lever into reverse, not forgetting to kick the clutch down twice. For the second time that day he selected the gear without trouble. Steadily he opened the throttle and, after a moment's juddering and grinding, the panzer moved backwards, shaking the enemy shell clear.

'Well done, driver. Now take her forward again. Quick!'

Helmut responded like lightning, knowing all their lives depended on the speed of his action. To his overwhelming relief the machine moved away, gathering speed by the second.

'Good, driver. Weave to the right. Now left. Edge round so we can take that outside Rusky on the flank.'

Activity and clear orders, the best antidote to fear and panic, helped Helmut to keep his head during this, his first taste of battle. Nevertheless, a sense of hopelessness kept threatening to overwhelm him as he glimpsed the odds against them. He knew they had hit another Russian, because black smoke was belching from a brown hull. They were speeding towards the T34 as three scrambling figures emerged from its turret and slid down the side of the tank. The enemy soldiers scattered hither and thither. One, who must have been blinded in the attack, ran straight into the path of the oncoming panzer. Helmut swung the wheel to avoid him, but it was too late. He just had time to glimpse the poor man's face – a frozen picture compounded of shock, terror and astonishment – before he disappeared beneath the tracks.

Five Soviet tanks had now been knocked out, but Ulrich's panzer had blown up, fired on simultaneously by two Soviet tanks attacking from either side. Two against seven. Not a chance. The Russians were reforming at around 2500 metres, ready for a concerted assault on the remaining pair of panzers. In a head-on confrontation the T34s would come off best without a doubt. They outmatched the Germans with a combined firepower of seven 76.2mm guns.

'You go right. I'll move left,' ordered the Company Commander. 'Each man for himself. At least we'll split the opposition and maybe knock out a couple more. Good luck!'

Tell-tale dust was rising behind the Soviet armour. The T34s were moving towards them.

'Advance right, driver.'

Shells were beginning to fall uncomfortably close. If the enemy's standard of gunnery had in any way equalled that of the Germans, they would already have been hit.

'Fire back at 1000 metres, gunner.'

Perhaps, as the Commander said, they would manage to get another of Ivan's tanks before they were destroyed themselves. The enemy force had split into two groups as anticipated. Four T34s were deploying in an obvious encircling movement. The panzers' situation was hopeless – two flies in a spider's web. Then the impossible happened. Out of the clear sky three rocket-firing stukas fell screaming on the unsuspecting foe. Within seconds three Russian tanks had been reduced to twisted heaps of scrap. The Stukas roared away, reformed and came in again, so low this time that the short grass of the steppe was blown flat by the slipstream. Deadly rockets slammed into two more enemy hulls, only one missile missing its mark. Ammunition spent, the dive-bombers flew in close formation over the two panzers, waggling their distinctive, crooked wings in greeting. Thiemann fired a bright green flare to express their gratitude to the Luftwaffe. Only two T34s remained intact and they were already heading for the north-eastern skyline.

When the two panzers finally reached Chuguyev, the crews learned that the flight of Stukas had been led by Squadron Commandant Rudel, Germany's highest-scoring ace. He had perfected the method of effectively destroying Russian tanks with cannon and had passed on his techniques to the young pilots in his squadron. Together they had achieved notable success. The JU87 or Stuka, which they flew, was virtually obsolete. Yet on the Russian front, against tanks, where opposition from the air was negligible, it had still proved to be a valuable weapon. By an incredible stroke of luck for Helmut and his comrades, Rudel's squadron had been posted to their sector of the front that very morning. When the Stukas came to the rescue, the flight was on its first operational reconnaissance since arriving in the area.

Helmut could hardly believe that so much had happened in a single day: the air-raid on the railway junction at Poltava in the small hours of the morning; the first sight of Soviet prisoners; his nerve-racking test as he drove the Panzer IV round the laager area; the destruction of the T34, and finally the desperate encounter with the Russian tanks. That night his mind was crowded with violent images and he knew that these images would be his close companions from now on.

He woke an hour before dawn, his body trembling from the shock of an oppressive dream of men, unable to escape, being burned alive inside a metal box. He saw, too, the vision of a blinded soldier stumbling, helpless beneath the crushing tracks of a tank in a war of gigantic, omnipotent machines against which creatures of flesh and blood stood no chance of survival.

A friendly hand descended on his shoulder. 'Have some coffee. Nothing better for chasing away the blues.' It was the veteran gunner, Manfred. He handed Helmut a tin mug.

'Well, you're one of us now – an old sweat! Don't worry. We've all been through it. You'll get used to things in time, like the rest of us – you'll see. Now, drink your bloody acorns while they're still hot!'

For Helmut this was a turning point. Over the weeks that followed the young trainee officer learned the value of comradeship in the German army. This, more than any other single factor, kept men steady enabling them to stand against an enemy of vastly greater numbers long after most other armies would have collapsed. It was no fault of theirs, or their commanders in the field, that they were let down so badly by an incompetent High Command back home.

Helmut felt a deep sense of pride at being accepted by the other members of his crew. The ordeal of fire had come early, yet he had not been found wanting. His happiest moment occurred while still at Chuguyev, about a week after their arrival. They had just returned from patrol when Thiemann used some pretext to send Helmut off on a minor errand. Feeling aggrieved at being given such a petty duty after a hard day's driving, he shoved open the door of the hut with his boot on his return. There he saw Thiemann and the three crewmen standing behind a small table. On the table was a little cake. On the cake a single candle spluttered.

'Do you know what day this is?' asked Thiemann.

'No, Sir,' replied Helmut.

'It is 14 August – your birthday!' Then the tankmen started singing, and clapping their hands. Helmut was staggered. He had completely forgotten the date – awareness of time had grown hazy at the front. But he would never forget the celebration that followed. Plenty of schnapps and a bottle of wine from the officers' quarters helped down a load of sausages, a roasted Russian hare, extra field rations and, of course, the cake.

Helmut's mood during the evening alternated between laughter and barely restrained tears. He wanted to know how on earth they knew about his birthday. Thiemann winked as he tapped his nose with his finger. 'German efficiency, Helmut, German efficiency. Date of birth, etc, etc – it's all there in your documents!'

When he turned in that night Helmut knew he had indeed become a man. After all he was now seventeen.

On 23 August, 1943, Kharkov fell to the Russians. Thanks to the panzers, the German army was able to extricate itself with a minimum of loss. Yet now the forces of the Third Reich were being pushed irrevocably westwards, particularly in the southern and central sections of the front. Chuguyev, their home of a few days before, was now well behind enemy lines. Poltava, where Helmut had detrained, had been threatened earlier. At the last moment III Panzer Corps and three SS panzer divisions arrived back from the south just in time to stem the tide which their depleted divisions on the spot could not have held alone. If Poltava had fallen at that time, Kharkov would have been encircled and the fate of the German garrison in the city undoubtedly sealed.

By September the situation was becoming stabilized, but not static. True enough the Russians, on the attack, were losing more men and equipment than the Germans. Yet the German losses were greater than they could afford, especially after the decimation of their forces in the ill-fated Citadel campaign two months before. Most seriously, the Soviets had crossed the Dnieper at no less than eighteen points along a stretch of sixty miles, a bitter blow to the German command, who had hoped to form a 'winter line' along its western banks. The panzer forces spread themselves even more thinly as they sped hither and thither in an attempt to contain these multiplying bridgeheads.

Helmut and his comrades were ordered to Kremenchug, sixty miles south-west of Poltava, on hearing news that the Russians had bridged the river at this point. It was in this devastated town that Helmut had a strange and moving encounter. Flanked by heaps of rubble the column of panzers approached through what had once been the attractive northern suburbs. The Russians were concentrating south of the town where the railway line to Kirovograd crossed the Dnieper. It was the panzers' task to disrupt them as quickly as possible.

Helmut's PzKw IV was third in a column of eight. The Commandant brought them to a halt in the cobbled square opposite what was left of the railway station. A pitiful collection of German foot soldiers from one of the Brandenburg Regiments was drawn up in ragged ranks. The men were emaciated, dirty, their uniforms in shreds. Many looked too old to take effective part in any military duties. They were in bizarre contrast to the well-dressed, healthy young tank crews. It would have stretched the credulity of an onlooker to learn that these two groups belonged to the same army.

It was time for the panzers to ready themselves for combat. Helmut helped to refuel the tank from the large metal drums lashed to the rear of the hull. The Commandant, *Hauptmann* Dr Heiermann, was standing in the middle of the square exchanging formalities with the officer in charge of the human scarecrows. At some point one of the scarecrows approached the officers, saluted and spoke a few words. A moment later Heiermann strode over to Helmut's tank and called up to Thiemann: 'You have a man named Steiner in your crew, I think?'

Thiemann pointed towards Helmut. 'Come down here, Steiner, I have something to tell you.'

Helmut followed his commandant across the square where Heiermann gestured towards a figure standing a little apart from the other men. 'Someone there wishes to speak with you, Steiner. I can give you ten minutes before we move off.'

The tattered figure started to move towards him. For a moment longer Helmut stood still, completely puzzled. Then the truth dawned. With a shout of emotion, Helmut rushed forward – to greet his father. It was a strange meeting in the depths of enemy country: the physically broken ex-politician and one-time shoemaker and his son, clad in the smart black uniform of an élite corps. What they said to each other was their secret. Only Erich's final words were heard by others as his son ran back to his panzer: 'Take care of yourself, Helmut. Take care.'

As he leapt onto the tank Helmut turned and looked across the square one more time. The father of whom he had seen so little stood on the cobble-stones, a sad, defeated wreck in an alien environment. Helmut lowered his head and clanged the metal cover shut. He did not then know that this was the last time he would see his father. Erich Steiner disappeared, leaving no trace. Like so many others, he was lost for ever in the infinite waste of the Russian war.

*

While at training school Helmut and his fellow cadets had been told by their officers: 'We can teach you a great deal, but none of it equals what you will learn through practical experience at the front.' After four months Helmut's knowledge of war as it was fought in tanks far exceeded that of any textbook instructor. Under training, for example, he had never been told that German tanks, though superbly engineered, often defied efforts to repair them in the field because of their intricate construction. Around 30,000 individual parts were involved in their assembly. By contrast the Russian T34 was a rough and ready machine of excellent design. It was often driven out of the factory and straight into battle. A single standard-sized bolt was used throughout. If one of these bolts had to be replaced in an emergency it could be 'borrowed' from the nearest dispatch-rider's motor-cycle! Sensibly, Soviet tanks were driven by diesel motors – simpler in concept than the German petrol engines, more reliable and much less likely to catch fire when hit.

Helmut soon heard that the new PzKw V – the Panther – although a superior tank in many ways to anything the Russians possessed at that time, nevertheless had an alarming tendency to burst into flames for no apparent reason. This again was the fault of the High Command, who insisted on rushing new models into the front line before they had been adequately tested and modified. What constantly amazed Helmut was how frequently the panzers were brought to a halt through lack of fuel. There was an occasion near Kirovograd when, after days of waiting, the tank crews at last received a supply of petrol. It turned out to be aviation spirit – quite useless in tanks.

He learned not only about machines, but also a great deal about the men who used them. As a potential officer, he had been set a superb example by his own tank commander and also by the remarkable Dr Heiermann, a rare combination of first-class soldier and thoughtful scholar.

The ordinary soldiers had taught him to control his emotions under fire. This was not so much through anything the men had said, but rather by their own behaviour in times of danger. Helmut knew that, once qualified, he would be leading the finest troops in the world. He had seen and admired their qualities at first hand. He was filled with an overwhelming pride and a feeling of deep gratitude to the Führer for giving him this wonderful opportunity. It was certain that the time was soon to come when the German army would throw back the Soviet barbarians and save Western civilization from destruction.

One thing, however, did worry Helmut. When the Wehrmacht had advanced through the Ukraine in 1941, the Germans had been welcomed by the inhabitants as liberators. Now, moving back over the same territory, this relationship had turned sour. The peasants looked at them either with fear or cold disdain. Marauding bands of partisans took every opportunity to harass the German troops by day and by night. Why had their one-time friends turned against them? It was the work of the bastard Gestapo, the veterans said, the scum who were never seen in battle, but spent their time tormenting old women and children far behind the lines. Helmut could not understand how such vermin were allowed to behave in this way. Why had the Führer not been told? Once Hitler learned of their behaviour, justice would be done quickly enough!

When his period of active service was over, Helmut felt downhearted at leaving his comrades. They advised him to hurry through the next phase of his training and come back soon. Meanwhile, the tankmen promised to keep old Ivan in his place until he returned. Helmut, having proved himself in the field, was appointed to an officer candidate course and promoted to *fähnrich*. Before recommencing his formal training, he was granted leave and managed to get home in time for Christmas. The family was overjoyed to see him. His mother cried when Helmut told her of the unexpected meeting with his father. He carefully avoided any reference to Erich's condition. Later, after Helmut had left for officers' school at Luckenwalde, the story filtered through to the Cologne newspapers. They wrote it up as an epic encounter, graphically describing how father and son stood shoulder to shoulder, heroically repelling the panic-stricken enemy!

Back in the classroom, Helmut settled down to what he expected would be six months' concentrated study. After this, unless he made a mess of things, he would become one of the youngest *leutnants* in the German army. At the back of his mind he remembered his comrades at the front and felt vaguely guilty. The feeling was shortlived, however. After only three weeks he was called before his commanding officer who said that Helmut's studies must be interrupted. His presence was needed back in Russia. He hoped that Helmut's tour of duty would be of short duration, but the situation was such that everyone had to make sacrifices. Helmut, who had just begun to adjust to his fresh way of life, was far from pleased.

Towards the end of an icy cold January he travelled back by train to the war he had so recently left. Now it was not so far to the front. Poltava was already a hundred and twenty-five miles behind the Russian lines. Melitopol, Drepropetrovsk and Kremenchug had all fallen to the enemy. The winter battle line in the southern sector was drawn from Kherson in the extreme south, bulging eastwards towards Zaporozhye, before sweeping back to Kirovograd, then heading north to a point west of Fastov. The conditions were as appalling as in previous winters, but now at least the tank crews were warmly dressed in heavy, generously cut uniforms, with long double-breasted overjackets complete with hoods. These garments were reversible, snow-camouflaged on one side, brown and green with 'rain' overpatterns on the other. Nevertheless, the most prized items of booty were Russian sheepskin coats reaching below the knee.

Many lessons too had been learned about how to protect machines and guns from freezing conditions. The panzers themselves were more rugged, better able to keep operating through the rigours of a Russian winter. Taking a tip from the enemy, tank tracks were now much wider, giving a firmer grip in soft snow. Although activity along the front was much reduced because of the conditions, the panzers were still mounting minor counter-attacks in the hope of gaining better positions as jumping-off points in the coming spring. During the lull, the divisions had been building up their armoured strength. Now there was a shortage of experienced tankmen to man the panzers, which was why Helmut had been recalled. He caught up with the 17th Division in the area of Krivoy Rog and by a stroke of good fortune he was reunited with his old crew. After his departure his comrades had been badly let down by an inferior driver. In fact they had been lucky to survive the experience. On hearing that Helmut was on the way, Thiemann had pulled every string to get him back into the team.

There was another surprise for Helmut. The old PzKw IV had run into a minefield and been wrecked, but the crew had escaped unscathed. Now they had a new PzKw V – Panther.

'She's a real beauty', Hans told Helmut. 'Don't worry about the early bugs in the machinery – like catching fire without warning. The engineers have sorted all that out and made a lot of other improvements too. You're going to enjoy driving her.'

The Panther was indeed a superior tank, superior to its main rival, the Russian T34, from which it had borrowed many of its design features, and armed with a long 75mm gun of considerable penetrating power – greater than that of the Tiger's larger 88mm gun. It could travel on roads at a top speed of 34mph, using nearly two gallons to every mile. Unlike the slab-sided hull of the Tiger I, the Panther had sloping armour which proved much less vulnerable. The chances of using her capabilities as an offensive weapon however, were now limited. Although undoubtedly the best designed tank of the Second World War, her qualities were largely wasted in a defensive role to which the heavier, slower Tiger was better suited.

The handful of Panthers in the 17th Panzer Division was therefore given the job of spearheading the counter-attacks mounted during the winter months in the southern sector. As Hans had predicted, Helmut found the Panther a pleasure to drive and easier to control than the old Panzer IV. After a few days he found it hard to believe that he had ever been away from the front.

Then the Soviets began to sweep forward again in strength. On 7 February they took Nikopol. Krivoy Rog, where their division had so recently been based, fell to the Red Army the following week. By the end of the month Helmut and his comrades had their backs to the River Bug. There was no let up; with the enemy's greater strength of at least six to one, the Germans were constantly forced to give ground. When Field-Marshal Walter Model took over command in the south from von Manstein in late March, the Wehrmacht had been pushed out of Russia, across the River Prut and into Romania. During these fierce onslaughts the panzers never yielded ground without a fight. In consequence the supply of new armour was once again decimated.

Thiemann and his crew appeared to lead charmed lives. Military skill, natural cunning, excellent teamwork and an instinctive sense of impending danger kept them out of trouble, when less experienced crews met with disaster. Yet even for them luck was running out. In the first week in May the Russians launched a heavy attack west of Jassy, down both banks of the River Siret. It was a battle involving no less than five hundred tanks and Helmut's Panther was in the thick of it.

They had been tracking a T34 for some minutes and had almost closed within firing range. Helmut had his foot hard down on the throttle when suddenly he heard Hans cry out: 'Christ! There's the biggest tank in the world bearing down on us to the right.' Although they didn't know it, because these monsters were new in the field, this was one of the latest Stalins. It mounted a 122mm gun, dwarfing even the mighty Tiger's 88mm and it was more heavily armoured.

'Forget the T34, driver. Turn to the right, and face that big tank,' Thiemann ordered. 'Then go into reverse. I'll guide you between those rocks. Gunner, line up and fire at will.'

This was a wise decision. Facing the giant presented a smaller target and exposed only the Panther's most heavily protected areas. Thiemann intended firing at the Russian while he simultaneously reversed behind the protection of an outcrop of large rocks. The Romanian terrain in the foothills of the Carpathian Mountains was very different from the flat steppe country of the Ukraine, where natural cover was at a minimum.

Those were the last words Helmut heard Thiemann speak. He remembered swinging the wheel hard to the right. At the same moment his ears were assailed by a shattering crash like that of an express train hitting a steel wall. He was aware of floating in space, unattached, weightless, no longer part of the world he had known. The rest was oblivion. When he recovered consciousness, he was lying on his stomach in a field service hospital. Bandages encased his body from neck to buttocks. His head swam with pain.

Later, when a fellow *fähnrich* came to visit him, he learned what had happened. Apparently, as the Panther started to turn, the Stalin tank fired.

The shell hit their panzer amidships. It tore into the turret compartment, decapitating Manfred, disintegrating the gun breach and filling the turret with flying splinters which killed Thiemann and Ludwig. A second shot hit the turret, knocking it askew. Meanwhile, Hans had managed to scramble out of his forward compartment and was running for his life towards the security of the rocks. He was cut down and killed by machine-gun fire.

The battle had ended in success for the Germans, which was fortunate for Helmut. After the Soviets had been repulsed, the area was combed for survivors and repairable machines. Helmut had been discovered hanging out of his hatchway, his head and arms drooping down the side of the tank away from the Stalin's attack. His back had been reduced to a pulp, showered by myriad steel fragments. At first he was assumed to be dead, but then a medical orderly detected a faint pulse. He was gently disentangled from the wrecked Panther – a difficult manoeuvre because his boot had somehow got caught up on a projection inside the tank. It was quite possible this tangle had saved his life. Instead of getting away from the panzer, in which case he would certainly have been gunned down, he had been pinned halfway out of the hatch. It seemed likely too that, in his efforts to struggle free, he was flung forward and took shrapnel in his back, rather than in his head.

He was sent to a military hospital near Dresden where he slowly recovered. Mentally he remained disturbed. Irrational thoughts filled him with guilt. Why had he survived when all his comrades had died? It was his fault. If only he had spun the wheel more quickly, the enemy's shell would have missed them and they would all be alive today. Day after day he lay in torment, longing to get back into combat, where he could forget his anguish in action.

Towards the end of August he was released from hospital and posted once more to Luckenwalde. The officer in charge of training told him that he was considered unfit for further active service, but in view of his front-line experience he would be useful to them as an instructor. Helmut was disgusted with this decision, but was unable to get it reversed. He spent long periods in the gymnasium every day trying to prove to himself and everyone else that he was as good as new.

His frustration was reflected in his attitude towards the pupils. This eighteen-year-old *oberfähnrich* treated them with a harshness excelling that of hard-bitten *stabsfeldwebels* more than twice his age. He sought no friends amoung the training staff. They were all older and mostly senior in rank to himself. He led a lone existence and spent his time brooding. For nearly six months he endured this alien life, fretting at the bad news from the fighting fronts, now coming in from both east and west since the Allied landings in Normandy.

Then, when he least expected it, his wish was granted. It was nearing the end of April, 1945. Germany's enemies were all around, deep inside her own borders. The situation had reached its last desperate stage. Orders had been issued for personnel in training establishments to play their part in defending the Reich in its dying hours. With a crew of instructors, Helmut drove a Tiger I, newly arrived from the production line, west to Dobritz. It was a journey of only forty miles. The roads were jammed with refugees all heading west, away from the Red Menace and all praying they would fall into the arms of the American forces now halted on the other side of the Elbe.

Helmut drove across fields as much as possible. Even so it took hours to reach their destination. They were acting as an independent unit, attached to no one in particular. Vague contradictory messages came occasionally over the radio. None referred to them or said anything that helped to clarify the situation. They had no idea why they had been ordered to Dobritz. Once a *hauptmann* drove up and ordered them to give assistance to a hard-pressed group of infantry fighting a desperate holding action in nearby Goritz. Helmut and his crew had the satisfaction of driving the Soviets out of the small town and relieving those of their German comrades who were still alive.

The relief, of course, was only temporary; the Russians would soon be back in overwhelming numbers. Nothing could be worse than getting caught up in street fighting. This was the situation when tanks were at their most vulnerable, as attacks could come at them from any angle, including upstairs windows. Bodies of German soldiers littered the streets as the Tiger slowly extricated itself. Helmut and his comrades looked on as a group of SS men discarded their own distinctive uniforms and donned those of the dead. If they were to be caught by the Russians, these onetime lords of the earth preferred it should be as ordinary front-line soldiers rather than members of an élite corps whose reputation was more than dubious.

Returning to Dobritz, they found the Red Army already forcing its way through the southern end of the town. Skirting round to the north, Helmut drove into a cemetery, away from overlooking houses. He stationed the Tiger behind an enormous tree. Studying the needle on the petrol gauge, he knew they had reached the end of their journey. From this vantage point they were able to look across to an impressive block of cavalry stables. Helmut guessed that sooner or later the Soviets would come round the far corner of those buildings.

They waited several hours and it was late into the afternoon before the first Russian tank nosed cautiously round the edge of the stables. Helmut and his crew waited until it was out of sight of other Soviets following behind, then blasted it at point-blank range. A moment later another tank appeared and suffered the same fate. Shortly after, a third tried to reverse back the way it had come. It crashed into the substantial iron railings surrounding the stables. Moving forward to disentangle itself, it was demolished by two of the Tiger's 88mm shells fired in quick succession.

'We can keep this going for ever,' thought Helmut, 'or at least until our ammunition is used up.'

They were preparing themselves for their fourth victim when the unexpected happened. Unknown to them, a Red Army infantrywoman had been creeping up on the Tiger from the rear, carefully dodging from one gravestone to another. When she reached her quarry, the crew had opened the hatches to take in a breath of fresh air. Seizing her chance, she leapt onto the back of the Tiger. Brandishing a PP Shpagin submachine gun, she screamed at them like an angry cat, motioning them to raise their hands above their heads.

The gunner unwisely reached up and tried to slam the lid shut. The woman was too quick for him. Wedging the hatch cover open with her boot, she fired straight down through the top of his head. After that, no one attempted further resistance. For Helmut the war was over.

Within a few days it was over for his country too. Germany lay a shattered ruin, deserted by her European allies, hated by most of the world, defeated by the combined strength of Russia, Britain and her Empire, and the United States of America.

Helmut, a prisoner of war in his own homeland, squatted in a muddy compound, soaked to the skin by incessant rain. He looked at his fellow prisoners. 'Why us?' he asked himself. 'What have we done to deserve this? Surely no men have ever fought so loyally against impossible odds, made such sacrifices, asked so little in return. Yet this is our reward.' He stared with ill-concealed contempt at the Russian guards – dirty, stupid-faced peasants in uniform, with the instincts of animals. Only overwhelming numbers and the boundless supplies of equipment provided by Britain and America had brought the Soviets victory.

He saw, with a spark of pride, how even on this Godforsaken patch his fellow Germans had organized themselves. Their captors had provided two tents to be shared among all of them – only enough to shelter a small percentage of those in the compound. Yet, without fuss, the sick and wounded had been laid under this cover as a matter of course. The guards had not bothered to dole out food, such as it was. Instead it had been thrown in a heap at their feet as though they were dogs. If Ivan had expected to be entertained by a scrambling, crowd of savages, all clawing for these scraps, then he was disappointed. The food was divided up fairly and every prisoner received an equal portion.

For a while Helmut contemplated escape. It would have been easy enough to slip away from the compound after dark. But what was the point? The Russians had taken his papers. How far would he have managed to travel on foot before being picked up. Without identification his position would be serious. He sank into a state of lethargy. His homeland was finished. So too was his army career. If he had been told then that he was to be shot at dawn, he would have received the news with complete indifference, almost with relief.

Instead, next morning he and many of the others were marched to the railway sidings and herded into cattle trucks. After days of travel they arrived at their destination. As Helmut jostled his way out of the wagon, he recognized the place at once – Poltava! Fate had brought him back to his starting point in Russia – but now how different the circumstances. He stared at the spot where he had first met *Leutnant* Thiemann. The prisoners were taken to a camp on the outskirts of the town. Here they were told the good news by some PoWs who had arrived before them: 'This is a "soft" camp. Do as you are told. Pretend to embrace communism, and you will be all right.'

The following morning the new arrivals were sitting in a classroom listening to a lecture. The tutor was German. He was dressed in a uniform of unusual design – Wehrmacht breeches and boots, but topped with an oatmeal-coloured Russian smock. The man himself was of medium height. With fine, pale features, he had dark staring eyes, slicked-back black hair and a small neat moustache like a dead caterpillar. At first he urged his audience to consider the evils of fascism and how they had all been duped by wicked leaders.

Later he extolled the virtues of communism and explained what fools the Germans had been to fight against their Soviet brothers. Finally he asked for questions. After an embarrassed shuffling of feet one or two of the prisoners made sycophantic noises, which brought a thin smile to the lecturer's face.

Helmut had been smouldering in a corner, writhing in agony at this heresy. He could stand it no longer. Jumping to his feet, he shouted: 'How can you say such things? You rotten bastard! Doesn't the memory of all your German comrades who died fighting the bloody communists mean anything to you? What about the folk back home, the ones who were killed in the bombing? Did they die for nothing? You are full of bullshit you dirty, lousy swine!' Then he rushed across the room and hit the man full in the mouth.

It was only a matter of hours before Helmut had been classified as an 'incorrigible'. He was transferred to a 'hard' camp nearby. Here prisoners existed in a state similar to that of battery hens. Crushed into small wooden huts, the men lay in rows on planked shelves fastened against the walls and reaching all the way up to the ceiling. There was just room between each layer of boards for a prisoner to lie on his back, but not to turn over or lie on his side. Facilities for exercise did not exist. Food arrived in two swill buckets per hut. As no bowls were available, the inmates had to thrust their hands into the indescribable filth in order to grab what they could. There was nothing left of hope. Most men stretched out in their allotted places, waiting for the end. Helmut had neither the desire nor the patience to prolong this pointless existence. When he discovered the rusty lid of an old tin can, he clambered onto his upper shelf, lay down and sawed away at his wrists. The end would probably have come quickly enough if Helmut's blood had not flowed down onto the occupants of the lower bunks. The ensuing shouts brought the Russian guards at a run. Helmut, now unconscious, was rushed to a hospital outside the camp.

When he came round he was filled with horror. Via a tube attached to his arm, blood was being steadily pumped into his body. The final humiliation – his pure Aryan blood was being inexorably tainted with inferior Bolshevik filth! He felt wretchedly unclean, tarnished beyond redemption. He reached up weakly to tear away the tube, but a burly Ukrainian orderly restrained him without difficulty. After a few days of steady, if unwilling recovery, Helmut managed to convince himself that the blood must have come from a fellow-countryman, otherwise his ideas and convictions would not have remained as German as ever!

During this time in hospital, a White Russian officer came to speak with him. He asked Helmut why he had tried to kill himself. The officer told him it was a crime against God for such an upstanding young man to contemplate taking his own life. Explaining that he was a follower of the Russian Orthodox faith, he imagined that Helmut too came from a Christian family. Begging him to think of his mother back in Germany, and to avoid doing anything that would cause her more anguish than she had already suffered. The officer assured Helmut that there was reason for hope and urged him to have faith in the future.

After release from hospital Helmut was returned to the appalling camp from which he had planned to escape through death. But now circumstances had changed. The White Russian had arranged for Helmut to come each day to his house to cook and clean. This routine was only broken occasionally when Helmut was ordered to remain in camp. This, he soon learned, was on occasions when the officer's girlfriend visited the house. These easy duties were the most fortunate thing that could have happened to Helmut, who showed his appreciation by doing his work conscientiously. In return he ate well. Food was so plentiful in his benefactor's larder that he systematically removed quantities for his starving friends back in the camp. Each evening he squelched past the guards on the gate, his shoes full of bacon, his trousers packed with bread!

One day, after he had attended to his routine housework, the White Russian told him that his services would not be required any more. 'No,' he said, smiling at Helmut's obvious dismay. 'I told you in the hospital you must live with hope. Tomorrow you will be returning to Germany – you are a free man!'

Helmut did not dare to believe what he had been told. It seemed too impossible. That night back in camp he scarcely slept, in case he woke up to find it had been a cruel dream.

Next day he was marched in to see the camp adjutant who issued him with a set of new papers. Following another nerve-racking delay, he was escorted to the railway terminal. With a stab of emotion, Helmut saw that his patron had arrived to bid him farewell. Just before the train steamed away on its long journey back to his homeland, the White Russian said: 'Take care, Helmut, and remember what I said about the future. It is there for you to grasp. You did your work well for me and I thank you for that.' Then he added, almost offhandedly: 'By the way, I hope your comrades in the camp enjoyed my food.'

After what seemed an age, Helmut arrived in the bomb-shattered city of Cologne. His mother, sister and brother Kurt had survived the holocaust and were rebuilding their lives under the comparatively paternal administration of the British Military Government. His sister Marlene staggered him when she introduced her new husband, a British sergeant in the Intelligence Corps attached to the British Army of the Rhine.

Within days of his return, a former colleague in the Hitler Youth denounced Helmut to his new brother-in-law as being an ardent Nazi! He was taken before a senior administrator in the miltary government in Cologne. After a lengthy session his interrogator, a Scottish Jew named Isaac Armitage, decided that young Helmut Steiner was just the chap he had been looking for to act as his personal driver. For several months Helmut helped Mr Armitage in his duties, including attempts to round up former Nazis. Helmut enjoyed his work very much. Apart from being well-fed and adequately paid, he was ideally placed to warn his friends of impending trouble.

ANTONIO BENETTI

ITALIAN SKI COMMANDO

WHERE IS IT that the Duce has led his trusting people after eighteen years of dictatorial power? What hard choice is open to them now? It is to stand up to the battery of the whole British Empire on sea, in the air and in Africa, and the vigorous counter-attack of the Greek nation; or, on the other hand, to call in Attila over the Brenner Pass with his hordes of ravenous soldiery and his gangs of Gestapo policemen to occupy, hold down and protect the Italian people, for whom he and his Nazi followers cherish the most bitter and outspoken contempt that is on record between races.

Excerpt from Winston Churchill's broadcast to the Italian people on 23 December, 1940.

This is the story of Antonio Benetti, a ski commando in the Italian Alpini, who was not called upon to stand up to the British Empire, or face the Greeks, or fall foul of the Gestapo. He averted the destruction of his men and himself on the Russian front by applying common sense and fostering good will among those people his leader insisted were his enemies.

It would be hard to imagine a more idyllic upbringing than that enjoyed by Antonio Benetti. To have been born on 4 December, 1913, in Venice; to move with the family after a few years to Padua, a city claiming to be the oldest in northern Italy; moving again later to Milan, and at last finishing up in Rome was certainly out of the common rut. Add to that frequent holidays in the beautiful region north of Verona, staying with relatives who owned handsome villas sited above sparkling lakes and backed by snowcapped mountains, must surely take some beating.

His father was a rich and well-connected lawyer, so Antonio had the opportunity to ride, to ski and to enjoy water sports. However, if the Benettis had not left Venice it is probable that riding would never have become part of Antonio's life. In a city where the streets are canals, waterborne traffic naturally takes precedence over the wheel and the hoof. In the Venice of Antonio's boyhood horses were scarce. It is said that in the eighteenth century Venetians actually paid to see a stuffed horse!

When his father made the final move and established what was to become a lucrative practice in Rome, Antonio was still young. The family lived in one of the city's smartest residential districts, in the Via Nomentana, almost within sight of the Villa Torlonia, a gift from the Prince of Torlonia to Mussolini.

Antonio's father, best described as a 'pale pink socialist', was not impressed with the fascist régime, but hoped, like most of his middleclass contemporaries, that a strong government might cure some of Italy's more obvious shortcomings: economic stagnation, corruption, poverty and bureaucratic strangulation of individual initiative.

Antonio was eight when Mussolini came to power in 1922 and was taken to see *Il Duce* as he stood on the balcony of the Palazzo Venezia. Mussolini was dressed in an ill-fitting frock coat, very different from the resplendent uniforms that later adorned his stocky frame. He was surrounded by black-shirted henchmen, some of whom wore slings or had their heads swathed in blood-stained bandages, for this was the day after the 'heroic march on Rome'. In fact, there had been no opposition. What blood had been spilled was due to scuffles between rival groups among the marchers themselves. Mussolini himself arrived in comfort at the last minute, by train from Milan! When he spoke, it was only a matter of moments before the crowd succumbed to his spell. With chest thrown out, head back, hands on hips, legs astride, his hoarse voice swayed the onlookers in an extraordinary fashion.

In later years Antonio could not recall anything he had said but he certainly remembered the effect of his words on the people around him. Antonio's mother muttered several times: '*Vigoroso! Vigoroso?* (a strong man) but he noticed this his father was in no way swayed by the common wave of emotion.

Antonio had managed, somehow, to escape being caught up in the activities of the Balilla, a quasi-military organization for boys from the age of 8 to 13. But when he was 14 he could not escape recruitment into the *Avanguardisti*, a set-up for older boys. Now, like it or not, he was forced to take some notice of fascist activities. Hating all forms of regimentation, Antonio dreamed up schemes to secure his absence during parades and other organized events. Often these tricks worked well enough, but not on every occasion. Once, he was ordered to be at the great Farnesina Sports Stadium at 6 o'clock on the following Sunday morning. The stadium was situated six or seven kilometres from his home, on the other side of Rome. Antonio said that it was impossible to walk right across the city and arrive in time for the start of the event, but what he was really dreading was the indignity of being seen in public, even at that early hour, in his fascist sports gear. The uniform consisted of black shorts, white shirt with loose-fitting sleeves, floppy black velvet hat and, worst of all in Antonio's opinion, a ridiculous cape with a sort of ruff collar. Although he tried every excuse, his officer was unrelenting and insisted that he must attend. Antonio sensed that something special was going to mark this occasion. So he pressed the Captain for further information. In the end the CO told him that, when they had completed their stint at the Farnesina Stadium, they would all be going in chartered buses to the Villa Torlonia for a treat. Beyond that he would say no more. Antonio saw this as a heavensent chance to get off the hook. 'Villa Torlonia!' he cried. 'The home of Il Duce. Couldn't be better. I live not two hundred metres from there. Tell me, Captain, what time you will arrive and I will be waiting outside the gates.' To Antonio it seemed a most logical solution – but his Captain thought otherwise. 'You are a miserable numb-skull, Benetti. You are not worthy to be a fascist.' Antonio nodded in agreement. 'We are trying to build a proud nation of warlike men – worthy

of Il Duce's brilliant example. But having to contend with slackers like you
. . .' The Captain swore that young Benetti would be in the direst trouble if
he did not show up at the stadium on time.

So next Sunday Antonio walked across Rome and kept the appointment.
Following a long session of disorganized gymnastic displays, the youngsters
were herded into motor coaches and driven to the Villa Torlonia. Although
situated in the city area, the gardens were extensive. The boys were lined up
on grass terraces overlooking an immaculately tended lawn. Then Il Duce
himself appeared and for the second time Antonio had an opportunity to
study the dictator.

On a signal from their leaders the *Avanguardisti* dutifully broke into an
enthusiastic chorus of '*Viva Il Duce!*' '*Viva Il Duce!*' over and over again, at
the same time throwing their hats in the air in a 'spontaneous' display of joy.

Il Duce marched purposefully on to the lawn, followed at a respectful
distance by members of his entourage. He was dressed in a white silk shirt,
well-cut riding breeches and shiny black leather boots. Antonio concluded
that he must be shortsighted and possibly deaf, because initially he gave no
sign that he was conscious of any onlookers until suddenly, and, apparently
for the first time, he became aware of his youthful audience bidding him a
tumultuous welcome.

Recovering from his 'surprise' with remarkable briskness, he sprang to
attention and treated his admirers to an energetic fascist salute. Generously
he invited them to remain and watch while he ran through his daily sporting
activities. Followed by a few Bersaglieri, he set off at a steady trot round the
grounds. After the 'warm-up', the show began in earnest. He put on a
spirited display of tennis, vigorously returning balls lobbed at him with the
greatest care by his coach. He then enthralled the onlookers with a dramatic
session of sabre flourishings. As a finale he mounted his magnificent black
horse and, to rapturous cries from the terraces, rode round in circles clearing
obstacles all of one metre high.

The effect on Antonio was decisive! From that day on, instead of a
lukewarm tolerance, he turned firmly away from fascism, not from any deep
political conviction, but because its chief exponent had revealed himself as a
posturing idiot. Back at school Antonio listened to the more ardent of his
fascist-inspired teachers with renewed cynicism. He was filled with contempt for such pearls as:

The eyes of the Duce are on every one of you. No one can say what is
the meaning of the look on his face. It is an eagle opening its wings and rising
into space. It is a flame that searches out your heart to light there a vermilion
fire. Who can resist that burning eye, darting out its arrows? But do not be
afraid; for you those arrows will change into rays of joy.
or:

How can we ever forget that fascist boy who, when near to death, asked that he might put on his uniform and that his savings should go to the party?

Antonio now spurned any activity that glorified the Party. Joining the ski and equestrian corps enabled him to avoid boring parades. When ordered to attend an equestrian event, he would explain that, unfortunately, he had a prior commitment to the ski corps. This ploy worked equally well in reverse.

Antonio's father was ambitious for his older son to follow him into his legal business in Rome, so he entered Rome University to study Law and Political Science. Naturally bright and gifted with a retentive memory, he had few problems with his studies. The pace was leisurely enough, leaving plenty of time for sport and amorous affairs. Antonio, always athletic, had grown tall and handsome, with a healthy tan, fair hair and a beard trimmed in the style of d'Artagnan's companions. He found little difficulty in attracting any girl who took his fancy.

Some of his professors were Jews. They, in common with most of the staff, had little respect for the fascist régime. Antonio enjoyed swapping 'Mussolini jokes' with his law tutor. The sharpest barbs, however, were reserved for those academics who had sold their names and reputations in exchange for honours and advancement.

Antonio tried not to let his thoughts dwell too much on the future. The prospect of actually earning his living as a lawyer filled him with foreboding. It would be impossible to sustain any enthusiasm for such a sedentary occupation. A hypocritical profession too, Antonio believed. Real justice had gone out of the window since the courts came under the jurisdiction of the government or, more accurately, under Mussolini's control. Enemies of fascism stood little chance of mercy from the law, while fascists themselves literally got away with murder. Yet he knew that his own feelings must take second place to his father's wishes.

Having completed the intermediate stage in his studies, at twenty-one he was called up for compulsory service in the army. This was midway through 1935. For seven months he trained at an officers' school in Rome. It was a pleasant enough existence, interfering little with his social life. He soon realized that it was important to volunteer for some interesting branch of the service. After some consideration, he narrowed his choice down to either the Cavalry or the Alpini. Fond as he was of horses, two factors weighed against his becoming a cavalry officer. For one thing, if war ever came, it would be foolish to imagine much could be done against tanks and twentieth-century artillery while mounted on a horse! Secondly, outfits such as the Cavalleria di Genova were truly the corps of the élite, reserved for the sons of dukes, counts and the exceptionally rich. Antonio fell into none of these categories, not even the third.

This left the Alpini – the ski commandos. It seemed the natural home for

Antonio. In wartime the Alpini would be engaged in theatres of war well away from all the nastier implements of modern battle. The principal enemy would undoubtedly be nature herself – the mountains, the weather, the freezing cold. Antonio understood and respected the elements, but did not fear them. He volunteered for the Alpini and, because of his experience, was accepted into the 7th Alpini Regiment, one of two regiments in the Pusteria Division. These divisions, of which there were six, had an honourable tradition dating back to 1872 when the Alpini were first formed. The Alpini battalions were named after the town, mountain, village or valley in that battalion's recruiting area.

It was not long before Secondo Tenente Benetti was posted to the most miserable, out-of-the-way place imaginable. San Candido, lost in the folds of the Carnic Alps on the Italian/Austrian border some eighty kilometres east of the Brenner Pass, was a dull little village, overshadowed by an ugly barracks built higher up the slopes.

Antonio reported to a seedy-looking adjutant who had obviously spent too long in this oppressive place. Patently resentful at being disturbed, the adjutant grudgingly detailed a soldier to show the new arrival to his quarters. As Antonio was leaving the office, he called him back: 'By the way, you are Orderly Officer tonight. You will find a list of your duties on the notice board in the Officers' Mess.'

During the evening, Antonio learned what he was expected to do: inspect the guard twice during the night; make sure that everything that should be locked up was locked up; turn off all things that could be turned off; visit the cells; inspect the kitchens; look in on each barrack block before lights-out; make sure all was in order. Apart from these routine formalities, the orderly officer was at liberty to spend the rest of the shift lying on his bed. He could read a book, listen to the gramophone, write letters, do anything provided he did not remove his uniform, pull off his boots or fall asleep.

During his rounds he tried to cheer up some unhappy recruits by telling them a couple of risqué jokes. Unfortunately, the reaction was not up to his expectations. Although they smiled politely, realizing the *tenente* was trying to be friendly, the young soldiers were neither in the mood, nor had the understanding to appreciate such sophisticated wit. They had been called up from local Alpine villages and bundled into the army to do their obligatory twelve months' service. None of them had been away from home before.

Depressed by his failure to communicate, Antonio returned to his room. There *were* no books, gramophone or writing materials. In defiance of the regulations, he hung his tunic on the back of a chair, kicked off his boots, lay down carefully on the rickety bed and within minutes was fast asleep.

The sound of the *fanfara* brought him to his senses. He looked at his watch. It was 1am. A strange time, Antonio thought, to hold a parade accompanied by a military band at full blast. Dressing quickly, he hurried out into the chilly night and made his way in the direction of the racket. The whole of one barrack block was lit up like a cruise liner on gala night and the noise was overwhelming. It was the building in which the recruits were quartered.

Striding along the corridor, he flung open the door of the main dormitory. Every one of the recruits, dressed only in long underpants, was down on his hands and knees. Sitting astride each were fully uniformed soldiers, with drawn swords, urging on their 'steeds' by kneeing them in the ribs and administering sharp slaps to their backsides. The *fanfara* added to the mood of the occasion. For one moment Antonio thought he had walked into a mass orgy, but quickly realized it was no more than a very noisy exhibition of boisterous horse-play. Moving over to the corporal in charge of the *fanfara*, he ordered him to silence the musicians. As the row subsided, he demanded to know what was going on. The hush that followed his unexpected appearance was dramatic. Antonio began to feel rather pleased with himself. He was master of the situation. He was about to assert his authority further when one of the 'riders' – a tall, distinguished man in his mid-twenties – quietly asked the intruder who the hell he was. 'I am the Duty Officer,' Antonio replied. 'In that case you have my sympathy,' smiled the officer. 'You may join our party. Be so kind as to get down on your hands and knees immediately!' Antonio had no time to consider the legitimacy of this order before the *tenente* leapt onto his shoulders and brought him crashing to the floor. The next moment the *fanfara* blasted off again and the fun was resumed.

During the night a large quantity of grappa was drunk and the light of dawn was beginning to appear over the mountains as the last bottle was emptied. Antonio eventually staggered back to his billet, exhausted but wiser. He had participated in the Alpini ceremony of 'Riding the Rookies'. He had learned too that even the gloomiest of places could be livened up with a little effort and the 'voluntary' cooperation of those involved.

Antonio had no idea how long he had been asleep; it seemed like five minutes. Someone was shaking him roughly and telling him to get up. Opening one bleary eye, he made out the solid form of a sergeant.

'Come on, Sir. The Colonel wants to see you at once!' A blurred vision of being put away for ever in the dungeons of this awful place floated through his fuddled mind. Slowly he pulled himself into some sort of shape and followed the sergeant.

Not having met the CO before, Antonio had no means of knowing whether the Colonel's face was permanently purple, or whether it only took on this hue at moments of exceptional stress. Two things were certain: first, the senior officer was very angry and, secondly, from the way he arranged his words in cliches Antonio was able to recognize him as a particularly thick-headed brand of fascist. It transpired that the Colonel had probably had even less sleep than his Orderly Officer. Although living in the village, he had nevertheless been woken by the noise around the same time as Antonio. Looking out of his window, he was appalled to see lights shining from a barrack block on the side of the mountain above him. He had spent the remainder of the night pacing restlessly up and down, wondering just how long it would be before the fool of an orderly officer, whoever he was, would get things under control. Now he demanded a full explanation and the names of those responsible.

Antonio, standing stiffly to attention, did his best to improve an unpromising situation. A few weak phrases fell from his lips: 'Only a bit of boyish fun . . . expressing loyalty to the regiment by taking part in traditional ceremony.' When it came to naming names, Antonio knew only too well the name of the ringleader – his own 'horse-rider', Senior Tenente Lombardini. In fact, Lombardini, with the other officers then in camp, including the surly adjutant, was standing behind the Colonel at that moment.

Antonio sensed that they had all had a severe grilling before he arrived and felt on firmer ground even remembering something of his lawyer's training, as he launched into his final defence: 'I only arrived at this place yesterday, Colonel. I know no one. I have yet to be introduced to my fellow officers.' Then, seizing an opportunity to get in a dig at the adjutant, he added: 'It was difficult coming to a strange camp and finding myself detailed as Orderly Officer straight away. As a newly commissioned officer, these duties were unfamiliar to me.' He had the satisfaction of seeing the Colonel throw a quick glance of reproof at the adjutant.

The Colonel growled: 'As for introductions, I am Colonel Felice Guzzoni and I promise you that you will never forget my name. You will be spending the rest of your time in the army here, at San Candido. During these coming months I shall go to a great deal of trouble to teach you your duties as an officer.' He paused for breath, then went on sarcastically; 'Although we have had the honour of your company for nearly twenty-four hours, you have so far come before me only once on a charge of indiscipline. A remarkable record. In view of this I am prepared to be lenient. You will be confined to your quarters for fifteen days. Antonio's look of dismay did more to assuage the Colonel's temper than anything else.

The days of Antonio's 'confinement' certainly did pass slowly and he sank into a state of listless boredom. One or two of the younger officers – including Lombardini – came to visit him regularly in his quarters, smuggling in the odd bottle of grappa. Lombardini stayed to talk on several occasions. He was entertaining company, but there were moments when Antonio felt irritated by his enigmatic air and his knowing smile. He told Antonio how he had joined the army as a career officer after taking his degree in Milan. In spite of his frivolous behaviour on the occasion of their first meeting, he took his profession very seriously. It seemed that most male members of the Lombardini family had close connections with the army. As for the officers in San Candido, Lombardini explained, they all longed to get away from the place. So far none had been successful. The adjutant had applied for postings himself on at least a dozen occasions to his knowledge, but without any luck.

Antonio asked Lombardini how *he* felt about being stuck in such a place. 'It suits me very well. I have certain "interests" in Austria which make this a convenient spot to live at present. When it ceases to be convenient, I shall leave. Meanwhile, I have a couple of phone-calls to make on behalf of a friend.'

Antonio woke on the tenth day of his incarceration to sounds of unusual activity that seemed to border on panic. Running footsteps could be heard all around, shouted orders rang out. When the orderly arrived with breakfast, he brought news that the camp was to be honoured by a visit from a general that day. No warning had been given, hence the urgent stampede to get things tidied up. For the first time since his arrival, Antonio glowed with satisfaction. He, at least, would not be involved in any parades or inspections! He spent the morning listening to the *fanfara*, the crunch of marching feet, the roar of the Sergente-Maggiore's voice and stretched himself out on his bed.

It was mid-afternoon and it was clear from the silence that all ceremonial had finished. He imagined that the general had either left or was sleeping off the effects of lunch. A knock at the door preceded the entry of a young officer with a message: 'Come on, Antonio, you are wanted by the general!'

Almost before he knew it, he was standing stiffly to attention in the Colonel's office. Instead of the CO, however, a very brisk little General sat behind the desk.

'So you are Secondo Tenente Benetti, eh?'

'Yes, my General,' replied Antonio.

'I understand you are a first-class skier.'

'Yes, Sir.'

'Then it seems to me,' continued the General, 'that you are being wasted here – you should be polishing your skills at one of our special Scuole Militari d'Alpinismo. Don't you agree?'

'I most certainly do!' replied Antonio.

'Then it will be arranged at once,' the General assured him in a tone that left no room for argument.

Before the end of the week, Antonio was on his way to a ski commando school near Cortina in the Dolomites. It was only thirty kilometres south of

San Candido, yet the contrast between the two places was so great it could have been on the other side of the world. Antonio certainly appreciated his extraordinary luck. He realized what a fortunate escape he had had by applying to serve as an officer in the Alpini. Like thousands of other Italians he might easily have become involved in Mussolini's war against Ethiopia where the dictator was trying to expand his ramshackle African empire and dreaming of sending millions of settlers to develop the country once it had been conquered. He wrongly believed that abundant deposits of gold, diamonds, copper, iron, coal and oil were waiting to be exploited. Nearly half a million troops were involved in subjugating a race of people completely lacking in modern arms. Yet it took more than twice as long to subdue the Ethiopians than the fascist experts had predicted. So impatient did Mussolini become that he ignored the Geneva Convention and sanctioned the use of poison gas. Once Ethiopia had been conquered and industrialized, he planned to raise a force of two million native troops with which he would dominate the rest of Africa. In all, it was a costly and wasteful affair that brought no benefit to Italy. Mussolini, previously thought of as a figure of fun – though admired in some circles – was now despised throughout the civilized world.

At home, however, by the use of unrelenting propaganda, he reached a new peak of popularity. Up to that time no citizens of a modern country had been so effectively cut off from the truth as were the Italians. This certainly applied to Antonio. But he had long ceased to believe anything he read in the newspapers, or heard on the radio. Fully committed to the ski school's rigorous training programme, going off for days on cross-country expeditions, divorced for most of the time from anyone but his fellow Alpinis, he had no time to think of much except his immediate activities. These were certainly agreeable and challenging enough for any young man of his adventurous temperament, without bothering about what was happening in other parts of the world. His skiing was being honed to perfection and he was learning how to survive in rugged mountain terrain under all conditions.

He was chosen to represent the army in the region's annual ski championships and given permission to move into civilian accommodation at a village near the course so he could get in as much practice as possible. Staying in a small house owned by an elderly widow, he could not have received better attention. The food was well cooked and plentiful, and he had a cosy little bedroom on the ground floor at the rear of the building.

Life had never been better – except for one thing. He found that even after a hard day's training, he was quite unable to sleep at night. This was a serious situation. Until then he had never missed a night's sleep in his life and now he was in danger of falling below his best performance through mental and physical weariness.

Seeing his plight, Antonio's hostess introduced him to Mosa, a gnarled old mountain guide dressed from head to foot in a hooded garment made from sheepskin. Mosa literally 'divined' the problem in no time. Using a forked witch-hazel twig, he discovered that the village drains ran beneath the floor directily under Antonio's bed.

'Move your bed to the other end of the room,' Mosa ordered, 'and you will again sleep peacefully.' Antonio did as he was told and thereafter had no trouble in sleeping.

Antonio won the trophy for the Alpini and established himself as an indispensable member of the corps. When the time came to say farewell, the old man wagged a finger at Antonio: 'Heed my words young fellow. You have friends and you have enemies, all these people will play a part in your future life. The mountains, although no friends of man, will always be kind to you. You will owe your survival to the mountains, many, many times.' Antonio had more than one occasion to remember Mosa's words.

After a further ten months at the Alpini School, Antonio was released into civilian life. However, he remained on the reserve of officers, subject to recall at any time. Back in Rome he completed his law studies and, once qualified, joined his father's firm. It was an unhappy experience. He derived no satisfaction from his legal work, finding it irksome and repetitive. He did have a little excitement when he went with fellow reservist, Rudolfo Rosselli, to hear Mussolini speak in the Via di Triumfe. It was a chance to have a laugh. After endless parades throughout the city the climax was reached when Mussolini jumped on to an armoured car. The Leader was resplendent in black tunic, grey breeches, black leather boots and on his shaven head, a black fez-like cap with the golden eagle, emblem of the Roman Empire. The crowd gave the customary cheer: '*Duce! Duce! Duce!*' Mussolini scowled back fiercely, clenched fists on hips, and Antonio was reminded of his childhood visit to the Palazzo Venezia. At last the dictator raised his hand, commanding silence. The speech contained all the usual ingredients: he extolled the glories of Rome, the greatness of Fascist Italy the might of his new Empire and the decadence of the Western Democracies. It was excellent entertainment.

Antonio and Rudolfo, like the rest of the crowd, enjoyed themselves immensely. Even those members of the Fascist party who had been summoned to attend seemed to be cheering more or less spontaneously. It was the period of Mussolini's greatest popularity. He was at the peak of his self-confidence, convinced by the flattery of the sycophants who surrounded him that he was a superman. Several foreign emissaries reported him to be slightly mad.

That evening the two friends were strolling through the crowded restaurant quarter near the Piazza di Spagna. As they passed a picture display-window of the *Giornale d'Italia*, Antonio spotted a photograph of Mussolini standing on his armoured platform, faced by the ecstatic mob. There also were Rudolfo and himself in the front row of the crowd. The camera had caught Rudolfo in the act of blowing a raspberry at the Great Man! Aware that his friend was in danger, Antonio rushed for the nearest phone. Quickly he contacted an acquaintance whose father happened to be picture editor of the *Giornale d'Italia*. Within half an hour the photo had been removed from the window. It, and the negative, were never seen again. By good fortune that particular picture had not been chosen for publication in any of the editions.

Now, in 1937, at the age of twenty-four, Antonio felt that the future held nothing but a dull, humdrum existence. Whenever he had time he jumped on a train and headed north to the alps and a spell of cross-country skiing.

When, later in the year, he received a summons to report to Army Headquarters, his hopes rose in anticipation that he might be needed for further service in the Alpini. Instead, the major who interviewed him pushed a paper across the desk, saying offhandedly: 'Just sign this note confirming that you volunteer to serve in Spain.' Antonio, who spoke good Spanish and had friends in that country, had no intention of becoming involved in the Civil War. He knew that many of his fellow-countrymen, mostly poor peasant lads without any say in the matter, had been conscripted to fight with the Italian contingent on the Iberian peninsula.

Antonio's insight into Mussolini's latest 'foreign adventure' was much sharper than it had been of events in Ethiopia. He was aware that Italian troops, both regular and militia, had moved north through Spain after taking Málaga. The contingent had been sent by Il Duce to assist General Franco. Mussolini intended to demonstrate to the world the might of fascism by taking Madrid unaided. Instead, at Guadalajara, the force was overtaken by catastrophe. In the mountains the Italian troops fell under the counter-attacks of Madrid's International Brigade. It was Italy's worst military defeat since the disastrous rout at Caporetto in 1917. Mussolini had since been pressing thousands more 'volunteers' into service in Spain.

'No thank you, Sir,' said Antonio, as he pushed the unsigned paper back across the desk, 'I do not wish to fight in Spain.'

During this period Hitler was clocking up one success after another: occupation of the Rhineland, the swallowing of Austria, which brought Germany to the Italian border, and the annexation of Czechoslovakia. Mussolini, chafing at being left behind in the 'conquest stakes', now embarked on his most futile invasion of all. Again without warning and with even less preparation than usual on Good Friday, April, 1939, he poured his troops into Albania. Of all the independent countries in Europe, this was the poorest, most backward and least desirable. It also had the smallest army.

Although the Albanians put up a stiff resistance, the country was subjugated in a few days. Confusion and maladministration brought chaos to a nation already hampered by an archaic system of government. On balance, here too Mussolini lost more than he gained. After this so-called conquest, the Balkan countries abandoned any trust they may have had in Italy.

Fortunately for Antonio he managed to avoid this fiasco as well, but his days as a civilian were numbered. He was recalled for service in August, 1939. Within a few weeks Hitler's invasion of Poland brought Britain and France into conflict with Germany. Mussolini, predictably, sat on the fence, waiting for events to unfold. In spite of 'The Pact of Steel' between Italy and Germany, he was far too timid to rush in on the side of his fellow dictator at this early stage. Although he desperately wanted to see the Democracies take a hammering, at the same time, such was his envy of Hitler, he would also have rejoiced at any military setback suffered by the Führer.

Meanwhile, Antonio found himself at his second Scuola Militare d'Alpinismo, about seventy kilometres from Turin and, more significantly, only an hour's skiing time from the French border. The school was set at the head of a valley, on the outskirts of a small town. Antonio, responsible for a troop of twenty-seven alpine commandos, was camped with his men on the slopes above the army base. Winter was still far enough away to make living in tents acceptable and bathing naked in mountain streams an invigorating experience.

During the first two or three weeks Antonio and his troops were engaged in a variety of medical experiments. They were made to swallow regulated doses of 'energy tablets'. Army medical staff accompanied them, checking pulse rates and blood pressure at prescribed intervals. The commandos reckoned that the tests were a bit of a bore; the pills appeared to have no effect on them, either one way or the other. As a medical officer said to Antonio: 'You guys are all so fit and healthy it is almost impossible to assess the real value of these drugs. They may only prove their true worth when you are run down and exhausted.' Antonio thoughtfully 'acquired' a few boxes of the pills as an insurance for the future.

The handsome Colonel in charge of the army establishment confided to Antonio one evening that he had a problem: he was being driven almost mad by the uninvited attentions of the local *tardone* (married ladies whose husbands held important positions in the community). It was flattering, the Colonel agreed, but it was also embarrassing.

'In spite of my protests these bloody women shower me with gifts,' the Colonel told Antonio. 'Believe me, if I hadn't put up a spirited resistance, they'd have given me a hell of a lot more than gifts!'

The Colonel said he needed Antonio to organize some sort of distraction that would give the ladies something else to think about. 'Your chaps up in the mountains are not a bad-looking bunch. I want to bring some of the local VIPs, including the *tardone*, up to the hills to see your lads in action. You can organize a show one evening as well.'

Antonio understood only too well the role he was being asked to play. His CO was under attack from a hungry pack of bitches and he had to produce some attractive bones to divert their attention. He knew that, if his efforts were successful, he would be ordered to carry out an endless schedule of entertainments. This was just one of those occasions in Antonio Benetti's army career when, in spite of his good intentions, things went decidedly wrong.

First of all, the Colonel and his entourage, including the Mayor and his lady, the Bishop and his Chaplain, the Chief Surgeon, the Veterinary Surgeon, the Secretario of the district, the Police Chief and a round dozen of the *tardone* and some of their daughters, arrived suddenly at the Alpini's mountain retreat unannounced. It was a glorious sunny day with clear blue skies. Antonio and his entire troop were happily splashing around in a large rock pool as naked as the fish they had disturbed.

The *tardone* were manifestly intrigued by so many muscular young bodies. Their daughters also appeared to be fascinated. The Colonel and the Bishop took a different view. But, as Antonio pointed out, if there were any objections on grounds of embarrassment, then they only had themselves to blame. They should have waited for the official invitation to a respectable ski display.

In the meantime, preparations went ahead for the big show. Antonio planned a full-blown musical spectacular, full of action and colour. The story was based on the Sheik of Araby and the fabulous Fatima. This ambitious production required painstaking rehearsal in order to transform soldiers into actors. It was not an easy task, but Antonio was able to pick out glimmerings of latent talent in a handful of individuals.

Abramo, a dark, heavily bearded peasant, well built and enormously strong, was cast as the Sheik. A slim youth, with fair hair and blue eyes, typical of the region of Il Veneto from which he came, was a natural choice for the role of Fatima. In reality his physical beauty made him no less of a man, as a number of the local girls would blushingly affirm!

The production then began to take shape. The 'theatre' was to be an enormous marquee, normally used as a canteen. Willing hands constructed props and scenery. For days the camp was filled with the noise of construction, hammering and banging, and shouts of advice. The racket mingled with the sounds of rehearsal, a twanging guitar, an accordion's repetitive wheeze and the concentrated blast of the *fanfara* which at times drowned everything else.

When the great day arrived, Antonio, in gleaming boots, smart breeches, immaculately pressed grey-green tunic and alpine headgear with feather, stood at the main entrance to welcome his guests. Once again they were all there – the Colonel, the Mayor, the Fascist *Federale*, the Bishop and, of course, the *tardone*, accompanied by their daughters. It was going to be a very special day indeed. Peppe, Antonio's batman, with due deference showed the people to their seats. The *fanfara* struck up; the spectacular had begun.

The first part of the show was filled by shouting, laughing acrobats jumping and tumbling their way through a series of intricate exercises, encouraged by a background of fast tempo music provided by the *fanfara*. The standard of performance was high and executed with near-professional skill.

Antonio then introduced a series of comedy sketches. The object of fun in nearly every act was the fascist régime. The stupidity and incompetence of Italy's rulers were highlighted with relish. Yet the theme was approached obliquely and, of course, the word fascism and the name Mussolini were never mentioned. If accused, the producer and his players could innocently have claimed that they were referring to the ancient Romans, even though the audience was left in no doubt at whom the darts were being aimed!

The guests, by and large, seemed highly amused by these innuendoes and applauded as each point was thrust home. Antonio could see, however, that the *federale*, the local agent of the Party, was furious.

Antonio heralded the second half of the show by explaining that they were about to witness a dramatic interpretation of the legend of the Sheik of Araby and the Shocking Rape of the Beautiful Fatima. He was aware of a combined movement from the onlookers as they sat up and slid forward to the edge of their seats. He now had no doubt that his troop's efforts would be crowned with success.

The scene opened to reveal the beautiful Fatima innocently sitting in her boudoir, combing her hair and singing to herself in a rather surprising baritone! Her maidenly reverie was rudely interrupted as the *fanfara* unexpectedly struck up with a vigorous cavalry movement. Right on cue the Sheik of Araby galloped into the young maid's chamber. He was mounted on something that almost resembled a horse. At least it had a leg at each corner and a tail not unlike an old goatskin. The 'steed' was in fact two sweating Alpini encased in yards of tent canvas surmounted by an approximation to a nag's head fashioned from an old coal sack. Even the ears wagged back and forth in time to the music.

It was great stuff and the crowd loved it! The black-bearded Sheik cracked his awesome whip several times, just to show how fierce he was. Poor Fatima broke into uncontrollable sobs, thereby showing she had got the message. 'Come with me, little maiden!' commanded the wicked Sheik. 'Never!

Never! NEVER!' cried the maiden, clinging desperately to the bedpost. 'Come with me you shall!' roared the black-bearded swine. 'I will take you to my gilded palace in far-off Araby. Once there,' he leered, 'I will make you mine!' With that he rode towards the terrified girl. Sweeping her up in one massive hand he raised her into the air and brought her by a dramatic circling movement on to his opposite shoulder. Then, to the accompaniment of cat-calls and hisses from the audience and a crescendo of noise from the *fanfara*, he galloped out of the tent.

Now came the big scene. The backroom boys had excelled themselves with a colourful interior of the Sheik of Araby's ornate palace. It was a tribute to the Alpini's ingenuity and only Allah knew where all the oriental-style ornaments had come from. They certainly created an authentic atmosphere of Eastern opulence. Poor Fatima was discovered prostrate on the palace floor, while the unspeakable Sheik stood over her, demanding that she should succumb to his wicked wishes. Being a well brought up Egyptian girl, she refused him time and again.

Losing his temper at the frustrating lack of progress, the Sheik again resorted to cracking the whip. In the end Fatima became so terrified, she agreed to meet this awful man halfway by performing the dance of the seven veils. So, to appropriate background music performed on a flute, the unfortunate maiden began her seductive act, moving sensually around the palace, slowly removing one veil after another. So well did the good-looking ski commando execute the voluptuous dance that the members of the audience had to keep reminding themselves that they were not watching a female performer. As for the *tardone* and their daughters, their eyes grew larger and larger as the time to remove the final veil drew closer.

By now some of the women were quite baffled as to the actual sex of the enigmatic Fatima. The climax of the dance was approaching fast and Fatima moved to centre stage where spotlights converged on the writhing figure. With a provocative flourish the remaining veil was discarded and Fatima stood naked for all to see, apart from a shapely flesh-coloured bra. A gasp of amazement went round the tent; the young Alpini, leaning slightly forward, had tucked his well-proportioned male appendages out of sight between his legs. From the back it was amply clear he was a man – but not from the front! They had reached the high point of the show and Antonio was delighted. Now it only remained for Fatima to shuffle slowly backwards and disappear behind the scenery.

Unfortunately Antonio had failed to discern a deep vein of exhibitionism within his leading player. Fatima had no intention of retreating. On the contrary, instead of backing away, the dancer moved tantalizingly forward until no more than one metre from the front row, mainly occupied by women. With a quick movement. Fatima leapt high in the air, then landed

legs wide apart and body thrust well back. In a moment all was revealed by
this most extrovert of 'flashers'. Dumb with horror, Antonio motioned a
sergente-maggiore to bundle the offender out of the marquee. But it was too
late. Led by the unsmiling bishop, the guests were already leaving in
shocked silence.

The Colonel sentenced the entire troop to a fortnight's 'hard labour' for
bringing the army into disrepute. They were ordered to carry baulks of
timber into the high mountains and then use them to construct a substantial
rifugio. Antonio felt the punishment was a little unjust. After all his CO had
wanted the minds of the *tardone* diverted – and that mission had surely been
accomplished! The penalty proved harsher than expected. On the first day
the weather broke and persistent blizzards covered the slopes in deep, fresh,
powdered snow. Almost every morning after that the site of the new *rifugio*
had to be re-dug before building work could commence. Yet the spirits of
the Alpini were always high and laughter often echoed down from the hills as
Antonio's men recalled the glorious night of Araby.

The winter of 1939/40 passed comfortably enough with the Alpini now
billeted in the town. Romantic attachments between the girls of the neighbourhood and the ski commandos inevitably flourished in the close-knit
environment shared by soldier and civilian alike. More of Antonio's time
was taken up solving problems arising from affairs of the heart than dealing
with military matters. On one occasion he was lying on his bed reading the
Osservatore Romano, when his bedroom door burst open and the town's
irate blacksmith stood before him. 'Where is that stinking *sergente* of yours?
I'll kill that son of a macaroni pedlar!' It appeared that Peppe, Antonio's
batman, had been paying far too much attention to the blacksmith's young
wife and the only possible solution in the blacksmith's view was that Peppe
should pay with his life!

The *tenente* was polite and sympathetic. He thoughtfully poured the
cuckolded husband a liberal measure of grappa and invited him to sit down.
For over an hour Antonio discussed the fickleness of women and the
brutishness of men, agreeing that it was indeed a wicked and unjust world.
Finally, Antonio persuaded the man that, as a highly respected citizen and
the only blacksmith in the district, he was far too valuable to the community
ever to risk his future by taking the law into his own hands. He assured his
uninvited guest that the *sergente* would be severely punished and never
allowed to come anywhere near the blacksmith's home again. The husband
left in much happier mood, resolved to restrict his actions from then on to a
more careful surveillance of his wife's activities.

'You can come out now, Peppe,' said Antonio, with mock sternness.
Sergente Peppe Giuseppe rolled out from under his officer's bed, stood up
and carefully dusted down his uniform.

'Grateful thanks, my *tenente* – that was a close one!'

When the spring arrived, the Alpini returned to the mountains, where Antonio put his men through a rigorous régime of retraining to clear away the cobwebs of the winter. He sometimes wondered if his troop, or any other unit of the Italian army for that matter, would ever be called upon to fight an 'enemy'. Neither he nor any of his men felt any animosity towards the people, or governments, of any other country. The Fascists' unremitting campaign to whip up public hatred against France and Britain was viewed either with puzzlement or blank indifference by the majority of easy-going Italians. Their leader had long ago revealed himself as the arch bluffer. Antonio believed that the dictator would grab whatever extra territory he could lay his hands on, short of actually committing his nation to war.

As a staunch monarchist, Antonio was sure his King would veto any foolish moves that Mussolini might be contemplating. At that time, in common with most Italians, he was unaware of Vittorio Emanuele III's weak character and his fear of making even the least important decisions. Much less did he realize that Mussolini was hell-bent on war, even though remaining a non-belligerent would have been far more in Italy's long-term interest. Il Duce, in fact, was waiting impatiently for the opportunity to sacrifice about two thousand Italian soldiers in battle. This would prove to Hitler how genuine were his intentions to uphold the Pact of Steel.

At the end of May, 1940, Belgium surrendered to the German panzer divisions, Calais fell and the British Army embarked on its perilous evacuation from Dunkirk. To Mussolini the outcome now seemed certain. Hitler's success was assured. Il Duce was determined to declare war on France and Britain before an armistice was signed. It was essential for Italy to invade France, now almost down and out, so that he could claim a share of the victor's booty.

On 10 June Mussolini made the greatest blunder of his life. He committed the Italian nation to war against Great Britain and France. Not surprisingly, no orders were received by the Alpini for several days. As usual, when Mussolini decided to go to war, muddle and chaos followed. Not only were the Italian people shocked, so also were the generals, admirals and members of the Senate, who had all been kept in the dark. Mussolini was confident that he was capable of directing the entire war effort himself. That being so, he considered it a waste of time to consult senior officers about plans of campaign. The last thing he wanted was to hear from the professionals that his country was totally unprepared for war.

It was 21 June before an attack on French territory began – the day *after* France had asked Mussolini for an armistice! Just before dusk on that first day a *maggiore* of the Tridentia Division informed Antonio that a detachment of French Moroccan troops was near and it was essential to neutralize it before the main Italian force in that sector could advance. It would undoubtedly be best to take it by force during the night. In reply to Antonio's natural query about the enemy's estimated strength, the *maggiore* merely shrugged his shoulders. Conscientiously the ski commandos searched throughout the night for Moroccans. The troops soon realized that they were at a disadvantage wearing alpine boots. It was early summer and no snow lay in the valleys, so every step they took over stony ground gave advance notice that they were on their way! Antonio, Peppe and three of the others had gym shoes in their packs. These they donned in place of boots.

About an hour and a half before dawn, they heard voices, and were just able to make out the vague shapes of about a dozen men crouched behind some boulders. Antonio sent Peppe back to bring up the rest of the troop as quickly and silently as possible. Unfortunately, before the reinforcements arrived, the men moved off and Antonio with his three remaining Alpini had no alternative but to follow them.

It was a difficult situation. In the dark it was impossible to leave clues showing those coming behind the direction they had taken. At the same time they could not afford to lose their prey. They tracked the men, more by sound than sight as they plunged into a forest of firs, for they continued to chatter among themselves. When the first light of morning began to filter through the branches, Antonio was able to pinpoint their position. With the dawn he also established contact with the rest of his troop and the enemy group was soon encircled. Antonio had no wish to see anybody killed, and, sensing that his victims were not particularly aggressive, he shouted out that they were surrounded and must surrender immediately. There was only a moment's pause before fifteen very weary and worried-looking soldiers rose out of the undergrowth, hands above their heads. They were not Moroccans but friendly Sicilian troops who had lost their way and were looking for their artillery regiment from which they had become separated! It was later established that no Moroccans were engaged in that campaign!

Five days later the armistice was signed and 'hostilities' ceased between Italy and France. Il Duce's last-minute participation in the war gained him no more than a strip of alpine territory, one hundred and ninety kilometres long, and from one to thirty kilometres wide. For years he had shouted about the return of Nice, Savoy and Corsica to Italy, but after the armistice these remained French possessions. This did not deter him from boasting in public that his timely intervention had swung the war in Hitler's favour! The Germans, full of contempt, now had the real measure of their posturing ally – from that time on Italy slid into the degrading role of a subservient state under the heel of the Third Reich.

Antonio now found himself involved as a small cog in the Mussolini 'myth machine'. 'The resounding victory' now being celebrated by Italy called out for heroes. The fact that none existed presented no problem to the fascist authorities – they could easily be manufactured. With full military pomp Antonio was paraded before his Colonel and awarded a medal for outstanding valour in the face of the enemy. His CO must have suspected that the battalion's 'hero' would dump his medal at the first opportunity so he took him aside and said: 'You *will* wear that bloody thing day and night, whether you like it or not.' Antonio did the only thing an Italian can do under such circumstances – he made a joke of it and called the award his 'Moroccan Campaign medal'.

Such was Mussolini's confidence that the war was as good as over – France defeated and Great Britain about to be invaded – that he took the unprecedented step of demobilizing vast numbers of troops. By releasing so many men he relieved the military of an acute supply problem and at the same time provided men for work on the harvest. But, still wanting to impress the Germans with his contribution to the war effort, he sent some Fiat bombers, complete with crews, to join the Luftwaffe in bombing England. When they arrived in Belgium, it was discovered that the machines lacked the range to take part in such raids, so they flew back to Italy.

At sea and in foreign ports Italian ships had not been warned about the declaration of war in time to return home. In this way the country lost a third of her merchant fleet overnight. No other nation made such a mistake.

In North Africa Mussolini had 300,000 men based in Libya. He was determined to march them into Egypt and in July told Hitler he would reach Suez by the end of the month. It was September before they even crossed the frontier. Marshal Graziani boasted of commanding 'the finest colonial army in the world', but he was too timid to advance far into Egypt. In December, a highly mobile, well-trained British and Indian force of less than 35,000 inflicted a catastrophic defeat on this Italian army.

To make matters worse, again without consulting his military chiefs, Mussolini had mounted an invasion of Greece in October. This was to be yet another 'push-over'. It coincided with the start of the rainy season, the worst possible moment to attack. The Greeks fought back fiercely and within a week had thrown the Italians back into Albania. For months after that Mussolini was obliged to fight a humiliating defensive action. The following spring the Germans took over and defeated the Greeks in two weeks.

Mussolini suffered another blow in his first six months at war. On 11 November half his battle fleet was put out of action at Taranto by a British carrier-based attack. The blame for these disasters can be placed squarely at the feet of Mussolini – not least for his insistence on running the war as a one-man operation. Apart from neither listening to nor seeking the advice of his generals or admirals, he caused chaos by sending his top administrators and ministers, the *gerarche*, to take over various commands at the front Most of these civilians had neither training nor experience to fit them for such jobs, while at home essential services ground to a halt for lack of control from the top.

Antonio began to believe that some guardian angel was watching over him and his men. It was remarkable that they had avoided involvement in any of Il Duce's disasters. Naturally they did not expect the Alpini to be needed in the sands of the North African desert, but the mountainous terrain of Greece and Albania was a different matter. Nevertheless, the nearest they came to that war was helping in the rehabilitation of Alpini from other mountain regiments who had been mentally and physically exhausted by the fighting in Greece. The instructions given to Antonio, quite ridiculous in the circumstances, were to give these men a stiff daily dose of parade-ground drill in order to toughen them up and 'bring them to their senses'. This he ignored and worked out a fairly leisurely schedule of swimming, skiing, shooting and sports. The men responded well and made good progress.

Then Antonio was posted to a sleepy little town in Il Veneto, a picturesque region of Italy north of Venice, dotted with lakes overlooked by villas. These villas, some more like palaces, had been built by the merchant princes of Venice.

Having spent his boyhood holidays there, Antonio knew the region well. The natives were in complete contrast to the people from the south of Italy. The Neapolitans and Sicilians often referred to them disparagingly as 'Polentoni' after polenta – a maize dish eaten in place of pasta. The Venetians called their detractors 'Macaroni'.

Almost as soon as he arrived Antonio met an old friend from his military academy days in Rome, Emilio Lois. Emilio was having coffee at a table in the corner of the piazza when Antonio joined him.

'This is a dreary, boring backwater,' grumbled Emilio. 'Nothing to do but nod politely at the old fogies who inhabit this place.'

'What about girls?' asked Antonio.

'Untouchable!' his companion grunted. 'The old women keep them under lock and key. There's no way of getting at the girls around this place. You may as well resign yourself to a life of celibacy while you're here.'

As Emilio was speaking, Antonio, only half-listening, concentrated on a pair of elegantly dressed young women, strolling across the piazza. Both were good-looking but one was strikingly beautiful. Her long, dark hair fell forward concealing part of her face. Yet what remained to be seen was more than enough for Antonio. In that instant he had fallen in love.

He turned to Emilio: 'What were you saying about this being a boring place? You must be crazy! I've just seen the most perfect girl in all the world and I won't rest until I meet her.'

'Just two perfect examples of those "untouchables" I was telling you about,' said Emilio. 'You'd be crazy if you pushed your luck in that direction.'

Emilio went on to explain that there were two all-powerful men in this part of the world, who ruled the community with unquestioned authority. One, an old bishop, dominated people's lives by divine right of the Catholic Church. The other, Emilio's Colonel of Artillery, put the fear of the devil into anyone rash enough to cross him. He was a mountain of a man, with an enormous black beard. A thick plaited leather whip was coiled across his left shoulder at all times. Before taking over command of his regiment in Il Veneto, this man had been in charge of thousands of negro troops in North Africa. It was there that he perfected the use of the lash as an instrument of persuasion. Not surprisingly he was known throughout the Italian army as 'il Leone Scudiscionte' – 'the Whipping Lion'.

'Now,' said Emilio deliberately, 'Maria, the girl with the Veronica Lake hairstyle, is no other than the daughter of the 'Whipping Lion' and the great-niece of the old bishop! If you want to stay healthy, take my advice and keep well away!'

Naturally, Antonio had no intention of taking his friend's advice. On the contrary, he was already making plans to meet the girl. During the next few days he struck up an acquaintance with a certain captain of artillery who was engaged to Maria's older sister. In no time at all he was introduced to the family circle and met the girl of his dreams.

She was even lovelier than he had imagined and her beauty was allied to a sparkling personality and ready wit which blended perfectly with Antonio's sense of fun. He was completely bewitched. Maria, it transpired, excelled as an athlete, being particularly good at sprinting and the high jump. She only lacked someone to give her expert coaching in order to achieve professional standards. Antonio was quick to emphasize his own interest and experience in all sporting matters and offered his services as an instructor!

At 18 Maria had sadly neglected the academic side of her education. To her mother it seemed as if fate had smiled on them when Antonio arrived, a young man with a degree, who could teach her daughter the intricacies of Italian grammar and the mysteries of Latin. From then on, whenever his far from onerous military duties allowed, Antonio was never away from Maria's side – conscientiously fulfilling his task as family-approved tutor. Although such things were never mentioned, Antonio was sure that Maria had fallen in love with him. It was impossible to put his intuition to the test, because they were never alone. Either the mother, the sister, or the old bishop was always present during lessons or on the sports field. The only person conspicuously absent was 'the Whipping Lion' himself – military duties apparently taking up almost every moment of his life. Antonio had only met him once, during his first introduction to the family. He decided then that the scourge of North Africa was indeed a very frightening man.

As the days passed Antonio began to despair of ever having his loved one to himself. Then one weekend the family decided to go to the country for two days. The party was to be made up of Maria's mother, her sister, the captain, the old bishop, and the 'Whipping Lion', who said he needed a break. Antonio suggested to Maria that she should feign a chill and ask to be excused. The ruse worked well enough and the family departed for its brief holiday.

Antonio feared that they might change their minds and return that same night. So, being doubly cautious, he arranged with Maria that he would come to the villa around midnight, well after the arrival of the last train from the country. When evening came, overwhelming excitement engulfed Antonio as he anticipated the delights that lay ahead. Just before midnight, dressed in his number one uniform, flowing alpini cape and headgear with a new eagle's feather he strode up to the darkened villa, accompanied by his faithful batman, Peppe.

They reached the large wrought-iron gate and discovered that it had been left slightly open. Antonio studied the luminous dial of his watch – it was already after midnight. 'Another five minutes, just to be sure,' he whispered. 'Then, Peppe, you can be off and I will keep my appointment!'

All remained quiet as Antonio edged his way through the gate and crept stealthily up the path leading towards the villa. His foot was barely on the doorstep when his ear caught the patter of feminine footsteps inside the building. This was the moment for which he had waited all these weeks. In seconds his lovely Maria would be in his arms. His trembling hand clasped the handle of the great front door – this too stood ajar in silent welcome. Then, just as he was about to enter the darkened hall, his body froze at the sound of voices coming from the direction of the garden. The family had returned. The bloody train must have arrived late. How to escape? To enter the villa and perhaps implicate Maria was unthinkable. To rush the gate impossible. Leaping down the steps, Antonio threw himself behind a small bush, the only available cover within reach. In doing so, he made enough noise to alert the approaching group to his presence.

'Who is there?' roared 'the Whipping Lion'.

'Come out in the name of God!' commanded the old bishop. The Colonel was standing little more than a metre from Antonio's hiding place. It was more than his nerves could stand. Maria's would-be lover leapt to his feet and charged headlong across the garden as fast as his booted legs could carry him. Only when he reached the extremity of the grounds did he realize that he was trapped. A high stone wall completely surrounded the villa – a wall topped with sharp pieces of broken glass. Now 'the Whipping Lion' had drawn his pistol and was firing wildly into the darkness.

Just when Antonio was sure that all was lost, he heard a voice calling from the other side of the wall. 'Hello, my *tenente*! It is Peppe here. I have thrown my coat over the wall to protect you. Quickly! Jump for your life.'

Without hesitation Antonio took a flying leap and cleared the wall in a style that would not have disgraced a pole vaulter! In an instant a badly shaken Antonio was standing beside his batman on the far side of the wall. 'Let's run,' gasped Peppe, tugging at his officer's arm, and they did not stop until they reached the barracks.

Early the following morning Antonio was summoned to the Artillery Headquarters on the other side of the town. Peppe went with him. On arrival he was told that the Colonel was waiting to see him. Antonio turned to Peppe: 'Be ready with a stretcher to cart me to hospital!'

As Antonio entered the office, the enormous man looked at him with an expression like thunder on his face. Antonio felt faint.

'Something terrible has happened,' said the Colonel. 'Last night our property was entered by an intruder. Fortunately we came back a day early because my wife was worried about our daughter's health. She has a bit of a chill. We disturbed the bastard just as he was about the enter the villa. I nearly got him – would have made mincemeat of him. But he managed to slip over the wall. Think he had an accomplice waiting on the outside.'

Antonio felt his knees beginning to tremble. 'Trouble is,' continued the Colonel, 'I can't spare much time to be at the villa. So the women and the old bishop are left there unprotected.' He broke off and looked at the young officer. 'You seem pale. Are you unwell? Sit down and have a glass of schnapps.'

Antonio was very glad to sit down and even happier to have a drink.

'Now,' the Colonel went on, 'I have an idea that will relieve me of a lot of anxiety. I want *you* to keep an eye on things for me.' He leaned forward across the desk and said almost pleadingly: 'Do me a favour and move into the villa right away!'

Following this episode Antonio enjoyed three months of perfect bliss. It was a constant source of wonder to him that no one in the villa appeared to suspect the warm relationship that he and Maria enjoyed. In the end, however, jealous tongues beyond the confines of the family began to wag. One day Antonio's own Colonel, a man of unusual perception, told him he had decided to post him away, for his own good and also because he wanted him to train up a fresh group of Alpini, this time for a special mission.

It was early 1942 and Antonio surveyed his new troop of Alpini ski commandos with some pride. After intensive winter training at the Scuola

Centrale Militare d'Alpinismo they were ready for anything. Their clothing and footwear were of the best, and white ski smocks worn over uniforms rendered the men virtually invisible in snow-covered terrain.

Only their weapons let them down. The previous November they had been on an exercise with some Austrian Mountain Jägers whose automatic rifles made them blink with envy. Antonio's men had Fucile model 91 rifles. The number actually referred, not to the model, but to the year of manufacture – 1891! The barrels were so long that they frequently became tangled up with the other equipment and impeded progress on skis. The General in charge of all Alpini regiments made personal representations to Mussolini and pleaded for more up-to-date weapons. The General emphasized that there was little point in training highly mobile, specialist mountain troops if, having tracked down their quarry, they then had no proper rifles. He explained that the Fucile model 91, with its impossibly long barrel, was an anachronism that should be relegated to a museum. Mussolini, with one of his inspirational flashes, snapped back, 'Saw 20cm off its length!' – and that is exactly what happened. Gunsmiths visited the Alpini regiments and the job was done in no time at all.

Antonio's troop was also equipped with Berretta light machine guns, but the lubricating grease invariably solidified and gummed up the gun in freezing conditions.

Not an official issue, but a personal weapon for which Antonio had a high regard, was an Austrian Schwartz Löser machine pistol from the First World War.

By now the German Afrika Korps, under the leadership of General Erwin Rommel, had taken over the battle for North Africa. All through the previous year the rival armies had moved back and forth across the desert, sharing almost equally in defeat and success. Now, at the beginning of 1942, it seemed at last that Rommel was gaining the upper hand. He had swept the British two-thirds of the way back towards the Egyptian frontier before they steadied on the Gazala line. It looked as if another onslaught would carry the Axis forces into Egypt itself.

In what was arguably the most significant event since the outbreak of war, Japan had attacked the American fleet at Pearl Harbor on 7 December and brought the United States into the war. Earlier Hitler had precipitated an event of equal consequence when he invaded the Soviet Union in June. All had gone well at first, as the German panzers roared east. Then the Russian winter brought the Wehrmacht to a halt. Within sight of Moscow the German troops were stopped by the freezing conditions and ever-increasing counter-attacks by the Red Army.

Now, with the coming of spring, the German High Command planned to return to the offensive. Mussolini had already committed large numbers of Italian troops to the Russian front, in spite of Hitler's suggestion that they would serve a better purpose in North Africa. Ignoring his fellow dictator's advice, he was determined to throw more men into the jaws of the Soviet Army. Antonio and his team of Alpini were to be a tiny part of this futile scheme. Few of the Italian soldiers who left for the Russian front at that time were ever seen again. Their fate is well illustrated by General Garibaldi's luckless Eighth Italian Army when it was overrun on the Don. Defenceless in the face of heavy armour, almost every man disappeared without trace.

Before entraining for Russia, Benetti and his commandos of the 7th Pusteria Alpine Regiment were chosen for a less arduous task. The authorities decided to commission Alessandro Blasetti, the well-known film director, to produce a 'documentary' about the daring feats of arms being performed by the courageous Alpini in Soviet Russia. The fact that the film was to be shot *before* they went into enemy territory was a mere detail! Fortunately, because one snow-covered mountain looks much like another, there was no problem in choosing a convincing 'Soviet' location.

The rail journey to Russia was cold, slow, cramped and unbelievably monotonous. Troops used to the open life of the mountains found being crushed day after day in stinking wagons nothing short of purgatory. They were finally tipped out at a place called Staraya Russia, a shell-pocked town overlooking Lake Ilmen. Antonio reckoned they were about 200 kilometres east of the Estonian frontier. The countryside was totally different from anything the Alpini had ever seen. To Italian eyes the flat swampy land seemed far from picturesque. Now in the early spring, although still cold, the ground was becoming softer underfoot. They were driven in a huge Opel lorry to a Wehrmacht camp not far from the town. A German corporal showed them where they could bed down for the night. Most of them felt more like stretching their legs after the interminable journey. Some of the more enterprising commandos carried out an after-dark reconnaissance to establish the whereabouts of the food store. To prove they had been successful, they came back with a carton of chocolate and a string of enormous sausages.

Next morning Antonio reported to the Commandant and asked for orders. The Major obviously wanted to be helpful, but he had not been warned to expect a group of foreign skiers wearing funny hats and carrying rifles from the last century. Politely he suggested that Antonio should hang about and he would try to get some information to him later in the day, after he had contacted Divisonal HQ by radio.

Antonio had no instructions from his own superiors beyond the assurance that they were on a 'special mission'. The troop had not been issued with radio equipment, so they were unable to receive orders or transmit information about their own activities. They were without maps and no arrangements appeared to have been made for the supply of ammunition, food or replacement clothing. Antonio, however, had every intention of getting what he needed from the Germans – after all, it was *their* war they were supposed to be fighting.

For a while the Italians spent their time watching the German soldiers performing their duties. The men of the mountains were impressed by their allies' efficiency and devotion to detail. They had never seen so much attention lavished on inanimate objects like rifles, machine guns and belts of ammunition.

'So serious are these people,' Antonio reflected, 'that they are natural soldiers; to them duty is everything. But is it possible to become such a soldier, and yet remain a human being?' He was to ask himself this question many times during his days in Russia.

After a time the Alpini grew tired of watching others at work and retired to the comparative warmth of their billet. Later in the day the German Major told Antonio he had been in touch with his HQ. Unfortunately they were equally in the dark as to why the Alpini had been posted to this part of the front. As the Major said, 'There seems to be an unfortunate lack of liaison between your army and the Wehrmacht.

The Major told Antonio as much as he knew of the current state of the war in that area. 'If you had arrived only a few weeks ago you would have found us in a perilous situation. North of here, in the Lake Volkhov region, we have just pinched off the bulk of two Soviet armies that broke through our lines and were streaming north towards Leningrad. Now they are surrounded and cut off, but it was a close-run thing. Incidentally, battalions of the Spanish Blue Division fought magnificently in helping us to close the gap. While all this was going on, we have been engaged in holding no less than five Russian armies in this sector. Our forces have been concentrated at Demyansk seventy-five kilometres south-east of here and in the town of Kholm a hundred kilometres to the south. It's been a hell of a time, I can tell you. Our lads at Demyansk, about 100,000 of them, were completely cut off. Then, in the foulest weather, the Luftwaffe flew supplies into them day after day after day. It was a wonderful effort – the biggest airlift the world has ever known. Now we have just broken through to them.'

Although the Major was in charge of a supply dump well behind the lines, he evidently took a personal pride in what the Germans had achieved. 'Those six divisions held off the Soviet armies all through the winter and now Ivan has lost his chance. The marshy ground is just beginning to unfreeze and soon he won't be able to move his supplies any more. Our line is becoming solidly re-established in this area. At Kholm our men are also having a tough time. A small force is holding this position and in a few days it is more or less certain that they will be relieved as well – and, by God, they will deserve it. You've timed your visit well. If you'd come here earlier in the year, you'ld have found the situation very different, apart from having your balls frozen off at temperatures of 50 degrees below!'

Antonio asked the Major what his troop should do now. The Commandant thought it would be a good idea if they were to go to Demyansk, on the slopes of the Valday Hills.

'It's an unbelievable dump, I can tell you, but our people might be glad of your specialized help if you could work your way up into the high ground beyond the town. Then you would be in a position to winkle out any Russian observation posts that may be established there.'

This was more or less how things worked out. At Demyansk they were regarded by the German troops with indifference, but no one objected when they put forward the Major's suggestion that they should climb into the hills. Someone pointed out that this was enemy territory and they would have to fend for themselves in the event of trouble. Antonio accepted this but asked that his troop be allowed to return to Demyansk when necessary in order to replenish their food supplies. The Germans agreed, but made it plain they would provide nothing more than rations. Replenishment of weapons, ammunition and clothing was the responsibility of the Italian authorities – wherever they might be!

'Nice to feel wanted,' said Antonio, as he and his men began their trek into unknown terrain under cover of darkness. They were glad to leave the marshland behind and breathe pure air again. They came to a small village nestling in a natural bowl in the hills. Because of its sheltered position, the little timber *baracce* (as they would have been known back home) were well protected from the worst of the elements.

All that day the Italians lay hidden, peering over the ridge and observing everything that moved in the village below. They had to be sure that no Red Army troops were using the village as a base. They saw only women and children and a couple of elderly shepherds keeping an eye on their flocks but still they approached the place with extreme caution as the evening light began to fade.

Pandemonium broke out when the Alpini entered the village – women screamed, children cried, a couple of mangy dogs howled like wolves, doors slammed shut and shutters closed. In vain the men shouted that they had no intention of harming them or of stealing their possessions. Then a solitary figure came steadily along the rough stone track that ran through the village. A tall, thin man of middle years, with close-cropped hair and greying beard, he was dressed in a threadbare black suit which gave him an air of respectability. He walked up to the Italian soldiers and they could see that he at least had no *paura* (fear).

As a natural linguist Antonio had few problems with French, Spanish, English or German, but Russian was beyond him. He wondered if the man might be some sort of village priest. If he were, then his religion would be Russian Orthodox, which in turn meant he probably had a knowledge of Latin, a language familiar to Antonio from his days as a lawyer. His hunch was correct and they were able to converse in Latin!

The outcome of this discussion was an arrangement which suited everybody. All the men of the village, with the exception of a few old shepherds and the priest, had either been called up or killed in the war. The women had therefore been obliged to do the work normally done by the men. The few cows, the goats, the pigs and the hens presented no problems. They could care for the animals, just as they looked after their children. The sheep were tended by the grandfathers. It was the sewing and harvesting of the oats, the rye and the potato crop that they found hard. Now the men fortunately could do this work. They set to with a will, lifting the potatoes and sowing the spring seed. The Alpini found nothing incongruous in what they were doing. On the contrary, here at last was some purpose to a meaningless incursion into a foreign country to fight a war they did not understand. In return, the troops were given shelter by the villagers.

The Valday Hills had none of the grandeur of the Italian alps. They were hardly mountains at all, but they rose high enough above the surrounding marshland to retain a thick covering of snow. Best of all, the hills were impossible terrain for tanks, troop-carriers or mobile guns – obviously the reason why the Alpini had been able to move up unmolested by the Soviets, after leaving the German stronghold down below.

One night, after they had been there about a week, they were woken up by the rattle of small-arms fire. Each man grabbed his rifle and took up position by a window. But then, as suddenly as it had started, the shooting stopped.

Next morning it was discovered that one of the village's precious pigs had been shot dead. Antonio, accompanied by Peppe and two other commandos, followed the tracks made by about a dozen sets of skis across the crest of the hill for about three kilometres until they reached a slope falling sharply away to the east. They could see the trail continue down through a wood and emerge on the lower side of the trees. The tracks then led to a small settlement, similar in size to their own village, overlooking a long narrow lake.

'Tonight,' said Antonio, 'we will return their visit!'

He learned from the priest that a reliable information network existed throughout the hill communities. It was run by the priests themselves, who walked almost daily to well-established meeting points between their respective 'parishes'. Here they exchanged the latest news and in this way even the most remote hamlets were kept in touch.

Before the Alpini carried out their reprisal raid Antonio was informed that a small force of Russian mountain troops, about equal in number to his own, was billeted there. After the raid they heard that the noise of the Fucile 91s had caused a certain amount of panic among both the civilian inhabitants and the troops. Yet, apart from a bullet-hole through a cooking pot and a sprained ankle sustained by an anxious peasant who leapt too hastily through his back window, there had been no damage. Antonio was relieved.

After two or three more of these pointless raids deaths had increased by two cows, a goat and another pig, and Antonio felt it was time to call a halt. He explained to the priest that he wanted to talk to the leader of the Russian mountain troops, and wondered if a meeting could be arranged by means of 'Pope Radio', as he nicknamed the church's unofficial communication system. The priest thought the scheme was fraught with danger but decided it was worth a try. The negotiations took several days, during which time Antonio's men tried to dissuade him: 'You can't trust these Russians, *tenente*, they'll stab you in the back first chance they have!' Antonio, however, had made up his mind.

At last a time and place for the meeting was agreed by both parties and on the actual day 'Pope Radio' sent messages far and wide announcing the momentous event that was to take place that night. As Antonio was about to set off with the priest, Peppe volunteered to go with them. Antonio said that there was absolutely no need for him to accompany them, but Peppe persisted and his company was accepted with gratitude. So it was that Antonio and Peppe followed the holy father into the darkness.

The rendezvous was in the forest near the rival village – not a place to their advantage if things went wrong. The Russian officer could easily have his men lying in wait. The three men arrived at the clearing well before the appointed time. It was a clear moonlit night and they had made quicker progress than expected.

As Antonio studied his watch for the twentieth time, there was a slight rustling from the undergrowth at the edge of the clearing. A shadowy figure emerged and walked steadily towards them. It was the priest from the other village. Formally he embraced his brother in God, then turned and nodded solemnly at Antonio and Peppe. After a moment he raised his hands level with his face and slowly clapped three times.

Two men slipped out from behind some trees and came across to where they were standing. Both men were dressed in long fur coats reaching almost to their boots; their heads were enveloped in fur caps. Each soldier was armed to the teeth with belts of ammunition, hand grenades, revolvers, knives and, strangely enough, long hunting rifles not unlike those of the

Alpini. It was clear that in their estimation the Italians were not to be trusted either! One of the men was tall, about Antonio's height; the other was a giant, towering over everyone. One of the priests introduced him as Comrade Batrakov.

Antonio spelled out what was in his mind: 'We have no wish to fight anyone and we certainly have no quarrel with you Russians. This war is not of our making and we want no part of it. We have cordial relations with the people of the village where we are living and have no intention of hurting them; nor do we want to see them hurt by others. Surely it is better to meet in friendship. As men of the mountains we share the same way of life, understand the same things.'

All this had to be translated from Latin into a form of Russian spoken by their priest, which all too clearly was not easy for the enormous Mongolian or his companion to understand. Antonio doubted whether the spirit of his message was getting through. 'Tell him,' he said to his priest, 'that we have a quantity of schnapps, some chocolate and other things to eat. We would be pleased to sit down and share these things with Comrade Batrakov and his men. In return, perhaps Comrade Batrakov would permit us to try a little of his famous Russian vodka.'

The mouth of the giant broke into a wide, toothy smile. Taking a stride forward, the fur-covered monster gathered Antonio in his arms and hugged him tight!

The plan had worked. Convivial get-togethers became a regular occurrence between the 'communist' and 'fascist' troops from then on. Many a Russian and Italian woke on mornings following these gatherings with his head splitting apart as a result of too much mutual hospitality. The German quartermaster never knew how much the contents of his store contributed to peaceful celebrations in the hills beyond the camp and the Germans were often encouraged by the sound of rifle fire that echoed down from the high ground. It seemed to show that the Alpini were dutifully engaged in routing out pockets of resistance. The truth was slightly different. Comrade Batrakov and his new-found friends were simply enjoying a good day's hunting!

Summer overtook spring and the Alpini began to gather in the harvest. One of Antonio's men, Enno, was a skilled woodcarver from the South Tyrol, and was putting the finishing touches to an exquisite statue of Christ he had carved for the tiny church. Antonio continued to give daily lessons to the children who were learning for the first time of a world beyond the Valday Hills.

But there was evidence of activity among the Germans in the lowlands. The roar of heavy guns was heard more frequently – a sure prelude to battle. On a recent visit to the camp to collect rations Antonio sensed an increased air of tension. The great armies were about to clash again. He was sure of it.

His duty was clear – to safeguard the lives of his men, while doing nothing to compromise the villagers. The more he considered the situation the more certain he was that the time had come for the Alpini to leave. If the little community was overrun by Soviet forces, it would do the people no good to be found harbouring enemy troops. Antonio told the Priest what he intended to do. As soon as the harvest had been gathered and as many provisions as possible filched from the depot for the benefit of the village, the Alpini would leave.

'Where will you go?' the priest asked. 'I am taking my men home to Italy,' Antonio replied simply.

He explained that they had had no contact with the Italian Army since they came to Russia. For all the Fascist authorities cared, he and his men could have starved to death.

It was with sad hearts that the Alpini said farewell to their friends and left the village that had been their home for several months. Each commando received some memento and a parcel of food. It was the people's way of saying that the Italians had found a place, not only in their hearts, but also in their history, leaving behind a small legend that would pass from one generation to the next – a story of how humanity survived in a sea of destruction.

Batrakov came over the hills to say goodbye. He embraced Antonio and then gave him a magnificent fur hat. The enormous Mongolian told him to wear it at all times to keep out the cold.

But the most valuable gift, one which probably saved their lives, was the letter which the priest gave to Antonio.

'This,' he told him, 'is to do with what you have always called "Pope Radio". I have written a message to my brother priests, telling them you are a good man, explaining how you have helped us and praying that they in turn will help you along the way. God go with you, my dear son.'

The Alpini's return to Italy, through Russia, Poland, Czechoslovakia and Austria was an epic journey. In the early days a number of diversions had to be made to avoid areas of conflict. Even so they were more than once in danger of being engulfed by fast-moving Soviet armour. The priest's letter brought them shelter and food and was of vital help in providing immunity from partisan bands.

The unhappiest event for Antonio concerned his own countrymen, whom they encountered in thousands near the Soviet/Polish border. Mostly Sicilians, they were reduced to shambling, half-starved wrecks. Their clothes were in tatters, their boots had long since fallen to pieces. Disowned by their own government, despised by the German 'super race', their useless weapons long since abandoned, they struggled on without hope – children of the sun, engulfed in the darkness of despair.

A Brigadier of the Bersaglieri rode up to the Alpini on his horse and shouted: 'This regiment is returning to Italy for re-equipment. You will join our ranks from now on.'

Antonio, standing smartly to attention and looking up at the Brigadier, said with all the confidence of a man who knew he was right: 'As a special unit operating independently, in no way are we permitted to join other forces.'

The Brigadier was staggered by his temerity. 'By the look of you,' he roared, 'you are all well fed and clothed. Why this should be, I will enquire later. Meanwhile, it is your duty to share what you have with your comrades.' This was meaningless claptrap; what little they had, distributed among so many, would be a pointless waste. Any way Antonio's first duty was to his men. The buffoon on the horse was merely trying to reduce them to the level of his own rabble. He left the Brigadier threatening dire punishment for insubordination, but there was nothing the man could do.

Winter descended on them when they were in the Austrian Alps. For some time Antonio had tried to hide from his men the fear that his sight might be failing, a complaint brought on by snow blindness. Some weeks before he had lost his goggles while chasing a hare along a *crinale* (mountain ridge). Peppe noticed it and mentioned it to Enno, who fashioned a pair of spectacles from a strip of pine, with nothing more than a pinhole for each eye. It was similar to those used by the Lapps and soon helped in restoring Antonio's vision.

But now, for the first time since setting out, the men suffered real hunger. This had hitherto been alleviated by chewing a concoction called pemmican. This consisted of a number of strange ingredients, including the flesh of a dead horse which they had stolen. It was brewed for some hours and then allowed to cool into an unappetizing mess which solidified. The 'cook' had been a student of chemistry before joining the army and he assured his comrades that the Norwegians had used it most successfully when exploring the Arctic! Each man had to stuff his ration into his underpants to prevent it freezing. When wanted, pieces could be broken off and chewed.

The year was nearly over when Antonio brought his twenty-seven Alpini through the Brenner Pass and up to the Italian frontier post. Although the place was swarming with Germans, it was the *Italian* officials who refused them entry. Only many hours later, after Antonio had managed to contact his old Colonel at the Scuola Centrale Militare d'Alpinismo, were they finally given permission to return to their own country.

The month that followed was not a pleasant one for Antonio. It started off well enough when he took his troop to the Scuola Centrale to receive a cordial welcome from his CO and other officers of the 7th Pusteria Alpini

Regiment to which he belonged. Everyone was anxious to hear his story, particularly how he had managed to bring his men back over such a vast distance. He told them he had simply set off on a south-westerly compass bearing, checking his position from the names of half-remembered places learned in school geography.

'I have been very lucky,' he said, with due modesty.

Then military police arrived from Milan and arrested him. He was taken before a tribunal on a charge of 'gross insubordination'. It was, of course, the Brigadier who brought the charge, having left his tattered regiment to fend for itself while he returned to Italy by train. The proceedings dragged on interminably. Conducting his own defence, Antonio was allowed to bring members of his troop to speak on his behalf. Other officers, including his Colonel, gave character references. It was the end of January, 1943, when he was finally acquitted with honour and congratulated by the chairman of the military tribunal on his outstanding qualities of leadership.

A few days later he was posted to his old Scuola Militare d'Alpinismo, but this time he was to be the Commanding Officer. Much to his amusement, he had become something of a legend. The film about the Alpini had received wide distribution during his absence and on his return newspapers gave lurid descriptions of how the courageous *tenente* and his brave ski commandos had fought the bestial enemy every inch of the way back to Italy. It was even suggested that they have survived by eating Russians!

Antonio plunged into his new job with enthusiasm. He had a mixed company, comprising his original troop, some new recruits and, as on a previous occasion, a number of other Alpini who had been badly shaken up in various theatres of war. He did his best to rehabilitate them by a combination of sporting activities and mental exercises. A small lake nearby gave him the opportunity to teach every man to swim. By breaking army rules regulating the use of pack mules, he was able to improvise a riding school. In an attempt to broaden his men's outlook towards their surroundings, he taught them something of the animals, the birds and the fishes living in the region.

After some months he decided to put on a show – a military show this time – that would demonstrate in an entertaining way the efficiency of his company. The day came and the visitors were seated alongside the lake. A General and his entourage had been persuaded to attend; the fame of Antonio's military school in the mountains was assured. Naturally, the VIPs were placed in the best seats, right on the water's edge.

The spectacular was on a scale of which Hollywood itself would have been proud. Antonio had recruited the help of an Alpine artillery battery who opened the show by thundering over the rise with horse-drawn cannon. As soon as the guns were deployed, they were charged by cavalry – mounted on mules. Every onlooker recognized the scene as the famous Charge of the Light Brigade. The cannon, loaded with blanks, flashed and banged alarmingly. The terrified mules stampeded, taking little notice of their inexperienced riders, some of whom were forcibly dismounted. Then, with a startling disregard for history, the 'tanks' attacked the artillery in force. The body of each 'tank' was made of cardboard, placed over a handcart propelled by two men. Some of this 'armour' disintegrated before reaching the objective, but the rest succeeded in overrunning the guns, causing the artillerymen to flee in well-simulated panic.

Finally it was time for a massed evacuation by sea. Rafts had been constructed onto which the soldiers clambered, while others swam alongside. Soon the enemy fleet was seen approaching to cut off the retreat – an impressive squadron of canoes. Each man was armed with an OTO grenade, quite useless for causing damage to people or property, but capable of creating an impressive fountain fifteen metres high, when exploded in water. Unfortunately the sea battle drifted nearer and nearer to the side of the lake where the distinguished guests were sitting and soon the General, the General's lady and all their friends were drenched.

Once again a 'Benetti Spectacular' ended in something less than popular acclaim. Rather vindictively, Antonio thought, he was reprimanded for disregarding a number of regulations, including the use of another company's men and facilities without first obtaining permission from the War Ministry in Rome; misuse of pack-mules; not seeking permission from Military HQ to hold military manoeuvres; irresponsible waste of OTO grenades – and many other previously unheard-of infringements. But he was saved from appearing before another tribunal by his country's preoccupation with more pressing affairs.

If the previous year had been a grim one for Italy, 1943 was a catastrophe. May marked the final defeat of the German and Italian armies in North Africa. In July Sicily was conquered. Early September saw the arrival of Allied armies on the mainland of Italy.

Mussolini had suffered serious ill health since the beginning of the year, his mental and physical condition deteriorating noticeably. After a vote by the Grand Council expressing no confidence in his prosecution of the war, he was at last deposed by King Vittorio Emanuele. Marshal Badoglio took over as Prime Minister. That was at the end of July. Under arrest, Mussolini was moved several times in the hope of fooling the Germans as to his whereabouts. Hitler was anxious to secure his release – a fallen dictator, even a third-rate one, hardly created a desirable precedent! In September, coinciding with the invasion of Italy by Anglo/American forces, Badoglio arranged an armistice with the Allies. Meanwhile, in a brilliant commando raid, a German unit, under the command of Colonel Skorzeny, snatched Mussolini from a hotel in the Apennines, where he had been held captive. The Nazis took control of Central and Northern Italy and persuaded Mussolini to set up a puppet government under their protection. This brought about the division of the country and led to eighteen months of civil war.

By this time there could hardly have been a family in the country that had not been deeply, often tragically, affected by the hostilities. The Benettis were no exception. Three of Antonio's male relatives had lost their lives in the Navy. When his young brother, Giorgio, a *tenente* in the field artillery, refused to obey the Germans, he was carted off to a PoW camp near Düsseldorf, where he remained for eighteen months until liberated by the Allies.

Soon after Mussolini's re-instatement Antonio received a telephone message from the War Ministry. He was informed that a Wehrmacht detachment would be arriving almost immediately to take over his establishment. The orders were to hand over all arms and ammunition and place himself and his men at the disposal of the German commander. Antonio called the entire company before him, read out the message and then told them: 'I want this place cleared by tonight. Each one of you must make your own way home. There is little I can offer you in return for your loyalty. I have no money to pay you. By all means take a pair of boots, a blanket and share the mules between you, leaving two for Peppe and myself. If you wish, you may also take a rifle and some ammunition for hunting. Now go before it is too late and God go with you.'

He said farewell to each man in turn until only he and Peppe remained. Next morning a group of miners, members of a local band of anarchists, came to the camp and asked them for weapons. Antonio explained that he now only had those of his *sergente* and himself but that, even if he had had any, he would not have handed them over. 'I would not let you have them on principle. Italians should not be shooting Italians.' He struck a bargain with them: if they brought him a pile of anti-personnel mines, which he knew they possessed, he would give them a supply of tinned beef. When the mines arrived, he and Peppe buried them in a row at the entrance to the courtyard. They had no intention of hurting anyone; it was just to make the German vehicles jump about a bit when they drove through the entrance arch.

It was early afternoon when the Germans arrived. They came in two lorries and halted outside the closed gates. The raucous voice of an impatient *hauptmann* yelled: 'Open these bloody gates, you stupid Wops.' Antonio stuck his head through the open window, smiled politely down at them and said in flawless German: 'I'm so sorry, but I don't understand a word you are saying.' A burst of machine-gun fire sent bits of masonry flying just above Antonio's head. He ducked inside the room and doubled towards the back of the building. From another open window at the rear of the barracks a ladder led down to a narrow cobbled street below. Here Peppe was waiting with two heavily loaded mules.

As the two men headed for the pass, they heard a lorry start up. There was a rending sound as it crashed through the big wooden doors of the Barracks they had just left, followed by a series of satisfyingly loud explosions.

A well-surfaced motor road led up through the pass, following the course of the river. On the farther bank a rough track also wound its way through the mountains and it was this harder route that the two men and their mules followed. Progress was slow and in the end they decided to cross the river and travel along the highway, but it was not long before they spotted a military convoy driving down the pass towards them. It included heavy armour, mobile artillery, trucks and an impressive Mercedes tourer.

'No time to dodge them,' muttered Antonio; 'they've probably spotted us anyway. We'll just have to bluff it out.'

Antonio must have presented an incongruous figure, in best uniform with eagle feather and long flowing cape, as he led his overburdened mule. Behind him came Peppe in *his* No 1 gear, sporting a crow's feather and the short cape of an NCO.

Soon they were abreast of the convoy, a detachment of SS troops. As the Mercedes drew near, Antonio jerked his head in the direction of the German officer in the rear of the car and then flung up the smartest salute he had ever executed. The German's puzzled expression turned to one of acceptance; he acknowledged the Italian's courtesy and nodded his head in recognition of a fellow officer. Antonio held the salute until the last vehicle had passed round a bend.

By late evening they reached their destination – a large hunting lodge buried in the depths of what had been, in peacetime, a private game forest. An old friend of Antonio greeted him warmly: 'My daughter and I have everything prepared; you may stay as long as you wish.' This was good news, as Antonio had only had time to phone him the previous day. Naturally, he had been unable to give any details. His friend, however, had assessed the situation accurately and made ready for their arrival.

Antonio and Peppe remained at this hideout for some while and before long everyone in the neighbourhood knew of their presence. Representatives of various groups – communists, monarchists, anarchists, even the neo-fascists – all came to see Antonio, hoping to persuade him to join them, but he refused all their invitations. Even so, another legend began to grow up around the 'Count' as he became known in that region. Rumour asserted that he was the leader of a large partisan band whose members, five hundred or more, were mysteriously concealed in the mountains. Antonio was well aware that, with all this unwanted attention, it was only a matter of time before other, more official, parties would be paying them a visit.

So one morning, as the first flakes of winter snow began to fall, Antonio and Peppe set out once more, now travelling light, with small packs on their backs. They were heading for the Swiss border. Up and up they climbed, the giant peak of Mont Blanc towering over to their left.

It was dusk when they came to the frontier. Snow was falling heavily, reducing visibility. In minutes now they would be safe in a neutral country. Suddenly a German voice yelled '*Halt! Wohin gehen Sie?*' Rushing forward, Antonio and Peppe flung themselves behind some rocks as a fusillade of bullets whined over their heads. They had stumbled into a German border patrol.

At that moment a flurry of snow gave them the cover they needed to crawl to a new position. Then they heard another voice calling softly: 'Quick! Come towards me.' It could have been a trick, but they had little choice. Slowly they edged in the direction from which the voice had come. Antonio felt a firm hand on his shoulder – it was impossible now to see more than a metre in any direction. He just made out the shadowy figure standing close beside him.

'Welcome to Switzerland, gentlemen,' said the Swiss Frontier Guard.

Author's Note

Sadly, since the writing of this book Antonio Benetti has died. It was a few days before his 75th birthday. I went to see him in hospital in Verona. He displayed qualities of courage, fortitude and humour until the end — those same qualities that had been his constant companions in life.